Adam Ferguson

Adam Ferguson

His Social and Political Thought

David Kettler

With a new introduction
and afterword by the author

Transaction Publishers
New Brunswick (U.S.A.) and London (U.K.)

Library of Congress Catalog Number: 2005043703
ISBN: 1-4128-0475-2
Printed in the United States of America

Library of Congress Cataloging-in-Publication Data

Kettler, David.
    [Social and political thought of Adam Ferguson]
    Adam Ferguson, his social and political thought / David Kettler ; with a new introduction and afterword by the author.
        p. cm.
    Originally published: The social and political thought of Adam Ferguson. Columbus : Ohio State University Press, 1965.
    Includes bibliographical references and index.
    ISBN 1-4128-0475-2
      1. Ferguson, Adam, 1723-1816. 2. Civilization—History. I. Title.

HM479.F47K48   2005
192—dc22

2005043703

FOR RUTH

Table of Contents

Introduction to the Transaction Edition

On the Personal History of the Project

I N 1954, with the encouragement of my teachers, Robert D. Cumming and Franz L. Neumann, I successfully submitted to the Rockefeller Foundation an application for a pre-doctoral fellowship for a grandiose "re-consideration of historicism," which aimed to respond to Karl Popper's *Open Society and its Enemies* and *The Poverty of Historicism*, not so much by arguing with his philosophy of science as by questioning his polemical account of the uses of historical periodization in social and political thought. As Cumming generously reformulated the design in his letter of support, the point was to examine "what exactly is under attack, which Popper is labelling 'historicism.'"[1] From the outset, the study expected to draw on a kind of sociological approach to the characterization of diverse forms of knowledge in order to ascertain the criteria appropriate to assessing one or another. "Adam Ferguson and the Scottish Historical School" was to have been only one of several chapters, beginning with Plato, continuing with Vico, and ending with Marx.[2] In the event, the puzzle of Ferguson absorbed all of my time and attention, yielding the book first published in 1965 and reprinted in the present edition. Ferguson seemed to be both remarkable and representative, and yet he could not be easily placed or defended as a philosopher, on a par with his contemporaries and friends, David Hume and Adam Smith. Simply put, the problem became how to explain the fact of his reception by thoughtful people at various times—without explaining it away.[3] The solution involved the search for an appropriate distance from the text, a workable framing.

My first introduction to Karl Popper had come a few years earlier in a course taught by Charles Frankel, who matched him with Karl Mannheim, whom he also taught us to read with pragmatic open-mindedness. Although the uncertain chapter on method was excised from the Ferguson book on the advice of the dissertation examiners, the influence of Mannheim's sociology of knowledge and theory of intellectuals is evident. The challenge was to draw on this mode of analysis without the reductionism and relativism with which it was generally associated at the time. Without grand meta-theoretical claims, then, the study offers a complex and pluralistic model of thought constituted by a paradigmatic syllabus of ethically charged conflicts, multiple uses, and characteristic rhetorical-cognitive strategies, imputed to the emerging social formation of urban intellectuals but by no means discredited by that imputation. De-

spite my unhappiness with many of Ferguson's political judgments, I recognized him as kin.

This outcome of my original encounter with Ferguson
led me to the first of several extended studies of Karl
Mannheim.[4] Ten years later, in 1975, strengthened in
method by work on previously unknown Mannheim texts,
informed by the fresh approaches of historians from Cambridge and elsewhere—notably J. G. A. Pocock—and inspired by an invitation to the Institute for Advanced Study in
the Humanities at the University of Edinburgh, I returned to
Ferguson, and specifically to the still unsettled question of
Ferguson's uses of historical stages.[5] The findings of this reconsideration are briefly signaled in the present preface and they
are extensively applied in the study published as the afterword
to this volume, which arose out of the current problem
constellation, where the concept of "civil society" rather than
the varieties of "historicism" is at the center of attention.

In the end, my conclusions about the bearing of
Ferguson's work on my own special subject of political theory
are more in the manner of Franz L. Neumann than in the
manner of Robert D. Cumming, but I want nevertheless to
dedicate this work to Cumming, who died on August 25,
2004, whose ability to hear what was being said and to give
it transformative recognition was unparalleled. That cour-
tesy was alas not always reciprocated.

Adam Ferguson among the Philosophers

Rarely mentioned by philosophers except as companion
of David Hume and Adam Smith, Adam Ferguson contributes a political consciousness to the moral philosophy
of eighteenth-century Scotland. In *An Essay on the History*

of Civil Society, Ferguson uses a comparative method to reflect on a commercial society distinguished by refined division of labor and to caution against its political dangers.
His elevated rhetoric belongs to Ferguson's strategy for coun-
tering his philosophical contemporaries' analytical aloofness
from the self-undermining consequences of the civility, commerce, security, and critical philosophy they prize.[6]
Ferguson's textbooks and Roman history deserve philosophical attention for their help with interpreting his distinctive
social diagnosis of the liberal political constitution.[7]

Ferguson's Highlands birth and knowledge of Gaelic were
unique among the figures prominent in the "Scottish Enlightenment," but he was unexceptionably Whig in politics
and Moderate in church affairs. Born 1723 in Logierait near
Perth, Ferguson moved to Edinburgh for divinity studies
after an MA from provincial St Andrews. An intimate of
the circle around Hume, he early abandoned a clerical career. Ferguson served five years as professor of natural philosophy in the University of Edinburgh, thanks to political
patrons of the literary set, and then, in 1765, he began a
popular twenty years as professor of pneumatics and moral
philosophy. The professorial office was more didactic than
scholarly, as witness Ferguson's effectiveness in the science
chair, but Ferguson's *Essay* gained him recognition beyond
admiring lecture rooms and appreciative salons. There were
French and German translations, and attentions from continental philosophers. Apart from four pamphlets in political controversies, Ferguson published two textbooks for his
course, the second a retrospective systematizing the changes
he made during his years of teaching, and a long-standard
but largely derivative *History of the Progress and Termina-*

tion of the Roman Republic. He died in 1815. His books were staples of instruction in American colleges well into the nineteenth century.

Neither Hume nor Smith was impressed by Ferguson as theorist. Philosophers have left his work to intellectual historians, who find there the epitome of republican misgivings (perhaps conditioned by a pre-Romantic Highlands sensibility) about the Scottish race to modernity after the Jacobite Rising of 1745, and to sociologists, who honor Ferguson as a science-minded progenitor of sociological theories of modernity. With his invocation of classical models and his alarms against corruption in nations dedicated to individual gain rather than heroic action, Ferguson amplifies the discourse of "civic humanism" or "Machiavellian moralism," as many historians emphasize, but he also fits in with a wider class of didactic rhetoricians who sought to bolster a religiously latitudinarian moral community in eighteenth-century Scotland.[8] Sociologists' claims to Ferguson are no less justified, especially by Ferguson's insistence that the study of human nature is an empirical study of humans in civil societies differing in design from one developmental stage to another and by his conjectural reconstruction of these designs to recognize not only political, economic, and ideological differences, in the manner of Montesquieu, but also such sociological mechanisms as integration through conflict, stratification and diverse forms of sociation. Karl Marx's incidental commendation of Ferguson as a materialist thinker with original insight into the harm done workers by a refined division of labor stimulated a tradition of commentary that emphasizes—and exaggerates—the extent to which Ferguson first identifies each historical period with a distinctive mode of subsistence, second, rationalizes the respective schemes of stratification, property, mentality, political formation by reference to this feature and, third, identifies a potentially explosive tension in the latest stage, a commercial society whose political order is progressively undermined by its own socioeconomic arrangements.

Although modest about the originality or rigor of his efforts, Ferguson counted himself a participant in the philosophical debates of his time, and, indeed, as Adam Smith's competitor in addressing what George Davie calls "the central problem of Scottish philosophy," that is, reconciling material advance with traditional moral standards in a "teachable philosophy of civilization."[9] Viewed from this perspective, Ferguson's writings appear as exercises in complementarity, seeking a reasonable strategy for coordinating two distinct modes of reflection. On one side is an analytical model of the progressive development of the human species through a sequence of stages in the history of civil society, with each stage conceived as a configuration of diversely formed productive, legal, moral, intellectual and hierarchical relations, some more systematic than others. On the other side is the evocation of a practical capacity to act in the diverse historical contexts, with the quality of actions assessed by standards of active virtue, especially manifest in political practice.

Ferguson submits the first level of study to Newtonian rules of method, in principle; and his work often offers but slight variations on themes from Hume and Smith. The second type of knowledge he distinguishes from the first as the knowledge appropriate to actors, not spectators; and he attacks Smith for neglecting this dimension, allowing moral psychology or economic laws to stand in for responsible decisions. Moral conduct is opaque without a science of the facts of human existence, but incoherent without practical understanding. Historical stages constitute scenes for actions subject to principles derived from a practical philosophy of elevated happiness. Political arrangements express modes of action to counter the defects of adventitious social circumstances. The essay form bypasses philosophical difficulties in interrelating these levels, but Ferguson's experiment gains in philosophical seriousness from his astute reflection on literary forms like the essay. In his moral philosophy class, as documented in the *Institutes of Moral Philosophy* and the retrospective *Principles of Moral and Political Science*, Ferguson grounded the "history of the species" in a psychological theory of the individual and elaborated a distinction between explanatory and normative theories. Although his decisive construct of "man's progressive nature" has the wobble of improvisation, the effort to constitute a structured connection between the distinct domains marks an advance in the literature of common sense responses to Hume. Put in the context of his activist conception of constitutions, taken as imperfect syntheses of conflicts, Ferguson's designs are suggestive for a period of philosophical experimentation.

Ferguson as Political Thinker

On a different level of analysis, however, Ferguson's writings are best understood as contributions to political and social orientation, properly challenged on evidence and arguments, but ultimately to be assessed in a practical context, on the responsibility of the person making the judgment, like all ideologies. That is the unpretentious normative frame of reference of the present study. A recent writer has distinguished between two kinds of approaches to the dilemmas posed by Max Weber's separation between scientific understanding and the search for meaning, given that intellectuals responding to the exigencies of political life are likely to seek some overview less paradoxical than Weber's own disillusioned realism. He distinguishes between those who seek formulas to "deproblematize" the issues and those who proceed in full awareness of complexity and tension to "reproblematize" them.[10] Ferguson reads Hume as posing almost the same difficulty as we find that Weber does for later generations, and he offers a model case of a thinker of the latter type. The denial of closure, I suggest, is the mark of responsibility.

As my brief comments suggest, I have found Ferguson a good counselor since I first published the book reproduced below, helpfully responsive to different questions at different times in the intervening years. My understanding of his contributions has naturally benefited from studies done by other scholars since I wrote the dissertation, between 1954 and 1959, as well as from my own subsequent work; but the original text has its own force and integrity—not to speak of a history of reception among specialists—and I could not begin to revise or to update it without writing an altogether new book. Framing it by my more recent reflections, then, I am happy to present my 1965 study in accessible form to a new generation of scholars and readers.

1. Robert D. Cumming to Joseph H. Willits, January 13, 1954. Rockefeller Archive Center: Columbia University, 200S. In his *Human Nature and History* (2 vols., Chicago: University of Chicago Press, 1969), Cumming promised a third volume that would in fact carry through the task that he had prema-

turely entrusted to me; but conditions led him to return instead to his work on Kierkegaard, Husserl, Heidegger, and Sartre in a series of brilliant books.

2. Cumming cited my master's essay, "Plato and the Problem of Social Change," as yielding results "which already seem to me disastrous for Popper." That study was written under the first impressions of reading Lukács and hearing Marcuse, but in fact it anticipated the pluralism of the Ferguson book.

3. This distinction is honored throughout the work by a consistent use of the term "explication," where "explanation" would appear reductionist.

4. The transition from Ferguson to Mannheim is attempted in "Sociology of Knowledge and Moral Philosophy: The Place of Traditional Problems in the Formation of Mannheim's Thought," *Political Science Quarterly* LXXXII (September, 1967), pp. 399-426. The many Mannheim studies are brought together in two recent books: David Kettler and Volker Meja, *Karl Mannheim and the Crisis of Liberalism* (New Brunswick, NJ: Transaction Publishers, 1995) and Colin Loader and David Kettler, *Karl Mannheim's Sociology as Political Education* (New Brunswick, NJ: Transaction Publishers, 2001).

5. "History and Theory in the Scottish Enlightenment," *Journal of Modern History*, 48 (March, 1976), pp. 95-100;

"Linking the Philosophical and Political," *Political Studies*, XXIV (September, 1976), pp. 334-338; "History and Theory in Ferguson's *Essay on the History of Civil Society.* A Reconsideration," *Political Theory*, 5 (November, 1977), pp. 437-460; "Ferguson's *Principles*: Constitution in Permanence," *Studies in Burke and His Time*, 19 (1978), pp. 208-222.

6. Kettler, "History and Theory" [fn. 3].

7. Kettler, "Ferguson's *Principles*" [fn. 3].

8. Istvan Hont and Michael Ignatieff, *Wealth & Virtue* (Cambridge: Cambridge University Press, 1983); D. Allen, *Virtue, Learning and the Scottish Enlightenment* (Edinburgh: the University Press, 1993).

9. George Davie, 'Berkeley, Hume, and the Central Problem of Scottish Philosophy.' in D. F. Norton et al. eds. *McGill Hume Studies* (San Diego: Austin Press, 1976).

10. Reinhard Laube, "*Bildung* as Reproblematization or Deproblematization: Max Weber, Erich von Kahler and Helmuth Plessner" in David Kettler and Gerhard Lauer, eds., *Exile, Science and Bildung: The Contested Legacies of German Emigre Intellectuals* (New York: Palgrave, 2005).

Acknowledgments

For financial assistance I am indebted to the Rockefeller Foundation, the Graduate School of the Ohio State University, and the Henry B. Spencer Fund of the Political Science Department of the Ohio State University.

It is more difficult to acknowledge all those who—in the spirit of intellectual comradeship—gave freely of their time and minds. I must, however, give special thanks to my teachers, Franz L. Neumann, John B. Stewart, and Herbert A. Deane, and to my colleagues and friends, Richard Falk, Myron Hale, Harry Jaffa, David Spitz, Maurice Stein, and Eugene V. Walter. Without their encouragement this study could not have been completed, and without their criticisms the work would have been more imperfect than it is.

D. K.

When the social feelings and reflections of men are committed to writing, a system of learning may arise from the bustle of an active life. Society itself is the school, and its lessons are delivered in the practice of real affairs. An author writes from observations he has made on his subject, not from the suggestion of books; and every production carries the mark of his character as a man, not of his mere proficiency as a student or scholar.

—*Adam Ferguson*

Introduction

ALTHOUGH he is today almost forgotten, Adam Ferguson held a respectable position among the eighteenth-century men of letters who were his contemporaries, and he enjoyed, for a time, great popularity and influence among the literate public. He was known as the professor of moral philosophy at the University of Edinburgh and as the author of a history of Rome, in addition to several books dealing with topics in moral, social, and political philosophy. That his reputation was not merely a provincial one is indicated by the fact that most of his writings were translated into major European languages almost as soon as the books appeared. Although he was never as highly regarded as his two famous Scottish friends, David Hume and Adam Smith, his books were favorably received in Paris and London as well as in Edinburgh; and his opinions were discussed in salons and drawing rooms as well as in class rooms. Yet his reputation suffered an abrupt eclipse at the beginning of the nineteenth century; until today his writings are known only to a few specialists.

Ferguson has been the subject of a book-length treatment, of several shorter monographs, and of chapters in a number of historical studies. In general, authors have considered him from one of three special points of view: sometimes as a minor representative of the common-sense school in ethical philosophy; most often as a pioneer of modern sociology; and, occasionally, as a second-rate conservative constitutionalist political philosopher. Although each of these vantage points reveals an important aspect of Ferguson's work, and although the quality of these studies is, on the whole, good, none of these authors has succeeded in carving out his special subject matter without doing some violence to the integrity of Ferguson's total production.

Two things are remarkable about Ferguson's work: the excitement it generated at the time of its publication among a few significant people, and the recurrent sense of timeliness which presents itself even to a modern reader if he should stumble on the books while in a patiently receptive mood. No existing study prepares one for the great respect accorded to Ferguson's writings by such leading figures as Schiller [1] and John Stuart Mill.[2] Even Marx's high regard for some of Ferguson's writings cannot be explained as simple admiration for the "scientific sociology" they contain.[3] But the most important shortcoming of the partial views is that they underestimate the importance of the issues raised by Ferguson—issues which excited his generation and which continue to concern men today.

A survey of the most striking of these will support this contention. Ferguson welcomed the advent of critical and analytical philosophy as an ally against superstitious credulity and confused obscurantism, but he was afraid that it might also dissolve the certainty of useful knowledge and virtuous judgment into incomprehensible technical complexity and ethical relativism. Although he was attracted by the manifest practical accomplishments of modern science, as well as by its masterful ordering of natural phenomena into a unified theoretical structure, he feared that its adherents would attack the dignity of the human spirit and debase the notion of man to that of a machine at the mercy of mechanical forces. Any study which focuses attention exclusively on the philosophical formulations which Ferguson devised or borrowed in order to balance his hopes and fears will fail to comprehend the passionate concern which drove Ferguson to seek *some* solutions, even if they were not formally correct.[4]

Ferguson thought well of ambition and was pleased by the energy engendered by the modern ethical code of achievement and success, but he also believed that modern man in a frenzy of ambition and frustration might tear at his own self-respect and peace of mind. Commerce he accepted willingly as a creator of unprecedented social well-being; yet he raised the question of whether a commercial society held together by contracts founded on private interest does not destroy the warm personal bonds of fellow-feeling which weld together a genuinely human community. While hailing the high level of technical skill and knowledge made possible by the division of labor on which modern society rests, Ferguson feared that intense specialization would deprive man of that versatility which has been significantly called virtuosity and would deprive mankind of its geniuses, leaders, and heroes. A value-free social science can catalogue the phenomena here discussed if it sees them, but it cannot, by definition, convey an urgent sense of human problems. Yet it is precisely such a sense which animates and distinguishes Ferguson's sociological observations.[5]

In Ferguson's political speculations, the same priority of

questions over answers holds true. He celebrated the security and ordered liberty produced by a constitutional and limited monarchy; but he also deeply regretted that such political institutions deny man the stimulation provided by heated conflict over the common good, and thereby fail to perform the vital pedagogical function of instilling a disinterested and active virtue. Finally, although Ferguson welcomed what he believed to be the elimination of totally destructive wars through humane codes, the newly discovered balance of power, and the distinction between soldier and civilian, he was afraid that the onset of professional and coolly calculating warfare would kill the high-minded spirit of patriotism engendered by the complete self-abandonment of a whole society to life-or-death struggle. The mild and inconsistent amendments which Ferguson offered to traditional constitutionalist theory and his energetic campaigns for military preparedness through a citizen-militia take on importance only in the light of the worries which evoked them. They can hardly be considered contributions to political theory worthy of consideration in their own right.[6]

Ferguson's philosophical writings bear throughout the marks of his eager involvement in society. Although they touch on a number of complex and technical philosophical problems, they do so mainly in order to push them aside. Metaphysics and epistemology, theology and natural philosophy—all of these are subordinated to the principal task: the accumulation of the knowledge he considered requisite for the conduct of a successful, virtuous, and happy life. "The aim is not novelty," he explained in the introduction to his most comprehensive work, "it is benefit to the student." And for Ferguson, success, virtue, and happiness are the concomitant products of a useful life dedicated to practical social activity.

As a teacher of the young, as a popular writer, and as an

intellectual, Ferguson was prepared to accept help from any doctrine which might further his aim, with the result that his writings frequently take on a patchwork appearance, sacrificing depth and consistency for utility. Epictetus and Lucretius, Marcus Aurelius and Machiavelli, Cicero and Locke, Reid and Hume, Aristotle and Bacon, Montesquieu and Hobbes, Shaftesbury and Newton, Rousseau and Grotius—he drew on them all for useful information and edifying principles. Philosophizing was primarily a social act for Ferguson, and as such it was governed by his conception of social responsibility.

It is for this reason that it is particularly important to understand his work in the context of his social position and environment. His philosophical work was an integral part of "what he *was*." In certain respects this can be easily seen. The two major books based on his class lectures explicitly avow their pedagogical function. They discuss all the topics which Ferguson deemed appropriate for the edification of young men about to venture forth on respectable public careers and exclude those which he considered inappropriate to this purpose. Similarly, the didactic style of all the works reveals the uplifter of public morality; the repeated admonitions that the poor ought to suffer their lot cheerfully indicate a desire to preserve public order as well as public virtue and thus manifest his commitment to the social status quo. But Ferguson was more than a pedagogue, edifier, and ideologist; his books are more than text-books, homiletic tracts, and propaganda. Ferguson was also, and above all, an intellectual: his work represents an attempt, characteristic of intellectuals, to develop an orientation towards the world of practice through the medium of ideas.

These considerations, then, suggest that the principles of the unity to be found in Ferguson's writings, as well as the sources of tension within them, are not to be sought in the doctrines of any one or combination of philosophical schools; they are rather derived from the school to which Ferguson pledged his allegiance—the school of society. The lessons communicated to a man in Ferguson's position were complex. His education and exposure to Western cultural traditions taught him to value universality, the life of the mind, and an ideal of man devoted to virtuosity and beneficent virtue; his connections with a bustling commercial society directed him to local pride, the life of practical achievement, and an ideal of man endowed with the special skills requisite for successful pursuit of private interests. On the political plane, he was influenced, not only by the classical model of the polity as a school for virtue, but also by the contemporary valuation of the state as a protector of material interests. The one taught the desirability of active and absorbing engagement in a politics of principle and conflict; the other taught the necessity of a limited political sphere dedicated to the preservation of individual liberty and secure order. Ferguson's search for "edifying" and "useful" ideas was impelled by a desire to reconcile these conflicting tendencies; and the criterion for a satisfactory reconciliation was less the philosophical adequacy of the synthesis than the performance of a complex social role.

Whatever hints of solutions to philosophical problems he may have offered, whatever contributions to sociological theory he may have made—the decisive phenomenon manifested by his writings is the emergence of an intellectual's point of view towards the conditions of modern society. Certainly many of the questions posed by Ferguson have been restated in more profound ways; some of the questions and most of the answers have been eliminated or transformed beyond recognition; and all of the issues are now expressed in harsh, new words. But, however formulated, Ferguson's concerns clearly foreshadow the problems of

over-rationalization, dehumanization, atomization, aliena-
tion, and bureaucratization which have been canvassed
again and again by intellectuals in the twentieth century.

It is a commonplace among sociologists that their discipline derives historically from "moral philosophy," particularly as developed in eighteenth-century Scotland. But this
recognition normally takes the form of a perfunctory obei-
sance before the image of the ancients prior to the celebration of the presumed steady liberation of the discipline from
the normative preoccupations of its founders. Similar tales
of "progress" occur in the standard histories of political
science, economics, and psychology; and the theme arises in
philosophy texts as well. The hunch animating the present
study is that the great figures in all of these disciplines can
best be understood as inheritors of the complex "moral-
philosophical syndrome" exemplified particularly well by
Ferguson. An understanding of Ferguson's strengths and
weaknesses, his concerns and aspirations, should illuminate
what we are ourselves about.

1. Ferguson's influence on Schiller constitutes an important topic in
itself, a topic which can only be suggested here. All commentators are
agreed that Schiller's earliest essays were flavored throughout by his
interest in Ferguson's moral philosophy, to which he had been
introduced (in Christian Garve's translation of the *Institutes of Moral
Philosophy*) by his teacher, Jakob Friedrich Abel. See Richard
Weltrich, *Friedrich Schiller: Geschichte seines Lebens und Charak-
teristik seiner Werke* (Stuttgart: I. G. Cotta'sche Buchhandlung
Nachfolger, 1899), pp. 234–35; Julius Petersen, *Schillers Gespräche*
(Leipzig: Im Insen-Verlag, 1911), p. 24; Oskar Walzel, "Einleitung,"
in *Schillers Samtliche Werke* (Säkular Ausgabe; Stuttgart und Berlin:
I. G. Cotta'sche Buchhandlung Nachfolger, 1910), XI, xv–xvi. In his
youthful writing, Schiller himself pays tribute to Ferguson as one of
"den grössten Weisen dieses Jahrhunderts," and again, "ein Weiser
dieses Jahrhunderts." See *ibid.*, pp. 12, 301; 20, 302.

More interesting for present purposes, if also somewhat more complex, is the nature of Schiller's continued interest in Ferguson's work
after the writing of his early schoolboy essays and dissertation. Some-

what unreliable (because inevitably biased) testimony occurs in Abel's own recollections of Schiller. "Ich kenne einen Mann von ausgezeichnetem Charakter," he wrote, "einst Mitschüler und durch das ganze Leben innigen Freund Schillers, der Uberzeugt ist, dass er die Bildung dem Häufigen Lesen Fergusons vorzüglich schuldig ist." See Petersen, *loc. cit.* But better evidence exists for believing that Schiller continued to rely on Ferguson well into his mature years. In a persuasive and careful study, a German literary critic has argued that *Die Räuber*—and in fact all of Schiller's plays until *Don Carlos*—bears strong marks of Schiller's reliance on Ferguson. See Wolfgang Liepe, "Der Junge Schiller und Rousseau. Eine Nachprüfung der Rousseaulegende um den Räuberdichter," *Zeitschrift für Deutsche Philologie,* LI (1926), 299–328.

For an example of Ferguson's influence on other Germans of his time, see Friedrich Heinrich Jacobi, *Waldemar* in *Werke* (Leipzig: Gerhard Fleischer, 1820), V, 69, 72–73. The intellectual hero of this philosopher's novel is quoted as saying that "Fergusons erste Werk . . . Epoche in seinem Leben gemacht hatte" (*ibid.,* p. 69).

The present author is indebted for information about these German references to Professor William C. Lehmann, whose courtesies to a younger critic exemplify the best traditions of academic scholarship.

2. See the letters to A. Comte, January 28, 1843, and October 5, 1843, in Francis E. Mineka (ed.), *The Earlier Letters of John Stuart Mill 1812–1848* (Toronto: University of Toronto Press, 1963), II, 566, 638.

"John Stuart Mill esteemed Ferguson highly, considering himself in the line of succession of 'this noble philosophic school' of Hume, Smith, and Ferguson, 'the most advanced of the eighteenth century.' " (Letter to A. Comte, February 27, 1843, in Roy Pascal, "Property and Society: The Scottish Historical School of the Eighteenth Century," *Modern Quarterly,* I, No. 2 (1938), 177. Although he has departed considerably from the interpretation and assessment of Ferguson presented in Pascal's article, the present author must acknowledge his general indebtedness to that challenging presentation, which was his first introduction to Ferguson and which stimulated his thought in more ways than he can specifically list. See also Roy Pascal, "Herder and the Scottish Historical School," *Publications of the English Goethe Society,* N.S., XIV (1938–39), 23–49.

3. On numerous occasions Marx approvingly cited Adam Ferguson, particularly in connection with the division of labor problem. For some reason Marx believed that Ferguson had been the teacher of Adam Smith, but, in any case, he repeatedly praised Ferguson's keen perception of the destructive consequences of specialization. See *Capital* (Moscow: Foreign Languages Publishing House, 1954), pp. 123 n., 354, 361–62, 362 n.; *The Poverty of Philosophy* (Moscow: Foreign Languages Publishing House, 1956), p. 145.

4. Cp. Umaji Kaneko, *Moralphilosophie Adam Ferguson's* (sic) (Lucka: Reinhold Berger, 1903).

5. Compare W. C. Lehmann, *Adam Ferguson and the Beginnings of Modern Sociology* (New York: Columbia University Press, 1930); Gladys Bryson, *Man and Society: The Scottish Inquiry of the Eighteenth Century* (Princeton: Princeton University Press, 1945).

See also Herta Helena Jogland, *Ursprünge und Grundlagen der Soziologie bei Adam Ferguson* (Berlin: Duncker & Humblot, 1959). This work, not available during preparation of the present study, presents a useful survey of literature and associates itself with the views put forth by Gladys Bryson.

6. For example, Sir Leslie Stephens, *History of English Thought in the Eighteenth Century* (New York: G. P. Putnam's Sons, 1927), VI, 215; Harold J. Laski, *Political Thought in England from Locke to Bentham* (New York: Holt, 1920), p. 174; John Snell, "The Political Thought of Adam Ferguson," *The Municipal University of Wichita Bulletin*, No. 21 (1950); William A. Dunning, *A History of Political Theories from Rousseau to Spencer* (New York: Macmillan, 1927), pp. 65–71.

PART I

ADAM FERGUSON'S SITUATION

Though words be the signs we have of one another's opinions and intentions; yet, because of the equivocation of them is so frequent according to the diversity of contexture, and of the company wherewith they go (which the presence of him that speaketh, our sight of his actions and conjecture of his intentions, must help to discharge us of): It must be extremely hard to find out the opinions and meanings of those men that are gone from us long ago, and have left us no other signification thereof but their books; which cannot possibly be understood without history enough to discover those aforementioned circumstances, and also without great prudence to observe them.

—*Thomas Hobbes*

CHAPTER I

The Transformation of Scotland

IF IT IS TRUE, as Adam Ferguson maintained, that literary talents "have most vigour when actuated in the mind by the operation of its principal springs, by the emulations, the friendships, and the oppositions, which subsist among a forward and aspiring people,"[1] then it should come as no surprise that his lifetime saw a great upsurge of literary activity in Scotland. The period of the "Scottish Renaissance" in literature, science, and philosophy was also a time of explosive economic change, accompanied by far-reaching changes and tensions in many other aspects of social life. Old habits and beliefs were called into question; changing practices required explanation; and new aspirations demanded new techniques. The eighteenth-century Scottish writers moved in an atmosphere of bustle, among men of affairs; and, with few exceptions, they were deeply interested in the happenings within their society. Disdaining the role of "closet-philosopher," they prided themselves on the practical relevance of their work and hoped to be taken as guides in the process of change. None of its participants doubted that the literary renaissance was an integral part of the "Awakening of Scotland" in the economic and other social spheres.[2]

Although Scotland had long had its merchant-adventurers, their activities had been marginal to Scottish life. Now, in the second half of the eighteenth century, Scotland became a commercial society. The mood of the time was captured by a correspondent in the *Scots Magazine* who wrote, "A spirit of industry and activity has been raised and now pervades every order of men, while schemes of trade and improvement are adopted and put into practice, the undertakers of which would, in former times, have been denominated madmen." [3] In the Highlands as well as in the Lowlands, in agriculture as well as in trade and manufactures, new possibilities for innovation and profit were recognized and exploited.

Well into the eighteenth century, the economic life of the Highlands was dominated by the needs of the clanship system and these were basically military. The land was owned by the chief of the clan and subdivided among his followers so as to recruit and maintain a fighting force.[4] Under this system, then, there was considerable security of tenure for the fighting holders of small plots of land, and Highlands agriculture was primarily an auxiliary of the basically predatory economy. The battle of Culloden and the suppression of the '45 Jacobite uprising marked the end of this system. Large tracts of land belonging to rebels were forfeited to the Crown, whose managers were not at all concerned with the traditions of clanship. The tenants were evicted, and the land was converted to cattle-raising and, somewhat later, to sheep-farming. The remaining Highlands proprietors followed the example.[5] In the attempt to eradicate the military threat of Highlands chiefs, Parliament deprived them of their heritable jurisdictions and reimbursed them for these lost rights. Many of the chiefs used the money thus acquired as capital, investing in stock and improvements. The agricultural economy of the Highlands was almost completely transformed within one man's lifetime: the "Highlands" of romantic folklore had ceased to exist by 1800.

Because Lowlands agriculture had long been liberated from subordination to military adventures, the changes here were not as revolutionary or abrupt. Nevertheless, progress in production and efficiency was rapid and widespread. Early in the eighteenth century, Scottish farms had a reputation for backwardness and poverty; by the end of the century, many Scottish farms were internationally known showplaces, and Scotland sent its agricultural specialists to all parts of Europe as teachers. Under the leadership of landlords interested in progress and profits, commons were enclosed, new crops introduced, and the runrig system of cultivation steadily eliminated. The scattered narrow strips of the tenants were converted into fields suitable either for pasturage or for proper treatment of the soil. The tenant farmers were displaced, converted into agricultural laborers, or, in the case of a few, raised to the status of professional farmer-managers and granted long-term leases.[6] The transformation of agriculture into a profit-making enterprise was accelerated by investments stemming from new commercial wealth.

Scottish commerce had suffered a severe setback from the failure of such speculative enterprises as the Darien scheme in the 1690's, and it was not helped initially by the Union with England. In fact, the free entry of English goods, better and cheaper than the Scottish, hindered recovery for a considerable time. From about 1740 on, however, Scottish trade

expanded greatly, soon surpassing the highest levels reached
in the seventeenth century. The key to this progress was
Glasgow's growing command of the tobacco trade. Thanks
to geographic advantage, excellent financial facilities, low
operating costs, and, perhaps, frauds (as was frequently
alleged by competitors), the Scottish port became the most
important center in Britain for this lucrative trade by 1758
and from 1768 to 1771 imported as much tobacco as all
other British ports combined.[7] Although Glasgow enjoyed a
virtual monopoly of the tobacco trade in Scotland, other
ports also grew in size and importance.[8]

Manufactures, too, were caught in the upsurge. Linen
production increased five-fold between 1728 and 1771 [9] and
many new industries were established. When the tobacco
trade collapsed at the onset of the American Revolution, the
new economy proved its resiliency and the solidity of its
growth. By 1791, total trade had almost regained its 1771
level and, most importantly, the trade had shifted from
tobacco, which had been only unloaded and reloaded for re-
export, to cotton and other raw materials which were
worked into cloth and other manufactured goods within the
country.[10] The awakening of Scotland was first and foremost

an awakening of tremendous economic vitality.

With the economic transformation of Scotland came
changes in established social patterns. Scottish culture had
in many ways been a more unified national culture than had
that of England: in the clan system (which had not been
confined to the Highlands, although it survived longer there
than in the Lowlands) the leader and his followers were
more closely tied than in a formal feudal relationship; the
Wars of Religion in Scotland had been far more national
wars against France, and later against England, than civil
wars; the rigid system of primogeniture and entail combined
with the general poverty of the nation forced the younger

sons of the gentry and nobility to enter into the professions and trades and so into the general population; and the system of almost universal elementary education assured widespread literacy and community of culture. Even the universities eschewed the social exclusiveness of English universities: students were drawn from many strata of the population.[11] The social and economic circumstances under which this spirit of national unity had arisen was now being revolutionized at an extraordinary pace.

While many of the Highlanders displaced by the agricultural revolution emigrated to America, others formed a mass of unskilled laborers uprooted from the means of their livelihood and from the symbols of their self-respect. During the early phases of the economic dislocation, there were even a few sporadic and scattered attempts to resist by force in southwestern counties,[12] but, on the whole, the new situation was accepted. More important in the long run than the original displacements were the gradual effects of the new agriculture on the social life in the villages. From communities of neighbors, more or less equal and independent under the benign and patriarchal eye of the local magnate, they became villages of employers, managers, and laborers. The commercial revolution drew thousands of laborers into towns which were not prepared to accommodate them. The unique Scottish system of education and social welfare, organized by parishes, could not cope with the new demands. As in the English cities, restlessness manifested itself in occasional destructive riots whose intensity and direction often bore little relationship to their ostensible causes.[13] But it was not until the last decade of the century that popular leadership emerged and organized opposition took shape. A certain measure of uneasiness and confusion was the main social symptom of the great changes taking place in Scottish society and of the strain they placed on established institu-

tions: even this was more manifest in the anxiety of the
preservers of order than in any public agitation.[14]

The economic transformation of Scotland, then, affected
the lives and expectations of many groups in Scottish society
but did not involve a fundamental alteration of class and
status relationships. At the end of the eighteenth century as
at its beginning, fewer than eight thousand proprietors
owned all the land in Scotland.[15] Under the leadership of
the great Lowlands families, the Scottish gentry retained
effective control of developments, pioneered in scientific
farming, and actively encouraged the expansion of commerce.[16] Although there was a slight infusion of nabobs and
commercial adventurers into the higher orders and some
genteel withering of recalcitrant Jacobite families, the
power of the traditionally dominant groups was not less-
ened. But the undermining of the traditional sources of
authority, the disappearance of paternalism and *noblesse
oblige,* did lead to an increased reliance on such alternate
instruments of power as politics and control of church
affairs.

To speak of "politics" in eighteenth-century Scotland is to
speak of access to the jobs, force, and favors at the disposal of
the British Crown and the House of Commons. This access
was limited to a small group of prominent landed families
which, at least in the second half of the century, operated
harmoniously under the guidance of some leading figure,
usually the Lord Advocate. Oligopoly was guaranteed by an
electoral system which was an anomaly even by the tolerant
standards of the times. The fifteen burgh representatives in
the House of Commons were chosen by the town council of
Edinburgh and by fourteen other assemblies, each composed
of delegates from four or five "royal burghs." Since the town
councils which thus had a monopoly of elections were self-
elected, and since in many cases the charters of the royal

burghs were only the dim remnants of an importance lost five or six hundred years before, it is not surprising that, as one writer notes, "In practice, the burgh electors . . . were in almost every case the mere tools of some great noble, political manager, or man of wealth." [17] The county franchise, which in England was the most independent, was even more easily controllable in Scotland than the representation of the burghs. The unusually high property qualification, combined with the irresistible opportunities for fraud presented to large landlords by the anachronistic wording of the relevant statutes, created a situation in which there were fewer than three thousand county electors in 1790, of whom about one-half possessed fictitious qualifications created by their masters.[18] In a letter to Christopher Wyvill, leader of the Yorkshire Association, Adam Ferguson neatly summed up the condition of the Scottish county franchise: "Persons having extensive superiorities in this part of the kingdom parcel them out to their retainers and friends in such a manner as to multiply Voters without increasing the number of Votes, the person who confers these qualifications being understood to dispose of these Votes as he pleases." [19] Thus, several hundred men effectively controlled Scottish election returns.[20]

Aside from occasional personal rivalries, no major issues divided this group. The furor and glamor surrounding Jacobitism must not obscure the fact that the Jacobites constituted an isolated and marginal group, and that the men of substance, respectability, and power never wavered in their allegiance to the Glorious Revolution. The Stuart cause was much less a Scottish political issue than it was a last rallying cry for forces irrelevant (except for a brief military foray) to the main current of power in Scottish life. In Scotland as well as in England, the Jacobite army, even while victorious, found itself a stranger in an alien land. Over and above the essentially bogus issue of Jacobitism, the dominant principle of eighteenth-century Scottish politics emerges: virtually undivided loyalty to whatever government was in power at Westminster in exchange for concessions and assistance to the dominant groups in Scotland, prime movers of the transformation of Scotland.[21] Scotland's forty-five members in the House of Commons could be counted on to vote *en bloc* with the government under the direction of a political manager for Scotland, not because of any unusual Scottish venality (as was heatedly asserted by opposition politicians), but because Scottish politics was, for the most part, an instrument of the ruling groups—an instrument for extorting advantages for Scotland from the government of the day and for maintaining domestic control.[22] Elie Halévy has remarked that the system of corrupt franchise and controlled politics "was one of the means which [Scotland] employed for the conquest of England"; he might well have added that it was also one of the means by which the dominance of the leading families was maintained in Scotland in the face of decisive socio-economic changes.[23]

The use of political leverage to further commercial progress in Scotland can be traced throughout the century. The Act of Union itself was jammed through the Scottish parliament largely in the interest of commercial advantage, and Article XV of the treaty allocated considerable sums of money for the encouragement of Scottish industry, particularly the manufacture of linen.[24] Once the Scottish representatives to the House of Commons overcame their original internal division and isolation, they were able to secure numerous laws for internal improvements, elimination of feudal restrictions on agriculture and manufactures, and assistance to Scottish trade.[25] The economic progress of Scotland owed much to the adroit use of political influence, and the security of gentry rule was enhanced by its contributions to Scottish prosperity.

In general, then, the upper orders successfully repaired with the cement of interest any breach that might have been created in their traditional authority. Only when they attempted to compromise the commercial interest (as when some political leaders tried to support the government during the Stamp Act crisis) or when some emotional issue caught the attention of the educated public and the urban mob (as in the Porteous Riots of 1736, the Scottish militia controversy of 1760, and the Catholic Relief Act of 1779) was their authority challenged at all during most of the century, and then the threat was easily averted by minor concession or diverted into harmless channels.

The first serious challenge to the political structure came during the 1780's with the rise of a movement for parliamentary reform in Scotland. As long as the English reform movement had been led by John Wilkes, it had been vehemently anti-Scottish; but after 1780, when Christopher Wyvill and the Yorkshire Association came to play a central part for a while, the English looked hopefully to Scotland—where abuses were severe, the population literate, and political experience in kirk government widespread. And in fact the appeals from Yorkshire found response: in 1782 the movement for burgh reform was supported in numerous Scottish towns, and a meeting for county reform was attended by representatives from twenty-three out of the thirty-three counties. Henry Dundas carried his alliance with Pitt to the point of supporting his moves toward parliamentary reform during 1783, and the Earl of Buchan acted as patron for the Scottish movement. Nevertheless, as the historian of the Yorkshire Association puts it, "Wyvill's hopes of Scotland were sadly disappointed. . . . [The]

burgh and county reformers in Scotland remained aloof
from each other and from the English associators." [26] The
Scottish Convention for Burgh Reform remained active
throughout the decade of the eighties, but it is basically
correct that, during this time, "Scotland . . . caused little
anxiety to the successive 'managers' who controlled its politics in the interest of the English cabinet." [27]

One primary reason for this may well be that, in the
towns, the reform movement overlapped with the antipo-
pery groups composed of "bitterly reactionary clergymen
and tradesmen," and thus frightened away a good deal of
influential, potential support.[28] Merchants and progressive
agriculturists were doubtless disgusted with the dull and
corrupt narrow oligarchies administering local governments
(a primary source of discontent with burgh government),
but they were not prepared to solve this problem at the risk
of undercutting the structure supporting prosperity and progressive change.

Reform had great potential support in Scotland: the potential was so great, in fact, and the consequences of mobiliz-
ing it so unpredictably dangerous, that the respectable pro-
ponents of reform exercised the greatest caution and abandoned reform at the very point when the movement began
to gather momentum. This was in 1789. News of the
French Revolution heartened the reformers, here as in
England, and hitherto unpolitical elements appeared to
show themselves newly aware of their stake in political life.
With the influx of supporters from among weavers and
other artisans and the coincidence of widespread outbreaks
stemming from economic dissatisfaction, the political reform
movement itself took on an ever more radical appearance,
and the authorities encouraged this view of the matter. By
1791, most respectable groups had left the reform move-

ment, and the whole was being portrayed as an offshoot of the French Revolution. This paved the way for a policy of vigorous and effective suppression through patriotic societies and a series of prosecutions. There is no basic difference between the unfolding of events in England and in Scotland, but it should be noted that it was Dundas who had charge of the prosecutions and that it was the Edinburgh prosecutions of 1793 which secured convictions. Established authority was vindicated throughout Britain during the crisis of the French Revolution, but the Scottish developments testify especially well to the efficacy of the political apparatus.[29]

Repression succeeded and reform movements disappeared until after the Napoleonic Wars, but the new structure of authority cemented by interest had revealed fatal cracks. It could only be held together by the baling wire of coercion and unity against an external foe. Yet even in the earlier part of the century, the oligarchy had been drawn to reinforce its position with means other than economic interest and control of politics.

Since the Church of Scotland was one of the most influential forces in Scottish society, it is not surprising that the attempt was made to enlist it on the side of economic progress and political stability. But this was no simple matter. At the beginning of the century, the leaders of the church were stern Calvinists, disdainful of the "luxuries" produced by economic progress and hostile to the intrusion of concern with profit upon the preoccupation with sin. Furthermore, this group enjoyed the enthusiastic support of the populace. In its attempt to displace the orthodox Popular party in the church, the social elite found its natural ally in the so-called Moderate party and its natural weapon in the patronage. The Moderates were cultured, sophisticated, and eager partisans of gentility and progress; the patronage enabled the influential gentry to impose Moderate clergymen on Populist congregations.[30]

The major step in the transformation of the church, then, was the reassertion of patrons' rights. The titles of "patron," with the attendant right to designate ministers, originated in the redistribution of Catholic Church properties at the time of the Reformation and were, for the most part, divided among the Crown, the nobility, and the higher gentry.[31] Despite the antiquity of these titles, however, it had become universal custom since the time of the Covenant to let congregations choose their own ministers. When Parliament in 1712 passed a patronage act reaffirming the rights of patrons, and particularly when after 1730 the patrons began a concerted drive to exercise their rights, there broke out a bitter fight which lasted for most of the century but ended in a total victory for the patrons and their Moderate protégés.

There were many patronage disputes, but the issues between the parties were stated most clearly during the controversy over the stage play, *Douglas,* in 1757. The theater had led a precarious existence in Presbyterian Edinburgh through most of the eighteenth century; but its extralegal existence was not seriously challenged until the performance of this play, written by John Home, minister of Athelstaneford, and attended by several other ministers, notably Alexander Carlyle of Inveresk. Considering themselves directly affronted, the orthodox Populist leaders of the Presbytery of Edinburgh mounted a sharp attack against the theater and against the Moderate divines who had so openly aligned themselves with the forces of sin. However, when charges were placed before the General Assembly, the annual meeting of lay and clerical representatives from the presbyteries of Scotland and the supreme legislative and judicial body of the Church of Scotland, the Populists encountered unexpectedly heavy opposition and had to be satisfied with a token victory.[32] In the debates and in the attendant pamphlet literature, the controversialists repeatedly linked the theater question with the questions of patronage and economic improvement, the one side pouring scorn on the minions of luxurious modern corruption and the other asserting its cultured superiority to the prejudices of the vulgar.[33]

The increasingly Moderate church of the second half-century, then, provided important support for the authority of the dominant groups in Scottish society. Alexander Carlyle, one of the most articulate and charming leaders of the Moderates, claimed as much when, in an appeal for higher wages, he wrote:

> It is observable that no country has ever been more tranquil, except the trifling insurrections of 1715 and '45 [*sic!*], than Scotland has been since the Revolution in 1688 . . . while, at the same time, the country has been prosperous, with an increase of agriculture, trade, and manufactures, as well as all the ornamental arts of life, to a degree unexampled in any age and country. How far the steady loyalty to the crown, and attachment to the constitution, together with the unwearied diligence of the clergy in teaching a rational religion, may have contributed to this prosperity, cannot be ascertained; but surely enough appears to entitle them to the high respect of the State. . . .[34]

Despite these obvious bonds of interest, it would nevertheless be unfair to both parties to view their alliance as a crass marriage of convenience. The Moderate clergymen and the social elite were also drawn together by a common love of science, classical learning, and culture. The liberal preconception—which equates the popular side in any conflict with progress and knowledge and the oligarchic side with reaction and obscurantism—is simply false when applied to eighteenth-century Scotland. At that time many sincere, disinterested, and humane men (and the Moderate party contained many such) saw their choice as one between a return to cultural barbarism and a conscientious support of the social status quo. The objects of the alliance between the Moderate clergy and the aristocratic gentry, therefore, included more than the pursuit of jobs and the maintenance of power. Among both partners were many who eagerly sought to create a truly civilized society, many who undertook to expand the intellectual horizons of Scotland.

1. Adam Ferguson, *An Essay on the History of Civil Society* (2nd ed. [Corrected]; London: A. Millar and T. Cadell, 1768), pp. 272–73.

2. William Law Mathieson applies the title *The Awakening of Scotland* to his history of Scotland from 1747 to 1797 (*The Awakening of Scotland. A History from 1747 to 1797* [Glasgow: James Maclehose and Sons, 1905]). Adam Ferguson lived from 1723 to 1815; Adam Smith, from 1723 to 1791; Henry Home, Lord Kames, from 1696 to 1782; Thomas Reid, from 1710 to 1794; William Robertson, from 1721 to 1793; and David Hume, from 1711 to 1776. Of all the prominent eighteenth-century Scottish writers, only Frances Hutcheson (1694–1746) failed to live the greater part of his adult life during this period of "awakening." See also Agnes Mure Mackenzie, *Scotland in Modern Times* (London: Longmans Green and Co., 1921), p. 37.

3. Quoted by Henry Hamilton, "The Economic Evolution of Scotland in the 18th and 19th Centuries," *Historical Association Leaflet*, No. 91 (1933), p. 36.

4. *Ibid.*, p. 31.

5. Mathieson, *op. cit.*, p. 293.

6. Hamilton, *op. cit.*, p. 37.

7. Jacob M. Price, "The Rise of Glasgow in the Chesapeake Tobacco Trade, 1707–1775," *William and Mary Quarterly*, 3rd Ser., XI, No. 2 (1954), 179–99. See also Hamilton, *op. cit.*, pp. 4–5.

8. The population of Dundee rose from 5,000 in 1746 to 20,000 in 1792; Perth doubled its population from 1750 to 1796; the shore dues from Edinburgh's port of Leith rose from £580 in 1763 to £4000 in

1783 (Mathieson, *op. cit.*, pp. 267, 256). Alexander Fraser Tytler of Woodhouselee in his *Memoirs of the Life and Writings of the Honourable Henry Home of Kames* (3 vols., 2nd ed.; Edinburgh: T. Cadell and W. Davies, 1814) II, 93–94, presents the following indices of Scotland's growth:

	1706	1800
Total revenues:	£160,000	£1,790,000
Income of the post office	1,194	89,817
Excise duties	33,500	833,000
Custom-house duties	34,000	578,000

9. Hamilton, *op. cit.*, p. 6.

10. The following statistics reveal the spurt in imports of raw cotton: in 1775, 137,160 lb.; in 1790, 1,757,504 lb.; and in 1810, 9,962,359 lb. (*ibid.*, p. 146).

11. See especially Laurence James Saunders, "The Parochial Tradition," and "The Academic Tradition," in *Scottish Democracy 1815–1840: The Social and Economic Background* (Edinburgh and London: Oliver and Boyd, 1950), Part IV, chap. I; Part V, chap. I.

12. Mathieson, *op. cit.*, p. 278. For a revealing account of the trend of change in a fictitious Lowlands village, see John Galt, *Annals of the Parish* (Chicago: A. C. McClurg and Co., 1911). Through the diary of a pastor, the author describes the effects of the introduction of scientific farming, coal mining, and, finally, cotton manufacturing between 1760 and 1810.

13. For a description of the Edinburgh riots in 1779 anticipating the London Gordon riots, see Eugene Charlton Black, "The Association: The Growth and Development of Extra-Parliamentary Political Organization from 1779 to 1793" (Unpublished Ph.D. Dissertation, Harvard University, 1958), pp. 113 ff.

14. Lord Bute expressed this uneasiness when, at the time of the Gordon riots in London, he stated his conviction that the riots sought to "establish some wild scheme of democratic government" (Black, *op. cit.*, p. 161).

15. Saunders, *op. cit.*, p. 14.

16. The dominant families in Scotland must not be confused with the kilted Highland chieftains of romantic fable. The Highlanders had been Jacobite, Episcopal (or Roman Catholic), and politically impotent even before they were completely smashed at Culloden. The really important group, the group which had engineered the union with England over widespread Jacobite and popular opposition, was progressive, hard-headed, and deeply immersed in capitalist enterprise, as well as in the Georgian politics of position. See L. B. Namier, *England in the Age of the American Revolution* (London: Macmillan and Co., Ltd., 1929), p. 39; and Tytler, *op. cit.*, ii, p. 84.

17. Holden Furber, *Henry Dundas, First Count Melville, 1742–1811* (London: Oxford University Press, 1931), pp. 187–88. For the Scottish franchise, see Mathieson, *op. cit.*, pp. 19–23; Elie Halévy, *A History of the English People in 1815*, trans. E. I. Watkins and D. A. Barker (New York: Harcourt Brace, 1924), pp. 102 ff.

18. Mathieson, *op. cit.*, pp. 17–18, 20.

19. "Letter from Professor Ferguson to the Rev. C. Wyvill, 2d. December 1782," in Christopher Wyvill, *Political Papers, Chiefly Respecting the Attempt of the County of York and Other Considerable Districts to Effect a Reformation of the Parliament of Great Britain* (London, 1794–1808), IV, 215.

20. Furber, *op. cit.*, p. 188.

21. In avoiding opposition to the government and principled competition among themselves, the Scottish politicians did not differ as markedly from the general practice of eighteenth-century politics as some liberal critics have supposed. See L. B. Namier, *The Structure of Politics at the Accession of George III* (2 vols., London: Macmillan and Co., Ltd., 1940), especially Vol. I, chap. IV. The Scots were unusual only in the consistency with which they adhered to the political maxims of the time, the degree of internal discipline of the parliamentary delegation, and the sizeable rewards they were able to win for their loyalty.

22. In the first half of the century, this system was less clearly established than in the second. The competition between the followers of Argyle and the Squadrone group divided the voice and vote of the Scots and led to some disregard of Scottish interests in the House of Commons. Even then the internal conflict revolved primarily around prestige and places, with the parties frequently switching sides on substantive issues. After 1746, however, such competition virtually ceased, both in Parliament and at home. The parliamentary delegation voted for the government, and the Lord Advocate gained favorable legislation for Scotland in Parliament and ruled the country. See P. Hume Brown, *A History of Scotland* (Cambridge: Cambridge University Press, 1909), III, 199 ff. Mackenzie, in *Scotland in Modern Times*, points to the end of the independence of Scotland's parliamentary contingent and to the rise of good government and favorable legislation under the "benevolent despotism" of individuals like Robert Dundas but does not see the connection between these two developments, believing that the improvement of Scotland's position was due to a "lucky chance" (*ibid.*, pp. 55–56). In a work prepared after completion of the present study, John B. Stewart comes to identical conclusions about the meaning of eighteenth-century Scottish politics in *The Moral and Political Philosophy of David Hume* (New York and London: Columbia University Press, 1963), pp. 2–6.

23. Halévy, *op. cit.*, p. 104.

24. Hamilton, *op. cit.*, p. 78; Mackenzie, *op. cit.*, pp. 4–5.

25. Herbert Butterfield, *George III, Lord North and the People, 1779–80* (London: Bell, 1949), p. 79. See also P. Hume Brown, *op. cit.*, pp. 337–46.

26. Ian R. Christie, *Wilkes, Wyvill and Reform. The Parliamentary Reform Movement in British Politics, 1760–1785.* (London: Macmillan and Co., Ltd.; New York: St. Martin's Press, 1962), pp. 173–74.

27. Philip Anthony Brown, *The French Revolution in English History* (London: Crosby Lockwood and Son, 1918); see also H. W. Meikle, *Scotland and the French Revolution* (Glasgow: James Maclehose and Sons, 1912), pp. 14–31. Eugene Black tends to credit the Scottish movement with rather more vitality during the late eighties than the evidence reveals (Black, *op. cit.* p. 329).

28. Black, *op. cit.*, p. 138. Sir James Grant led the Edinburgh Society for Protestant Interest, whose agitations precipitated the 1779 riots and anticipated the Gordon riot of the following year. Grant was also *praeses* of the 1782 meeting on county franchise reform.

29. Meikle, *op. cit.*, and P. A. Brown, *op. cit.*, best tell the story of the reform movement and prosecutions in Scotland. P. Hume Brown, the liberal historian of Scotland, presents the reformist account, according to which the prosecutions were altogether drummed up as a way of getting rid of moderate reform (*op. cit.*, pp. 378–79). Several contemporaries went so far as to explain the whole war with France as a ruse to justify suppression of reform (see *infra*, pp. 95 f.). It is almost certainly correct that the frame of reference of the earlier reform movement had become irrelevant after 1789 and that Pitt and Dundas followed sound political instinct in seeing the new reformers as mortal enemies of the established system, whether the reformers intended this or not. This assessment doesn't justify the repressions, of course, but it makes them appear less shabby and unworthy than does an interpretation of events guided altogether by a reading of Braxfield's odious charges to the juries. See Meikle, *op. cit.*, p. 134.

30. Henry Gray Graham, *The Social Life of Scotland in the Eighteenth Century* (London: A. and C. Black, Ltd., 1928), pp. 362, 374–75.

31. In 1769 the benefices were divided as follows: The Crown held 334; the nobility, 309; the gentry, 233; the Royal Burghs, 45; the Colleges, 18; and five elsewhere (Mathieson, *op. cit.*, p. 146 n.).

32. Mathieson reports that Home was permitted to resign his charge without censure and that Carlyle was let off with a "decision so favourable to Carlyle that a fanatical opponent could say that he had been dismissed with a playhouse clap" (Mathieson, *op. cit.*, pp. 160 ff.). The following description helps to account for this result: "In the General Assemblies met the men most conspicuous for worth and ability, both lay and clerical; and in the debates, ministers of distinguished talents, and elders who were the most accomplished and brilliant Scotsmen, took their parts. . . . Advocates, eminent at the

bar, like Wedderburn (an elder at 23) and Henry Dundas, lords of session like President Dundas, statesmen like Sir Gilbert Elliot and Lord Marchmont, were members of the Court. The roll of Assembly for 1754 includes amongst its elders nine peers and five lords of session; the rest chiefly consist of baronets, lairds, and advocates of high standing at the bar and in society" (Graham, *op. cit.*, p. 359).

33. In a satirical pamphlet called *Votes of the P——y of E——h*. the anonymous author ascribes the following "resolutions" to the anti-*Douglas* Edinburgh Presbytery:

Resolved, That Improvements of all Sorts are hurtful to Society.

Ordered, That no Alteration be ever attempted to be made of the Principles, the Customs, and the Manners of Men.

Ordered, That the Method of improving Land by inclosing and fallowing be immediately laid aside because . . . it is offensive to the People.

Quoted in Alice Edna Gipson, *John Home. A Study of His Life and Works* (Caldwell, Idaho: Claxton Printers, 1917), p. 109.

Twenty-five years later, the strands were somewhat more twisted. Sir James Grant, leader of the ultra-Protestant "no popery" movement in Edinburgh and *praeses* of the 1782 meeting which brought together delegates from twenty-five of the thirty-three Scottish counties for discussion of franchise reform, combined the following issues: "Large farms—High Rents—Laws of Patronage—Encouragement of French Cambricks—Neglect of the Fisheries" (Black, *op. cit.*, pp. 57, 133 n.). Still, the Populist movement continued to speak for small tradesmen and others hostile to innovation. See also Graham, *op. cit.*, pp. 161–62.

34. Alexander Carlyle, *Autobiography* (Boston: Tichnor and Fields, 1861), p. 408.

CHAPTER II

The Emerging Intelligentsia

MODERATE clergymen were among the main-stays of the "Scottish Enlightenment." Together with lawyers, professors, and one or two individuals who can best be characterized as professional writers, they constituted that circle of intellectuals which Scottish patriots and some others have likened to the Paris *philosophes*.[1] The rhetorician Hugh Blair, the historian William Robertson, and the playwright John Home were active clergymen; Lord Kames and Lord Monboddo, writers on legal and social philosophy, were prominent judges; Adam Smith, Adam Ferguson, and Thomas Reid were professors; and David Hume, although he held various governmental posts throughout his life, was primarily a professional writer. With few exceptions, these men had lowly social origins and owed whatever promi-nence they possessed to their professional and intellectual achievements. Needless to say, they welcomed and received aid from influential patrons; but, as a group, they formed

something approximating the modern intelligentsia, which
depends for its livelihood on professional skills and acceptance by the literate public. Except when visiting London or
when temporarily employed by some nobleman as tutor or
secretary, their most intimate and constant associations were
within the group itself. The Scottish writers of the eighteenth century, then, were allies of the ruling group, not its
servants: [2] they constituted a distinct, self-respecting element in society, no mere assemblage of clients.[3]

The universities were the recruiting grounds for members
of the professional intellectual class. Promising youngsters
of fourteen or fifteen years of age came there from all parts
of Scotland and from all levels of society to receive training
for professional careers. Unlike their English contemporaries, these students were often earnest and poor, working
hard and eating little to earn the certificates which would
enable them to practice at the bar or to enter divinity school.
The emphasis was on class attendance, diligence, and learning, rather than on examinations, brilliance, and scholarship. Because of their youth and the methods of instruction,
the students did not get a profound education, but, at best,
they did get an interest in learning and respect for knowledge. Furthermore, during the eighteenth century, there
grew up student discussion groups whose importance a recent historian assesses as follows:

> [One] of the most important educational agencies devel-
> oped outside the class altogether. In contrast to the conven-
> tional bias of the English universities and to the politically
> controlled European schools, the Scottish students were
> left free to associate and discuss at their pleasure. In the
> numerous student societies which met in the university
> buildings and in which a member of the university faculty
> appeared only as an invited guest, there was something
> more than a practice of good fellowship. The young law-

yers, doctors, and divines met for debate; wits were sharpened on contemporary issues; a less rhetorical style was formed and was expected to support its display of dialectic by an appeal to evidence. . . . [4]

Such organizations as Edinburgh's Select Society grew out of these student groups and in turn contributed greatly to the high period of Edinburgh culture. In the universities, then, the Scots were deeply initiated into the intellectual life.

If the Scottish renaissance produced no profound scholars and very few original thinkers, it did produce a number of learned, well-read men and quite a few capable speculative writers. Many read the great Romans despite the weakness of their classical training; they read the English philosophers—Bacon, Hobbes, Locke, Berkeley, and Shaftesbury; they kept abreast of French developments and knew Voltaire, Rousseau, Holbach, Helvetius, and Montesquieu; they worked on scientific writings, especially those of Newton; a considerable proportion (particularly among the lawyers) studied in Holland for a year or two, and others, too, read Grotius and Pufendorf; and all prided themselves on their good taste as they read Shakespeare and Milton, Racine and Corneille. In short, the Scottish intellectuals remedied the defects of their youthful schooling with a lifetime of serious reading.[5] Moreover, the range of their writing was almost as wide as that of their reading. They ventured into physics and literary criticism, mathematics and drama, philosophy and history: they produced creditable works in all of these fields.

But the characteristic concern was with the science of human nature and moral philosophy, and it was in these areas that the most important work was done. Although Francis Hutcheson was the pioneer, David Hume was the dominant figure. An intimate member of the intellectual circle, he provided the stimulus for their work and the target for their attack. Reid, Kames, Ferguson, and others struggled with him about epistemology, ethics, and social philosophy, in writing and in conversation. He was the lion of the group, and they made lion-hunting their favorite sport.[6] While they never caught him, the hunt was worthwhile—productive of much muscle and a good deal of other game. Hume's work excited and disturbed them so because they believed that he had questioned man's special and superior position in a beneficent universe. That Hume was one of them in every respect except epistemology and that he shared their lives and conventions did not weaken their objections. It was not enough to *be* a specially pleasant person in a specially pleasant time in a specially pleasant world: one had to *know* it for certain. Despite the dedicated optimism of these writers, the very intensity of their affirmations reveals an undercurrent of doubt. They acclaimed John Home as the Scottish Shakespeare, James Macpherson's Ossian as the Scottish Homer, and Thomas Reid as the Scottish Aristotle. But they could not rest until they had silenced the questions they persisted in ascribing to Hume, no matter how frequently he insisted that he too was firmly committed to the life of civilized men in a civilized society. The placidly academic tenor of Scottish moral philosophy cannot disguise the tensions and discomfort which underlay it.[7]

The roots of these tensions can be traced to several sources: Scotland's provincial position vis-à-vis the metropolitan centers of Paris and London; the intellectuals' ambiguous and novel situation in a society which emphasized practical achievement; and the anti-humanistic pressures generated by the very process of socio-economic progress which helped to spur the cultural revival. A consideration of each of these factors in turn will explicate the complex

lessons which the school of Scottish society taught its
scholars.

Although the intellectual life of Edinburgh was certainly
the most lively in eighteenth-century Britain, no one
doubted that London was the metropolis and Edinburgh a
provincial town. The "great life" was lived in the capital,
and Edinburgh had lost that standing at the Union. The
Scottish writers were cosmopolitan figures, with national
and international reputations; but they were also provin-
cials, with gruff manners and outlandish speech. About the
last point the Scots were particularly sensitive, as witnessed
by Hume's incessant preoccupation with Scotticisms and
the eager audience of notables who attended Sherman's
lectures in 1761 on rhetoric and correct speech. Two historians, likening Scotland to America in this respect, have
indicated the importance of the cosmopolitanism-provin-
cialism duality:

> The provincial's view of the world was discontinuous.
> Two forces, two magnets, affected his efforts to find ade-
> quate standards and styles: the values associated with the
> simplicity and purity (real or imagined) of nativism, and
> those to be found in cosmopolitan sophistication. . . .
> The complexity of the provincial's image of the world
> and of himself made demands upon him unlike those felt
> by the equivalent Englishman. It tended to shake the mind
> from the roots of habit and tradition. It led men to the
> interstices of common thought where were found new
> views and new approaches to the old.[8]

Whatever sense of "rootlessness" the ambiguity between
provincialism and cosmopolitanism may have engendered in
the intellectuals was reinforced by the uncertainties attendant upon the role of intellectual as such. The dominant
attitudes of the time, as well as those of the Roman tradition
in which the intellectuals were reared, placed a heavy pre-

mium on effectiveness in achieving practical results. The
writers supported and developed this emphasis. But, except
for the lawyers, all were pretty well cut off from the world
where decisions were made and things done. No matter how
frequently the ministers and teachers persuaded themselves
that their inculcation of morality and science served useful
purposes, they were uneasy and could never intermit such
persuasion. Particularly since the Scottish intellectuals were
not inclined to social reform, they were uncomfortable in
the position into which they had been thrust by their inclinations and experiences. They found it necessary to reject
Hume's playful and aloof conception of at least a part of
philosophy; to insist on the practical implications of that
portion of his work; and to essay a moral philosophy which
would, at once, avoid the deleterious consequences they
ascribed to Hume's work and serve the practical needs of
their society. And always they wished they could act.

The final and most important source of perplexity (and
stimulus to thought) stemmed from the tendency of social
change itself. Perceiving that culture, "refinement," and
civilization could flourish only if the narrow world view of a
backward nation of pious countryfolk were destroyed, the
Scottish writers supported the progress of commerce and,
therefore, the continued domination by a progressive ruling
class. But, increasingly, they feared that progress in profits
might impinge on progress in learning and that the aristocratic patrons of culture might become crass materialists.
Furthermore, they knew that the stable hierarchy which
they were defending precluded the kind of vigorous political
life which, their classical texts taught them, was essential to
a truly civilized society. These fears and this knowledge,
however submerged under cheery optimism, lent urgency to
the search for a science of man and society which would

reveal the unifying and benevolent *logos* underlying the contradictory appearances.

To admit doubt into a situation so loaded with dangerous perplexities could threaten the whole structure of their lives. No wonder the Scottish intellectuals struggled so hard against it—they were at the same time trying to resist the perplexities. The Scottish Renaissance, then, takes place among a "forward and aspiring people" engaged in a basic transformation of their society. It is lent "vigour" by the "friendships" and "oppositions" of that time, partaking of the glories and problems of its friends and experiencing both internal and external "oppositions." [9] But, most importantly, it is the achievement of men increasingly forced to clarify their own positions as intellectuals in a practical world.

1. Mathieson writes: "Moderation was, indeed, the master spirit; for it ever insisted that a creature so variously endowed as man has other faculties to develop than that which is technically termed his soul; and all the divines who distinguished themselves as philosophers and historians belonged, without exception, to this school. If the Church had continued to be ruled on the principles of those who wrote against *Douglas,* there would have been no more toleration for Hume; Robertson, instead of adhering to his motto, *Vita sine Literis Mors,* would have been absorbed in what Shaftesbury called 'the heroic passion of saving souls'; and the General Assembly would never have listened to such a speech as this: 'Who have wrote the best histories, ancient and modern? It has been clergymen of this Church. Who has wrote the clearest delineation of the human understanding and all its powers?—a clergyman of this Church. Who has written the best system of rhetoric and exemplified it by his own creations?—a clergyman of this Church. Who wrote a tragedy that has been deemed perfect?—a clergyman of this Church. Who was the most profound mathematician of the age he lived in?—a clergyman of this Church. Who is his successor in reputation as in office? Who wrote the best treatise on agriculture? Let us not complain of poverty; for it is a splendid poverty indeed! It is *paupertas fecunda virovum!*'" (Mathieson, *op. cit.,* p. 203). It is not necessary to share the enthusiasm of the anonymous orator—or even that of Mathieson—to note that, com-

pared to London and all other European capitals, eighteenth-century Edinburgh stands second only to Paris in intellectual achievement.

2. There were exceptions even to the unanimity of political conservatism. Adam Smith was as notoriously heterodox in his politics as in his religion, and his brilliant pupil, John Millar, Professor of Law at the University of Glasgow, was a radical reformer. See Carlyle, *op. cit.*, pp. 228, 339.

3. In writing to patrons and prospective patrons, of course, the literati frequently adopted a self-deprecating tone. But this manner, born of the conventions of the time and of constant poverty among the intellectuals, does not negate the general sense of independence.

4. Saunders, *op. cit.*, p. 310. Although Saunders' study deals primarily with the early nineteenth century, he presents excellent surveys of the eighteenth-century background.

5. Graham's enthusiastically modernist description of eighteenth-century improvements in the universities suggests that the account given here may give inadequate credit to the classroom: "By the year 1730," he writes, "came signs of a revival of philosophy and science; there was a shaking of the dry bones of mediaevalism. . . . Even before Oxford and Cambridge had awakened from stagnation, from 'port wine and prejudice,' Scottish schools had begun to show intellectual life in spite of their poverty. Antiquated systems died out. The Aristotelianism and the scholasticism of Ramus . . . disappeared, and Bacon, Locke, and even Pufendorf and De Vries, were welcome textmen for the students in their stead" (Graham, *op. cit.*, p. 464). Given the youth of the students and the available evidence from lecture notes, it still seems probable that the main achievement of the universities was to instill intellectualism.

6. While it is true that many of these writers placed their debate with Hume at the very center of their interest, their intellectual disputes never interfered with their personal friendship for him. In a letter to Adam Smith, Adam Ferguson wrote: "I am told that Dr. Beaty [pious author of a vicious attack on Hume], or his party, give out that he has not only refuted but killed D. Hume. I should be very glad of the first, but sorry for the other" (quoted in John Small, "Biographical Sketch of Adam Ferguson, LL.D., F.R.S.E., Professor of Moral Philosophy in the University of Edinburgh," in *Transactions of the Royal Society of Edinburgh*, XXIII, Part III [1864], 614 n.). When, in 1755, a group of Popular clergymen sought to have Hume in effect excommunicated on the grounds that he taught that justice has no absolute foundation, that adultery is lawful although not expedient, that religion is prejudicial to mankind, and that Christianity has no evidence of divine revelation, the Moderate clergymen, led by Hugh Blair, firmly defended him. See Robert Morrell Schmitz, *Hugh Blair* (New York: King's Crown, 1948), pp. 30 ff. Upon Hume's death, Adam Smith wrote a famous encomium, which was published at the time, much to the dismay of the orthodox. Smith wrote, "Upon the

whole, I have always considered him, both in his lifetime and since his death, as approaching as nearly to the idea of a perfectly wise and virtuous man, as perhaps the nature of human frailty will permit" (Letter to William Strahan, quoted in C. R. Fay, *Adam Smith and the Scotland of His Day* [Cambridge: Cambridge University Press, 1956], p. 32).

7. Thomas Reid, the best-known serious contemporary critic of Hume, stated the typical reaction thus: "The little I know of the planetary system; of the earth which we inhabit; of minerals, vegetables, and animals; of my own body, and of the laws which obtain in these parts of nature, opens to my mind grand and beautiful scenes, and contributes equally to my happiness and power. But when I look within, and consider the mind itself, which makes me capable of all these prospects and enjoyments; if it is indeed what the *Treatise of human nature* makes it, I find I have been only in an inchanted castle, imposed upon by spectres and apparitions. I blush inwardly to think how I have been deluded; I am ashamed of my frame, and can hardly forbear expostulating with my destiny; Is this thy pastime, O Nature, to put such tricks upon a silly creature, and then to take off the mask, and shew him how he hath been befooled? If this is the philosophy of human nature, my soul enter thou not into her secrets. It is surely the forbidden tree of knowledge; I no sooner taste of it, than I perceive myself naked and stript of all things, yea even of my very self. I see myself, and the whole frame of nature, shrink into fleeting ideas, which, like Epicurus' atoms, dance about in emptiness" (Thomas Reid, *An Inquiry into the Human Mind on the Principles of Common Sense* [London: A. Millar; Edinburgh: A. Kincaid and J. Bell, 1764], pp. 30–31). Later in the same work Reid wrote: "This opposition betwixt philosophy and common sense, is apt to have a very unhappy influence upon the philosopher himself. He sees human nature in an odd, unamiable, and mortifying light. He considers himself, and the rest of his species, as born under a necessity of believing ten thousand absurdities and contradictions, and endowed with such a pittance of reason, as is sufficient to make this unhappy discovery: and this is all the fruit of his profound speculations. Such notions of human nature tend to slacken every nerve of the soul, to put every noble purpose and sentiment out of countenance, and spread a melancholy gloom over the whole face of things" (*ibid.*, p. 147). See also Tytler, *op. cit.*, I, 282.

8. John Clive and Bernard Bailyn, "England's Cultural Provinces: Scotland and America," *William and Mary Quarterly*, 3rd Ser., IX, No. 2, pp. 212–13.

9. The words in quotation marks are taken from the Ferguson passage quoted on page 15 above.

CHAPTER III

Adam Ferguson: Biography

ON JUNE 20, 1723—one year after the last witch was burned in Scotland and in the same year which witnessed the founding of the "Honourable Society of Improvers in the Knowledge in Scotland"—Adam Ferguson was born in the manse at Logierait, Perthshire. The small village is located fifteen miles from Birnam Wood, at the junction of the rivers Tay and Tummel, in the foothills of the Scottish Highlands. His father, also named Adam, was the local minister and had himself been born, in his own words, "of poor but honest religious parents, at the Bridge end of Bernoch, near Faskelie, in the parish of Moulin, in Athol [about five miles from Logierait], upon the 4th day of August 1672; being the third child of Lawrence Fergusson and Janet Fergusson." "In a year or two after his birth," continues the elder Ferguson's autobiographical sketch, "his parents being, through a dearth then prevailing, unable to pay their rent, did remove to Moulin, where his father's predecessors lived for several generations practicing the smith trade, in very good reputation."[1] The philosopher's father had attended parish schools, apparently learning English only in his last year of school from a highborn schoolmate; and, having failed to secure a bursary at the college in Aberdeen, finally succeeded at St. Andrews through the patronage of a namesake.[2] After a varied career as parish school master, tutor, and minister in a poor parish, Reverend Ferguson was presented to the relatively prosperous parish at Logierait by the Duke of Athole, elder brother of his schoolfriend. He married Mary Gordon, daughter of an Aberdeenshire farmer, who presented him with a large number of children, the last of whom was young Adam. Despite some family connection to the gentry—the Ferguson family owned the small estate of Dunfallandy in Athole and the Gordons claimed a distant relationship to the Duke of Argyll—the boy, therefore, grew up in a setting of respectable, fecund poverty.

To judge from the father's adult remorse over his childhood depravity in profaning the Sabbath with song and play, the manse must have been a place of piety, prayer, and a Calvinism as rigid as was compatible with the Highlands background of the father and the Highlands location of the parish.[3] But the atmosphere in the Ferguson household was also one which encouraged intellectual enterprises. Although the elder Ferguson was himself a man of very limited attainments, he soon recognized his son's abilities and transferred him from the local parish school to the better known grammar school conducted by James Martin at Perth. At this school, which had trained the future Lord Mansfield eighteen years before, the boy distinguished himself in the study of Latin and the writing of essays after classical models. In 1738, at the customary age of fifteen, he won a competitive examination for a bursary and matricu-

lated for the degree of master of arts at his father's college,
St. Andrews. This provincial university had no great reputation at the time, and Ferguson undoubtedly attended rou-
tine classes in moral philosophy, natural philosophy, Latin,
metaphysics, and mathematics taught by undistinguished
clergymen. He also picked up a smattering of Greek, although, like most of his countrymen at the time, he was
never at home with that language. After four years of class
attendance, he was granted the degree of M.A. "with the
reputation," according to his biographer, "of being one of
the best classical scholars, and perhaps the ablest mathematician and metaphysician of his time at the university." [4]

In keeping with his father's wishes, Ferguson enrolled in
Divinity Hall at St. Andrews to prepare himself for the
ministry. But he seems to have become tired of the narrow
horizon of the small town because he shortly undertook to
continue his theological studies at the University of Edinburgh. This important move brought him to the center of an
exciting intellectual atmosphere, and he soon became an
accepted member of the elite student group which included
John Home, William Robertson, Hugh Blair, and Alexander Carlyle. They read and discussed Shaftesbury,
Hutcheson, and Montesquieu; they explored liberal theology; and, together with such older friends as Lord Kames,
formed the Speculative Society for the study of science and
philosophy. Although Ferguson seems to have thrived in
this setting, he eagerly seized an opportunity for adventure
which presented itself when he had completed only two of
the normal six years at the divinity school.

The Athole family had continued its patronage of the
Fergusons; and when in 1745 the twenty-two-year-old Lord
John Murray was appointed colonel of the newly formed
Forty-second ("Black Watch") Regiment, his mother, the
Duchess Dowager of Athole, eager to provide her son

with a companion of his own age who would exercise a wholesome influence, arranged to have Adam Ferguson installed as deputy-chaplain of the regiment. Although he had not been ordained a minister, he accompanied the regiment during the Flanders Campaign of the War of the Austrian Succession. In nineteenth-century Scottish literary folklore, there exist numerous stories describing his courageous conduct at the decisive Battle of Fontenoy. Even discounting some of the more lurid tales of fighting daredeviltry, it is clear that Ferguson acquitted himself well—if also in an appropriate clerical manner—on that occasion and, in general, relished the military life.[5]

The General Assembly, citing Ferguson's knowledge of Gaelic, a skill rare among Presbyterian ministers but essential for the chaplain of a Highlands regiment, and influenced by the appeal made by the powerful House of Athole, granted a special dispensation so that Ferguson could be ordained a minister of the church upon the return of his regiment from Flanders on July 2, 1745.[6]

Ferguson had accordingly just been ordained and promoted to the rank of chaplain of a Highlands regiment of the British Army when Charles Stuart's return to Scotland touched off the '45 Rebellion. Although Ferguson's regiment was carefully kept out of that campaign, Ferguson was, like his father and his friends, anti-Jacobite and sought to make a contribution to the struggle.

During the '15 Jacobite rebellion, the Earl of Mar, then commander of the Stuart forces, came to the village of Logierait. When the Reverend Ferguson asked the Earl, an acquaintance, whether he would be permitted to conduct services, the Jacobite assured him that so long as he prayed for the King there would be no objection. According to the old man's memoirs, the Reverend then insisted that he always prayed for the true king—George II—whereupon

permission to hold service was refused.[7] The elder Ferguson
also figures in a report from Colonel Yorke to his brother,
later Earl of Hardwick. Commenting on the Jacobitism
encountered among the inhabitants of the Highlands after
the '45 Rebellion, Yorke wrote:

> The presbyterian ministers are the only people we can
> trust, and to give you an idea of one small part of the
> country, I mean the county of Athole, the minister one
> Ferguson of Loggerite, told me that if you were to hang
> throughout all that country indiscriminately, you would
> not hang three people wrongfully.[8]

Carlyle tells the story of the participation of the Speculative
Society members in the Edinburgh volunteer brigade which
bravely took up defensive positions outside the city at the
news of Charles' approach and prudently ran without firing
a shot at the sight of Charles' army.[9]

A sermon Ferguson preached to the troops in 1745
brimmed with patriotic fervor and sharp denunciations of
the Stuart pretender, and his patroness had published an
English translation of the Gaelic (Erse) text.[10] All of his life
Ferguson retained a slightly patronizing identification with
his Highlands schoolmates and comrades-in-arms, and he
never lost his command of their language; but he never
shared their enthusiasm for "the good old cause," and did
what he could to secure the loyalties of the Highlands
troops.

Despite his apparent enthusiasm for the martial life, Ferguson applied, after the Peace of Aix-la-Chapelle (1748),
to the Duke of Athole for the prosperous living at Caputh.
His application was rejected, however, and he rejoined his
regiment. He was with them for a year or two in Ireland
and served in the disastrous expedition to Brittany under
General St. Clair, as did David Hume. When in 1754 the

"Black Watch" was ordered to America, Ferguson declined to accompany them and resigned his commission, thus concluding his nine-year military career.

He brought his clerical career to a close in the same year. The reasons for this step are obscure. When he left his Edinburgh friends for a vacation in Holland, they had, apparently, no intimation of his intentions: the first news came in letters he wrote to his friends, urging them to address the reply "without any clerical titles, for I am a downright layman." [11] His biographer speculates that Ferguson abandoned the ministry because he was disgusted with his patron's failure to provide him a parish and particularly with the Duke's unwillingness to present him to the church at Logierait when the elder Ferguson died in 1754.[12] Although there is nothing inherently improbable in this speculation, the evidence suggests a deeper reason. Ferguson's departure from St. Andrews, his failure to complete his theological studies, and his failure to apply actively for his father's post argue that the prospect of a life as a country preacher never really appealed to him. Perhaps the death of his father liberated him from the obligation to pursue such a career and gave him leave to try his fortune as a man of letters in Edinburgh.

Ferguson's application for the Caputh parish and his famous temper do support the view that he ended his clerical career in a fit of anger at his patron's disregard. The anonymous reviewer of Small's biography explains the refusal to apply for the Logierait living by saying that Ferguson felt that the position should be offered to him as a matter of course and that he was "too proud" to ask for it when no such invitation was presented.[13]

Yet Ferguson's correspondence is filled with requests for favors, occasionally phrased in almost abject terms. Like his contemporaries, he knew how to play the game of favor-seeking which was necessary for a decent life, if not for survival. They accepted this necessity as a matter of course and never felt that they were demeaning themselves when they sought a position or gift from those who commanded them. This consideration makes it unlikely that Ferguson would abandon a chosen and valued career out of pique or pride. As his subsequent success indicates, he had established contact with men of influence other than Athole, and a determined search would certainly have uncovered some other clerical appointment.

Small maintains that the Duke of Athole refused to exercise his patronage rights in Ferguson's behalf because Ferguson's sermons tended to bristle so with classical allusions and philosophical niceties that the plain country people could not understand anything.[14] Although it seems strange that Ferguson would have been retained as a military chaplain if he was quite so abstruse, it is possible that the Duke hesitated to give too egregious an affront to the Popular congregations who despised the Moderate clergymen as irreligious moralizers, and that this consideration would not enter with regard to the Highlands soldiers who, in all likelihood, were really Episcopalians or Catholics anyway. But if Ferguson sinned in this respect to an extent remarkable even among his Moderate colleagues, it would tend to confirm the argument presented here—that Ferguson left the clergy with a sigh of relief rather than with a groan of angry despair.

The question of Ferguson's motives in departing the ministry is canvassed here at some length for two reasons. In the first place, the question relates to—although it could under no condition decide—the issue of Ferguson's adherence to Christianity in any but the most formal sense, an issue which will be discussed below.[15] Secondly, the interpretation here offered supports the assertion that Ferguson experienced strong internal conflict between a desire for practical usefulness (and the dutiful country minister—acting as spiritual guide, social agency, auxiliary policeman, and even sometimes schoolmaster—did lead a busy and practical life) and a desire for a life of the intellect. Although Ferguson may have decided in favor of the latter option at this time (and, by the way, in his resignation from the military as well), the conflict recurred throughout his life.

Whatever considerations may have entered into Ferguson's decision to return to Edinburgh as a "downright layman," assurance of financial security was certainly not among them. The five years between 1754 and 1759 were filled with an assortment of unpleasant makeshifts and unsuccessful schemes to solve his financial problems. He had no source of income at all until David Hume vacated the position of keeper of the Advocates' Library and clerk to the faculty; and when in January of 1757, with the help of influential friends, he succeeded Hume in this position, he earned a salary of forty pounds per annum, a pitiful sum for even those frugal times.[16] A short time after this inadequate stroke of fortune, a significantly better opportunity presented itself—a position as tutor to the sons of Lord Bute, the future prime minister and the friend of the Prince of Wales. Although this position was more remunerative and Ferguson's acquaintance with Bute opened other possibilities, his abrupt departure from the Advocates' Library aroused some hostility and was, in general, a slightly distasteful affair. Furthermore, as a tutor he enjoyed little status, security, or leisure.

His friends, therefore, led as usual by David Hume as projector and chief tactician, launched an involved scheme in 1758 to gain him an academic appointment. Counting on the good offices of Lord Milton, Andrew Fletcher of Saltoun, who was at that time the political "doer" for Archibald, Duke of Argyll, and therefore the most powerful person in Scotland, they planned to bring Adam Smith to the University of Edinburgh to occupy the sinecure chair of the Law of Nature and Nations and to locate Ferguson in the post of professor of moral philosophy at the University of Glasgow thus vacated by Smith. Hume's proposed tactic was to have Lord Milton induce the Edinburgh Town Council, the governing body of the university, to press the incumbent (a Mr. Abercromby) to present regular lectures (which, Hume knew, he would not and could not do) or to turn the position over to Adam Smith (who would, of course, pay him the £800 which the position cost). Hume tried very hard to persuade Smith to agree to the proposal, assuring him that his income from public subscription lectures in Edinburgh would far outweigh the investment and the loss of the Glasgow salary, that his Edinburgh friends were very eager to see him there, and—lest Smith hesitate to expose himself in such a vulnerable position to attacks from the orthodox clergy—that "Lord Milton can with his finger stop the foul mouths of all the roarers against heresy." [17] Nevertheless, the Glasgow professor refused to jeopardize his pleasant and secure position, and Hume attempted, despite little hope for success, to secure the Edinburgh professorship for Ferguson. In any event, the whole enterprise foundered when Abercromby—resisting persuasion, pressure, and even the threat of a lawsuit—insisted on a £200 profit of his investment, and the Ferguson advocates refused to pay the £1000. Ferguson had to wait until the following year for an academic appointment.

When, in 1759, the Edinburgh Town Council finally elected Ferguson to a professorial chair, it was in so unlikely a subject that even the sophisticated Edinburghers, accustomed to every sort of jobbery, were astounded. Ferguson was designated professor of natural philosophy. A commentator well described Ferguson's relationship to the material he was now called upon to teach when he wrote: "The subject was one which he had never studied since he left college, for which he had neither special taste nor special aptitude, and of which he must literally have known nothing." [18] Despite these obvious disqualifications and although there was available at least one obviously qualified candidate, somehow Ferguson's friends and patrons persuaded, bribed, or duped the Town Council into making the appointment. Everyone, including those who had sponsored him, was even more surprised when Ferguson prepared adequate lecture notes in the three months between July 4 and October 1 and embarked on a successful five-year tenure as a popular teacher of natural science. However lacking in depth his treatment may have been, and the schoolboys who received their first introduction to the subject in his classes could not have been very critical or demanding, Ferguson's achievement ranks as a genuine *tour de force* and was acclaimed such by his contemporaries.

Even Hume, who was always ebulliently optimistic in assessing the prospects of his friends, doubted whether Ferguson would get the appointment. In a letter to William Robertson, he expressed his misgivings and cited the superior qualifications of Ferguson's competitor (and, incidentally, relative), Mr. Russel; but, characteristically, he hoped for Ferguson's success "because of his need." [19] Faced by Ferguson's triumph over competitor, town council, and subject matter, he eagerly bestowed the laurel wreath—although he may have set it on Ferguson's head just a little crookedly. Carlyle reports that "David Hume said Ferguson had more genius than any of them, as he made himself so much master of a difficult science—viz., Natural Philosophy, which he had never studied but when at college—in three months, so as to be able to teach it." [20]

Hume was so much impressed with Ferguson's newly

acquired specialty that he was a little wary when Ferguson
finally had an opportunity to return to his first and major
love, moral philosophy. Hume wrote to Hugh Blair, "Between ourselves, I know not whether I ought to rejoice at
Ferguson's getting the class of moral philosophy: He succeeded perfectly in his former Department. . . ." [21] This
comment lends itself to at least two interpretations: either
Hume doubted Ferguson's intellectual ability and meant to
say, in effect, that Ferguson was lucky once and might not
be so lucky again; or he might have meant that Ferguson
had done so well in the difficult and important subject of
natural philosophy that he should have continued working
in that area. The available evidence points to the second
interpretation. Although Hume was, at a later time, to criticize Ferguson's work in moral philosophy quite sharply, he
had been enthusiastic about the only one of Ferguson's
productions in this field which he had seen at the time of the
letter. In 1759, he discussed with friends to whom he could
speak frankly—Adam Smith and William Robertson—a
short essay entitled "A Treatise on Refinement" which Ferguson had sent him. To Robertson he wrote, "Ferguson's
book has a great deal of genius and fine writing, and will
appear in time"; and his letter to Smith spoke even more
firmly: "Ferguson," Hume wrote, "has very much polished
and improved his Treatise on Refinement; and with some
amendments it will make an admirable book, and discovers
an elegant and singular genius." [22] There is, therefore, no
reason to suppose that Hume's reluctance to see Ferguson
give up natural philosophy implies anything other than his
regard for that field and his respect for Ferguson's endeavors
in it. But since Hume was in many ways a very simple and
warm person, it is equally possible that none of the above
interpretations is relevant and that he was only concerned to
spare Ferguson strain and trouble attendant on preparing a

new course. This is a perfectly acceptable reading of the following excerpt from a letter to Ferguson, particularly if the last two sentences are considered together and the whole is taken to be only mildly sarcastic:

> I am glad of the change of your class [from natural to moral philosophy] because you desir'd it, and because it fitted Russel. For otherwise I shou'd have lik'd better the other Science. The News of your great success in teaching has reach'd me in Paris and has given me Pleasure; but I fear for your health, from all these sudden & violent applications.[23]

Although written much later in his life, Ferguson's essay on the life of his relative, Joseph Black, the noted chemist, doubtless reflects his general approach to physical science. The central concern is with the moral implications of "the system of nature." Accordingly, Ferguson concludes his description of Black's work on heat with the observation: "It is no doubt a mighty increment in science, to have found such powerful substances operating . . . without gravitation, inertia, or impenetrability, *the great bases and columns of the mechanical philosophy.*"[24] He also disclaimed expertise, at least with regard to chemistry.[25] Nevertheless, it would be an error to confuse Ferguson's attitude towards physical scientists with disrespect or disregard for their concerns and disciplines. Fear of materialism (which for Ferguson, as for many of his contemporaries, takes the form of hoping for the irreducibility of familiar substances) combines with respect for the work of physical scientists in the following wistful comment: *"If in science there might be any choice of truths,* I would willingly hope that the decomposition of water might be found a mistake."[26]

Ferguson never became a physical scientist, but there were no "two cultures" in eighteenth-century Edinburgh. In

fact, Ferguson was very close to both Black and James
Hutton, the geologist. Unfortunately, the precise extent of
mutual influence must remain a matter for speculation. The
question is given particular piquancy by several considerations. Black's father, a wine merchant in Bordeaux, was an
intimate friend of Montesquieu; Ferguson and Black were
cousins; and the two of them lived in the house of their
relative, James Russel, after Ferguson's return to Edinburgh.[27] While Ferguson was teaching natural philosophy
and preparing his essays on moral philosophy, then, he
remained in constant and intimate communication with
men who stood at the very center of investigations into
questions of natural science. During these years, Hutton
developed his theory of the earth, stressing the continuity of
physical development; and when Ferguson, at the end of his
career, accepted a nominal appointment as professor of
mathematics at the university, he hired as his assistant James
Playfair, who was Hutton's most important disciple.[28] Many
other connecting links can be cited, but nothing can reveal
exactly what was said in the course of the long, innumerable
conversations among these men.[29] There can be no doubt,
however, that Ferguson shared with these friends the "uncommon activity and ardour of mind, upheld by the greatest
admiration of whatever in science was new, beautiful, or
sublime." [30]

But Ferguson never abandoned his basic commitment to
moral philosophy. There is no evidence that he himself ever
undertook any research in physical science or planned any
publications concerning this subject during the five years he
taught it. On the other hand, there is much evidence that
Ferguson continued to work on problems of moral and
political philosophy and that his planned writings dealt with
this area. Accordingly, it is not surprising that, when the
professor of pneumatics and moral philosophy, James Bal-

four, won an appointment to the chair of the law of nature, Ferguson sued for the vacated position. With his election to this professorship in 1764, Ferguson attained the goal which he had undoubtedly sought during the ten years since his return to Edinburgh and which may even have lured him back there in the first place.

During those ten years Ferguson had become one of the prominent intellectual leaders of the community, had established a number of significant friendships with a number of important men, and had participated with his cronies in the controversies and enthusiasms of his time. When he returned to Edinburgh in 1754, he found his former Speculative Society friends risen in their professions as ministers and lawyers and joined together with other men of note and promise in the Select Club. As an old friend of many of the members, he was soon accepted into that company of Hume, Robertson, Kames, Smith, Monboddo, and Home (as well as a considerable number of influential gentlemen) and began to take an active part in their debates and discussions.

As a professor, he met and befriended a number of students who later became his most influential friends: foremost among these was John Macpherson, the son of a poor Highlands minister. Ferguson brought him into his house, hired him as a tutor for wealthier students, and, in general, took the boy under his charge. When, in later years, Macpherson succeeded Warren Hastings, as governor-general of India, he was able to repay his teacher in many ways—with friendship, influence, and even outright gifts of money.[31] Ferguson's professional activities also introduced him to the sons of noble families, long arrived at positions of eminence. Even his work as a tutor had been productive in this respect: he was known throughout Scotland as "Bute's Ferguson." Since it was customary at that time for professors to supplement their income by accepting wealthy boys as boarders, Ferguson sought such assignments and frequently, as in 1763 when he took charge of the sons of the Earl of Warwick, exercised the mixed functions of guardian and servant of the scions of the nobility. Ferguson experienced directly the ambiguous mixture of privileges and limits which characterized the relationships between the Scottish intellectuals and their social superiors.

His easiest and happiest times, therefore, were spent in the company of his cronies. Many of them were Select Club members too, and a number occupied quite important positions in the church, on the bench, and in the university; but no one was so high in rank that he could threaten or promise to patronize the others. It was in this company that Ferguson and the others enjoyed their robust meals, accompanied by much alcohol, practical jokes, and lusty squabbles; it was here they planned strategies for professional schemes and pamphlets for their favorite causes—like the *Douglas* dispute, the militia controversies, the General Assembly fight about Hume and Kames, and the national defense against English slurs upon the authenticity of Ossian; and it was here that they sometimes seriously discussed the new books from France, Reid's attack on Hume, Kames's theory of literary taste, and anything else that they could reach. Ferguson was deeply involved in all these things and became one of the mainstays of the group. He ate and drank and joked and fought with the best of them; he shared in scheming and planning, wrote a pamphlet in behalf of *Douglas* and a pamphlet at each stage of the militia fight; he took the lead—as the Gaelic expert of the group—in supporting James Macpherson against mounting skepticism about the genuineness of his "translations"; and, finally, he was perhaps the best-read member of the group and always prepared to examine serious topics.[32] By 1762, the Select Club had disbanded, and the clique of cronies decided to organize a new club around the theme of their preoccupation with the English refusal to let the Scots have their own militia. Ferguson proposed that the club be called "The Poker," and so it became. The "literati of Edinburgh and its neighborhood" lived a decisive part of their lives around the Poker Club and its informal antecedents and extensions.[33]

Outside of the inner circle, Ferguson's greatest success came during his years as professor of pneumatics and moral philosophy at the University of Edinburgh. Students flocked to his classes; prominent men attended his lectures; and the leaders of politics and "society" in London as well as in Edinburgh praised his writings. For a time he became the most approved philosopher of the age—a sort of "court philosopher" to the establishment. This status was not achieved through prominent connections or popular lectures alone: it rested on his published writings. Apart from the pamphlets and two brief course outlines for the use of his students, Ferguson's first book was *An Essay on the History of Civil Society,* published in 1766. An expanded version of a ten-year-old unpublished "Treatise on Refinement," the book sought to explain, through a comparative treatment, the character of a "polished society" as distinct from the "savage" and "rude" stages of social development. In addition, the book directed attention to the steps necessary to preserve "national felicity" under advanced conditions and to the dangers of "decline." Despite mixed critical notices, the book was enthusiastically received by the Edinburgh and London *haut monde.*

Learned opinion was divided. From Baron d'Holbach came friendly words of praise; and the Edinburgh circle, filled in any case with loyal admiration for their friend, acclaimed the work as a masterpiece of literature and philosophy.[34] The only dissenter among them was David Hume, but although his was the judgment they most respected and feared, he could not dampen their enthusiasm for Ferguson's essay.[35] Hume's dislike for the piece was strong, lasting, and unequivocal. In a letter to Hugh Blair, he attempted to forestall publication of the manuscript, writing:

> I have perus'd Ferguson's Papers more than once, which had been put into my hands, some time ago, at his desire. I sat down to read them with great Prepossession, founded on my good Opinion of him, on a Small Specimen I had seen of them some Years ago, and on yours & Dr Robertson's Esteem of them: But I am sorry to say it, they have no-wise [sic] answer'd my expectations. I do not think them fit to be given to the Public, neither on account of the Style nor the Reasoning; the Form nor the Matter.[36]

This opinion, based on an examination of sections selected by the author, was not changed by the passage of time, a reading of the whole book, or the widespread success of the publication: Hume wrote to the same correspondent a year later:

> The success of the Book, Dear Dr, which you mention, gives me great Satisfaction, on account of my sincere Friendship for the Author; and so much the rather, as this success was to me unexpected. I have since begun to hope, and even to believe, that I was mistaken; and in this Perswasion [sic] have several times taken it up and read Chapters of it: But to my great Mortification and Sorrow, I have not been able to change my Sentiments.[37]

Hume concluded his original letter of disapproval by saying, "It is needless to enter into a Detail, where almost everything appears to be objectionable." [38]

Hume thus left no statement detailing his objections to the work, and the omission has given rise to numerous speculations about them ever since. One commentator has

believed that Hume's antipathy stemmed from an "insistence upon the inevitability of progress, upon the principle
of perfection" allegedly found in the essay; [39] another has
seen the cause in Ferguson's reliance on Montesquieu, a
writer whose works Hume allegedly saw doomed to merited
oblivion.[40] Neither of these explanations seems altogether
convincing. Although Ferguson was mildly optimistic in the
Essay on the History of Civil Society, the fear of tyranny
and decay which runs through the book precludes any "insistence upon the inevitability of progress." As for the "principle of perfection," it is, in the first place, not synonymous
with a principle of inevitable progress; and it was, in the
second place, expressly developed by Ferguson only in his
later writings. Furthermore, Hume was not in the habit of
denying the merit of books to the extent of counseling
against their publication simply because he disagreed with
their authors' principles.[41] This last objection also holds
against the speculation based on Ferguson's affinity to Montesquieu, except insofar as Hume's prepublication advice
rested on concern for the market success of the book.
Despite serious reservations about *L'Esprit des Lois,* Hume
respected Montesquieu's work.[42] However uncomfortable
some of Ferguson's ideas may have made Hume (and the
important differences between them will be examined in a
later chapter), this feeling cannot account for Hume's reaction to the book. His objections must have rested first, and
probably foremost, on defects which Hume believed he
found in Ferguson's style; and, second, although this speculation cannot be supported by documents, in Ferguson's
evasive imprecision when confronted with problems which
Hume considered vitally important. As a self-consciously
professional writer, Hume placed very heavy emphasis on
purity of diction and polish of style. His belief that Ferguson's book was deficient in both of these respects would have

provided sufficient reason for him to counsel against publication, particularly because he believed Ferguson's faults to be
characteristically provincial (and Scottish) and because he
was so patriotically eager to protect the good name of Scottish letters.[43] When to this powerful motive is added his
probable disdain for what he must have considered Ferguson's vagueness and uncritical reliance on moralizing
truisms, then an explanation emerges which is both adequate to the facts and consistent with Hume's known character.[44]

But Hume's professional judgment against Ferguson's
book in no way restrained the pleasure with which he
reported its successful reception in the London salons. In a
series of letters written in the spring of 1767, he traced its
triumphant progress: from Lord Mansfield's initial approval, through the enthusiastic acclaim of Lords Shelton,
Chesterfield, Lyttleton, and Bute, to the culminating judgment of the Archbishop of York, who said "that in many
things it surpasses Montesquieu." [45] Ferguson also received
more material indications of his success: a second edition
was published in 1767, and by 1814 the book had gone
through nine English editions and reprintings; a German
translation was published in Leipzig in 1768; and a French
one in Paris in 1793.[46]

In every way, the year 1766 was an auspicious one in his
career. Not only did it mark the beginning of his literary
prominence, but it also saw his marriage to Katherine Bur-
net (a niece of his relative and close friend Joseph Black),
the highly complimentary news that he was being considered for the governorship of West Florida, and the award
of an honorary LL.D. degree from the University of Edinburgh.

Although Ferguson enjoyed considerable recognition for
the remainder of his life, he never again aroused such a

flurry of favorable notice as he did with his first literary production: his future prizes and advancements were such as normally appertained to the position he had gained. In 1768, he published the *Institutes of Moral Philosophy,* an expanded summary of his lecture notes. The book was a fairly standard compilation of the doctrines then prominent in Scottish universities. In it Ferguson referred his students to Bacon's *Novum Organum* as the authority on "knowledge in general"; to Buffon's *Natural History* on the physical characteristics of man; to Wallace's *Numbers of Mankind* and Hume's *Populousness of Ancient Nations* on population; to Harris' *On Coins* on arts and commerce; to Montesquieu's *L'Esprit des Lois* on political institutions; to Reid's *Inquiry into the Human Mind* on the functions of language and perception; to Shaftesbury's *Inquiry into Virtue* on the origin of moral approbation; to Smith's *Theory of Moral Sentiments* on the harmony between self-preservation and morality; to Hutcheson's *Of the Ideas of Beauty and Virtue* on the objectivity of aesthetic standards; and— with his characteristic preference for classical models— to the writings of Epictetus and Marcus Aurelius on the harmony between true virtue and true happiness and to Cicero's *De Officiis* on virtue in external actions. Intended primarily as a guide to his students, the book contained none of the attempts at eloquence or originality which had distinguished his first work, and, therefore, it aroused relatively little interest in the circles which had acclaimed the essay. Nevertheless, it enjoyed a considerable vogue in schools in many parts of the world. The *Institutes of Moral Philosophy* went through four Edinburgh editions, including an enlarged revision in 1785; it was translated into French and Russian; and, in 1772, it was published in German, with a long critical appreciation by Christian Garve.[47] With this book, then, Ferguson established an international academic reputation as an earnest and substantial pedagogue, if not as a brilliant or original thinker.

In 1773, the guardians of young Charles, the Earl of Chesterfield, offered Ferguson an opportunity which promised to let him collect the rewards of this reputation throughout Europe and to strengthen his always precarious financial position and which, in the event, threatened to wreck his academic career at Edinburgh. They proposed to him, on the recommendation of Adam Smith, that he accompany the Earl as tutor and companion on an extended trip through Europe at a stipend of £400 per annum during the Earl's minority and a pension of £200 per annum for life. Finding the offer irresistibly attractive, Ferguson applied to the Edinburgh Town Council for permission to hire a substitute to teach his class during his absence. The council—perhaps because it was loath to lose such a popular teacher, perhaps because it was determined to assert its authority against the whole tribe of professors which treated it with such cavalier disregard, but most likely because it contained members "who aim[ed] at filling the vacancy with a Friend," as Hume put it—denied Ferguson's request and warned him that he would be dismissed if he left without permission.[48] Ferguson submitted to their decision insofar as he agreed to complete the 1773–74 school term, but he defiantly persisted in his decision to absent himself for the following year.

Upon his departure in the following autumn, the council undertook to make good its threat: in an official vote it declared that the position of professor of moral philosophy had been vacated. With Ferguson away on the Continent, the remaining members of the Poker Club swung into the fight for his reinstatement. They pleaded Ferguson's virtues, they cited long and not dishonorable precedent, and they mobilized influential friends in his behalf. Although the struggle lasted for a whole year, their power—if not their arguments—finally proved too strong for their opponents, who were divided among themselves over contesting candidates for the position, and the council rescinded its resolution, thereby reinstating Ferguson.

Either because his escape from dismissal had been so narrow or because his duties with the Earl had become wearying, Ferguson unexpectedly returned to Edinburgh in time for the following school year. He had lived for a time in London; his European tour had taken him through France, Germany, Switzerland, and Italy; and, although there exists evidence only of his visit to Voltaire,[49] he had undoubtedly met other literary men. But, like Hume and Smith before him, he had resisted the lures of London and Paris to return to provincial Edinburgh. In fact, he had spent a good part of his time in Europe anxiously urging his friends to secure his return to Edinburgh, and he had departed from London so abruptly that he had jeopardized the promised pension from Chesterfield. Although his eagerness can be accounted for, partially, by a prudent reluctance to risk the fortunes of himself and his now growing family in novel surroundings, there remains a balance of feeling which must be ascribed to the provincial's distrust of the "great world," despite its brilliant attractions.

Nevertheless, he seized another opportunity to expand the range of his activities beyond the narrow horizons of professorial Edinburgh. Of the pamphlet literature called forth in London by the outbreak of the Revolutionary War, one of the earliest influential works favoring the American cause was that written by Dr. Richard Price, a well-known English reformer and publicist; Ferguson undertook to write a reply.[50] Whether on commission or on his own volition, he dispatched to Grey Cooper, one of the secretaries of the Treasury (whom Ferguson did not know), a long letter in

which he granted Price's contention that Parliament had
pursued a faulty colonial policy but in which he heatedly
denied the right of the colonies to gain a redress of grievances through coercion. This argument—more moderate
than the offensive strictures laid down by some of Price's
other opponents and therefore more likely to appeal to the
uneasy but law-abiding English merchants—was welcomed
by the government, and Ferguson's message was published
as a pamphlet at government expense.[51] Later in the war, the
government manifested its gratitude for his services by appointing him secretary to the Carlisle Commission, sent to
negotiate with the American colonists.[52] He easily secured
permission to leave the university for this mission, departed
from Edinburgh in the spring of 1778, and, after some delay
in London, arrived at the Delaware River in June of that
year. The mission was a total failure, and Ferguson's role
thoroughly unspectacular. The commissioners quarreled
among themselves; they offended the government at home
by relaying to England the protests of Philadelphia loyalists
against Howe's order to evacuate the city; and they were
unable to enter into any negotiations at all with the Continental Congress, which would only treat with them on a
sovereign basis. When, as a last resort, the commissioners
sent Ferguson under a flag of truce to try to deal directly
with Washington, the American commander, asserting the
authority of Congress, refused even to grant him a passport
through the American lines. Ferguson's letters from America strike a note of disillusionment and are largely given over
to querulous inquiries into the emoluments to be granted
him.[53]

One year after he had left, Ferguson returned to his
teaching duties at the university, but he was soon prevented
from resuming his accustomed mode of life. In the fall of
1780, at the age of fifty-seven, he suffered a nearly fatal

paralytic stroke. He was treated by Dr. Black, who prescribed unusual dietetic therapy in this case, and he recov-
ered his health. Contemporaries were astounded at his recovery and, ascribing it to Black's treatment, hailed the
doctor as a medical genius. Ferguson apparently shared their
astonishment and judgment, since he remained on a sparse
vegetable diet for the rest of his life.[54] Although he restricted
his convivial activities, he continued his pedagogical and
scholarly careers; and, in 1783, he brought out a multivol-
umed *History of the Progress and Termination of the
Roman Republic,* the book which retained its reputation
longer than any of his others and which one Victorian critic
called "his principal work." [55] Written on the model of
Tacitus and relying heavily on standard classical sources as
well as Montesquieu, the study encompasses the period
between the beginning of the First Punic War and the end
of Augustus' reign. Despite long moralizing excursions into
the motives of Pompey, Caesar, and Augustus, Ferguson
pioneered in critical historiography when he refused to consider Livy's tales about the monarchy and early years of the
Republic as evidence of anything except what later Romans
thought of their origins and when, in a later revision, he
sought to correct the notoriously inaccurate classical accounts of battles on the basis of a personal inspection of the
battlefields. Although French and German translations of
the book became available within a year of its publication,
Carlyle reports that much Edinburgh critical opinion was
unfavorable.[56] Leadership was gradually slipping from the
hands of the old generation of Edinburgh intellectuals, and
in 1785 Ferguson resigned his position as professor of
moral philosophy at the University of Edinburgh.

His retirement was made possible, curiously enough, by
his appointment to a third professorial chair at the university, the chair in mathematics. This time, however, the un-

likely appointment was made *pro forma* only, so that he could draw the salary while a "junior professor" performed the functions of the office.[57] With this income joined to his small pension from the Chesterfield family, Ferguson was able to maintain his family and to give up the chore of daily lectures to large classes of young boys; yet his situation was never sufficiently secure to obviate constant worry about his family and repeated appeals to friends and patrons for financial assistance and career opportunities for his sons. Ferguson's old age, like all of his life, was shadowed by the fear of poverty.

It was, nevertheless, a productive and vigorous old age. He published in 1792 his *Principles of Moral and Political Science*, which was subtitled *A Retrospect of Lectures Delivered in the College of Edinburgh*. As a conscientious teacher, he had constantly revised his lectures; the new work, paralleling the *Institutes of Moral Philosophy* in subject matter, revealed a higher degree of internal unity and a greater measure of independence than the earlier work.[58] He still swore by Bacon, Reid, Marcus Aurelius, and Montesquieu; but he made some effort to devise formulations which would contain these diverse strands within a more coherent whole. Although his last work was therefore in many ways his most interesting one, his star as a philosopher had set and the book was never republished—except once, in a French translation, when his work enjoyed a brief vogue in the Paris of the Bourgeois Monarchy.[59] But Ferguson continued to work. He published no more on philosophy but, as revealed by the manuscripts he willed to John Macpherson, wrote a considerable number of philosophic essays in which he tried further to refine his conceptions.[60] To the very end he struggled to fulfill what he took to be his duty; viz., to make useful sense of the world.

Roman history also continued to occupy Ferguson's attention. This interest, in fact, occasioned his last trip abroad when, in 1793, he decided to visit the theater of the actions his study described. Undeterred by his age or by the less remote and more dangerous actions then present on the European stage, he toured through Germany and Italy. In addition to his impressions and notes, he brought back from the continent the title of honorary member of the Berlin Academy of Science. Returning to his home on the outskirts of Edinburgh,[61] Ferguson prepared an extensive revision of his book which was published in 1795.

The year of his last work for publication was also the year of his wife's death and of his departure from Edinburgh. In a move which he himself later characterized as foolhardy, he persuaded a wealthy friend to let him occupy the vacant and ramshackle castle of Neidpath on the Tweed, and the old gentleman spent a pleasant summer and an unbearable winter sharing tenancy of the place with animals from the field. Chastened by the experience but still determined on a bucolic retreat, he moved to the village of Hallyards, where he remained for the next twelve years.[62] He devoted those years to gentlemanly farming, philosophical meditation, and shrewdly attentive study of the exciting European events of the time [63] until, in his eightieth year, his sight began to fail; [64] and in 1808 he returned to the care of friends in his college town, St. Andrews. On February 22, 1816, four months before his ninety-third birthday, Adam Ferguson died. According to tradition, his last words were, "There *is* another world." Whatever may have been Ferguson's hopes for another world, certainly his most characteristic attribute was a zestful curiosity about this one. For this reason, if for no other, the epitaph most appropriate for him is not the florid one devised by Sir Walter Scott but that which he intended for himself: "I have seen the works of God; it is now your turn. Do you behold them and rejoice." [65]

This epitaph certainly captures an important truth about Ferguson's life. Particularly if one focuses on Ferguson's own most common perception of his own role, one could say that his was a life of warm friendships, serenity, and scholarship. But the present overview has also revealed discordant elements in the story. His friendships with those of higher station were always marked by a certain measure of strain born of inequality and need. His serenity was disturbed by conflicting desires and a constant struggle for economic subsistence. The life of the scholar repeatedly erupted into frustrated forays into the world of action. The role of aloof philosopher towards which Ferguson frequently aspired remained always beyond his grasp. External, social conditions thrust themselves between him and his goal; the story of Ferguson cannot be encompassed within the private and literary spheres. As an intellectual, he was to a large extent a public figure, and a full assessment of his experiences must await a description of his public and political character.

1. A manuscript, "Ms. Memoir of Mr. Adam Ferguson, Minister of Logierait," quoted in review of John Small's *Biographical Sketch of Adam Ferguson* . . . in *Edinburgh Review*, CXXV, No. 255 (1867), 51. The author speaks of himself in the third person.

Except where otherwise noted, general material concerning Ferguson's life is drawn from Small, *op. cit.*

2. Reverend Ferguson was taken under the protection of a Reverend David Fergusson in St. Andrews who, "being very clannish," reports the memoir, "was much inclined to be beneficial to any of the name of Fergusson that was thought worthy of a liberal education." This Fergusson was descended from one of the important Reformation divines and may have been a distant relative of Adam. At the time of his admittance to the college, the boy had had about eight years of schooling, the first four being, by his own report, almost totally useless and the second four being devoted to the study of Latin. It is noteworthy that the noble youth with whom "Adie contracted great familiarity" in the parish school was the youngest son of the Marquis of Athole ("Ms. Memoir," *op. cit.*, pp. 55, 53).

3. For the father's confessions, see *ibid.*, p. 52. There is some evidence that the parish at Logierait was unusually orthodox for the Highlands. In any case, the record of the presbytery of Dunkeild reveals that the elder Ferguson's "presentation [was] sustained after some delay on account of the right of Patronage being disputed" (National Library of Scotland, Ferguson MSS, No. 3434, hereinafter cited as National Library MSS).

4. Small, *op. cit.*, p. 600.

5. According to Sir Walter Scott, Ferguson threw himself into the heat of the battle with drawn broadsword and withdrew from the action only upon direct command. General David Stewart, a participant in the battle, in his *Sketches of the Highlanders and Highland Regiments,* drew a less dramatic picture of brave ministrations to the wounded and dying. Although Stewart's memory may also have been colored somewhat by Ferguson's later fame, the following tribute to Ferguson as chaplain sounds believable: "By his fearless zeal, his intrepidity, and his friendship towards the soldiers . . . ; his amiable and cheerful manner, checking with severity when necessary, mixing among them with ease and familiarity, and being as ready as any of them with a poem or a heroic tale, he acquired an unbounded ascendancy over them; and while he was chaplain of the corps, he held an equal, if not, in some respects, a greater influence over the minds of the men than the commanding officer" (Stewart, *op. cit.*, I, 292, cited in review of Small's *Biographical Sketch,* p. 63.

6. The records of the presbytery of Dunkeild contain a fairly extended description of the tests administered to Ferguson before he was recommended for ordination (National Library MSS, No. 3434). The unanimous presbytery vote in favor of his being licensed—although not conclusive—suggests that Ferguson's extraordinary advancement testifies to his orthodoxy and attainments as well as to his influential patron.

7. "MS. Memoirs," p. 58.

8. "Letter from Col. the Hon. Joseph Yorke to the Hon. Philip Yorke, February 13, 1746," ed. Philip C. Yorke, *The Life and Correspondence of Philip Yorke, Earl of Hardwicke* (Cambridge: Cambridge University Press, 1913), I, 500.

9. See Carlyle, *op. cit.*, pp. 124 ff.

10. The pamphlet, Ferguson's first publication, was issued in 1746 with the weighty title of *A Sermon Preached, in the Ersh* [sic] *Language, to His Majesty's First Highland Regiment of Foot, commanded by Lord John Murray, at their Cantonment at Camberwell, on the 18th day of December, being appointed as a solemn Fast. Translated into English for the Use of a Lady of Quality in Scotland, at whose desire it is now published* (London, 1746).

11. "Letter to Adam Smith, October, 1754," cited in Small, *op. cit.*, p. 603.

12. *Loc. cit.;* review of Small's *Biographical Sketch, op. cit.,* p. 63.

13. *Ibid.*

14. Small, *op. cit.,* p. 601.

15. Compare *infra,* pp. 171 f.

16. Hume's biographer believes that Hume resigned his commission at the Advocates' Library expressly to help Ferguson (Ernst Campbell Mossner, *The Life of David Hume* [Edinburgh: Nelson, 1954], p. 256). In view of Hume's good-natured concern for the well-being of all of his acquaintances and of the improvement in his own financial circumstances to a point where the small salary would not be missed, this generous act is not surprising, although Hume could not have known Ferguson very well at the time. Ferguson's name first appears in Hume's correspondence in a letter to Gilbert Elliott, dated August 9, 1757, where Hume describes him as a "man of sense, knowledge, taste, elegance, and morals," ed. J. Y. T. Greig, *The Letters of David Hume* (Oxford: Oxford University Press, 1932), I, 263); all quotations from this work are used by permission of the Clarendon Press, Oxford. This sounds a note of respect rather than intimacy. If, therefore, Hume left the Advocates' Library solely to help Ferguson, then he gave up a position he valued, for the access it gave him to books, to aid a needy member of the intellectual circle.

Although Hume and Ferguson came to be quite good friends, Hume's correspondence does not bear out Ferguson's recollection, late in life, that Hume was one of his three closest friends. In a letter to his constant correspondent, John Macpherson, Ferguson reminisced: "I often feast even in the midst of circumstances that are disagreeable to me on the recollection of three friends that have fallen to my lot & who have more than compensated all that has ever been adverse in my fate by the mere sense of having had and having them. You will guess I am persuaded that I mean David & John Home & yourself" (Edinburgh University Library, Ferguson Letters, No. 56 [January 15, 1799], hereinafter cited as Edinburgh University Letters). Aside from letters concerning Ferguson's professional career and reports on the progess of Ferguson's book, only two letters about or to Ferguson appear in Greig's collection of Hume's correspondence. In one Hume places in his charge the education of his favorite nephew, surely a mark of some consideration ("Letter dated November 9, 1763," Greig, *op. cit.,* I, 410). The other is really only a portion of a longer letter in which Hume forwarded messages to William Robertson, John Jardiner, Alexander Carlyle, Hugh Blair, and Adam Ferguson. For the most part, all of these sections are devoted to simple teasing. The section addressed to "Dr. Ferguson—Who by the bye, I believe is not a doctor tho' highly worthy from his Piety and Learning to be one: Then Mr. Ferguson" carries on in the same vein and concludes: "Ah! that you cou'd learn something, Dear Ferguson, of the courteous, and caressing and open manners of this Country. I shou'd not then have been to learn for the first time (as I did lately from General Clerk) that you have not been altogether ungrateful to me, and that you bear me some good will, and that you sometimes regreat [sic] my Absence. Why shu'd [sic] your method of living with me have born so little the Appearance of these Sentiments?" ("Letter to Hugh Blair dated April 6, 1765," Greig, op. cit., I, 496). Even through the facetiousness, a genuine reproach at Ferguson's apparent aloofness comes through the text. It is a friendly letter, but as the only intimate personal letter in the correspondence, it cannot sustain the weight which Ferguson's recollection places on it.

But Hume's correspondence is not an adequate evidence concerning the relationship between the two men during the last years of Hume's life, when both were in Edinburgh. Hume never missed an opportunity to further Ferguson's career; and, in Hume's will, Ferguson appears along with Adam Smith and Jean d'Alembert as beneficiaries of £200 tokens of friendship (Mossner, op. cit., p. 591). It is clear, in short, that while Ferguson never achieved the same measure of intimacy with Hume as did Robertson, Blair, or Adam Smith, he did develop close ties of friendship with Hume.

17. Greig, op. cit., I, 279; see also ibid., pp. 286–87; Small, op. cit., pp. 605 ff.

Hume seems to have entered this kind of activity with the kind of zest which suggests a sporting joy in intrigue as well as genuine sympathy. Furthermore, Ferguson was a favorite object of his attentions. In addition to the plan detailed above, Hume attempted to procure the chair of church history at the University of Glasgow for him in 1759 (Raymond Klibansky and Ernest C. Mossner [eds.], New Letters of David Hume [Oxford: Oxford University Press, 1954], pp. 55–56); he sought to persuade Adam Smith to act as substitute for Ferguson when Ferguson had trouble securing a leave of absence to accept a tutoring job in 1767 (Greig, op. cit., II, 285–86); and in 1772 enlisted all the influence his publisher, Strahan, could muster to secure Ferguson an appointment as secretary to the commission to investigate the East India Company (ibid., p. 260).

In 1773 Lord North wrote to King George III, listing "Dr. Ferguson, the author of a celebrated treatise on Civil Society" among the three "gentlemen" who have "offered themselves for an important position relating to government of India" ("Letter No. 1267, dated June 8, 1773," in Sir John Fortescue [ed.], Correspondence of King George the Third [London: Macmillan and Co., Ltd., 1927], II, 497–98). Ferguson's interest in India appears to have been quite serious, as witnessed by the surprising number of references to Indian examples in his books; but nothing further is known about his earlier contacts there. At this time his student and friend, John Macpherson, is rapidly advancing in his career with the East India Company. In 1791, Ferguson's intimate friend, William Robertson, published An Historical Disquisition concerning the Knowledge which the Ancients had of India. . . . with an Appendix containing Observations on the Civil Polity, the Laws and Judicial Proceedings, the Arts and Sciences, and Religious Institutions *of the Indians.* [London: T. Cadell *et. al.,* 1821 (8th edition)]

Loyalty to his group, concern for a friend, the fun of the chase—all of these factors entered into Hume's sincere, though uniformly unsuccessful, attempts to assist Ferguson. The letter to Strahan, written in 1772, sets forth the warmest and least complicated plea of them all: "I hear . . . that there is an intention of appointing Professor Ferguson Secretary to the Commission. Surely there is not a man of greater worth in all the world. If you have a vote or interest, I beseech you, employ it all in his favour as well for his Advantage as for that of Humanity" (Greig, *op. cit.,* II, 260).

18. Review of Small's *Biographical Sketch, op. cit.,* p. 65.

19. Klibansky and Mossner, *loc. cit.*

20. Carlyle, *op. cit.,* p. 230.

21. Grieg, *op. cit.,* I, 438.

22. *Ibid.,* I, 308, 304.

23. *Ibid.,* I, 496.

24. Adam Ferguson, "Biographical Account of the late Dr. Joseph Black," in *Transactions of the Royal Society of Edinburgh,* V, Part III (1801), 108 n. (emphasis supplied).

25. "The writer of this article has little more than heard of chemistry as a branch of general science, and fondly embraced any doctrine as it seemed to connect with the system of nature; but farther, his own studies have been so different, that he would not, if he could, charge his mind with any of its practical details" (*ibid.,* p. 110 n.).

26. *Ibid.,* p. 105 n. (emphasis supplied). Aesthetic considerations, as well as more narrowly moral ones, might enter into the evaluation of science for the Scottish moral philosophers. For a striking statement, see Adam Smith, "The Principles which lead and direct Philosophical Enquiries; illustrated by the History of Astronomy," in *Essays on Philosophical Subjects* (London: T. Cadell and W. Davies; Edinburgh: W. Creech, 1795), esp. pp. 20–21.

27. This is the same Russel who was Ferguson's competitor for the chair of natural philosophy in 1759. Ferguson probably lived in his house during 1756; Ferguson praised him as a man "whose singular correctness and precision of thought, in various branches of science, could not fail to be of use to all who approached him" (Ferguson, "Biographical Account," *op. cit.,* p. 103). For the tie between Black and Montesquieu, see *ibid.,* pp. 101–2 and Robert Shackleton, *Montesquieu* (Oxford: Oxford University Press, 1961), pp. 209–10.

28. For Hutton, see James Playfair, "Biographical Account of the late Dr. James Hutton, F.R.S.E.," *Transactions of the Royal Society of Edinburgh,* V, Part III (1801), 39–99; and "James Hutton. 1726–1797," in *Proceedings of the Royal Society of Edinburgh* (Edinburgh: Oliver and Boyd, 1950), LXIII, Part IV, sec. B—esp. S. I. Tomkeieff, "James Hutton and the Philosophy of Geology," 387 ff.

29. In addition to Ferguson, Russel, and Black, Hutton's closest friends were James Watt, Adam Smith, and two brothers named Clerk. Among Ferguson's unpublished papers, there is a discussion, "Of the Principle of Moral Estimation," in which the participants are Adam Smith, David Hume, and Robert Clerk (who is made Ferguson's spokesman). Hutton's patron and friend was the Duke of Athole. Hutton and Black were Adam Smith's literary executors.

30. James Playfair, op. cit., p. 91. Applied technologists as well as scientific reseachers were admitted into the inner circle. Hutton and Black were partners in a shop exploiting a joint chemical discovery; Hutton was a renowned scientific farmer; a man named Geddes, "an eminent manufacturer" with glass works at Leith, was an intimate of the group.

31. In 1788, Sir John Macpherson wrote to another student and intimate of Ferguson: "Ferguson has his farm for the philosophy which he taught us. Yes, he has it as his own ground, and is lord of it" (A. Aspinall [ed.], The Later Correspondence of George III [Cambridge: Cambridge University Press, 1962], I, 425).

32. For the reports of the eating, drinking, etc., of the group, see Carlyle, op. cit., passim; about Ferguson's irascibility, Carlyle wrote: "[Adam Ferguson's] wife used to say that it was very fortunate that I was so much in Edinburgh, as I was a great peacemaker among them. She did not perceive that her own husband was the most difficult of all. But as they were all honorable men in the highest degree, John Home and I together kept them on very good terms: I mean by them, Smith, Ferguson, and Hume; for Robertson was very good natured, and soon disarmed the failing of Ferguson, of whom he was afraid" (ibid., p. 229). Small asserts that Ferguson's stroke in 1780 was "probably occasioned by his free manner of living" (Small, op. cit., p. 630). He presents no evidence to support this contention, so there is no reason to suppose that Ferguson outdid his companions in this respect. He held his own, however, and that was no mean feat in the eighteenth century.

Carlyle is the best source for the schemes and plans of the group. The first of Ferguson's two pamphlets on the militia question was written in 1756, during the debate on Pitt's Militia Bill; the second, in 1761, after the defeat of a Scottish Militia Bill in that year. Both were published anonymously, the one as Reflections Previous to the Establishment of a Militia (London, 1756), and the other, an allegorical satire, as The History of the Proceedings in the Case of Margaret, Commonly called Peg, only lawful Sister to John Bull, Esq. (2nd ed.; London: printed for W. Owen, 1761). The authorship of the latter, incidentally, was never publicly known at the time. It was commonly ascribed to Carlyle, and Hume even teased Caryle by claiming to have written it himself. See Carlyle, loc. cit., and Greig, op. cit., I, 341–42, 341 n. 3. Ferguson's pamphlet on the Douglas controversy, also unacknowledged at the time, was entitled The Morality of Stage Plays (Edinburgh, 1757). The pamphlets will be discussed below (compare *infra,* pp. 83 f.). For the *Ossian* controversy and Ferguson's part in it, see Schmitz, *op. cit.,* pp. 42 ff.

33. Carlyle, *op. cit.,* p. 340. See also Harry A. Cockburn, "An Account of the Friday Club, written by Lord Cockburn, together with notes on certain other social clubs in Edinburgh," *The Book of the Old Edinburgh Club* (Edinburgh: T. and A. Constable, 1910), III, 145–54.

34. Baron d'Holbach, to whom Ferguson had presented a copy of the book, wrote: "I found [your book] answering completely to the high opinion I had conceived of your great abilities and ingenuity by the testimonies given of you by Mr. Andrew Steward, Colonel Clerk. . . . Tho' you don't seem to set a high value on theory, it must necessarily precede practice, and I think that given in your grand performance, by enlightening the human mind, may contribute to render their practice better; for I don't despair of the perfectibility of mankind; I believe they have been mere children in matters the most important for them. I am of opinion that the greatest part of our distresses arise from ignorance, and give me leave, Sir, to tell you sincerely, that I am persuaded that your valuable work is, and will be, very able to dispel the foggs [*sic*] that hang over our understanding" ("Letter dated June 15, 1767," cited by Small, *op. cit.,* p. 611). Henry Home, Lord Kames, was an enthusiastic supporter of Ferguson's book and strongly recommended it to his friends. See Tytler, *op. cit.,* II, 65 ff; the judgment of the others can be easily deduced from Hume's replies to their letters.

35. Still, Hume's influence is manifest in the plaintive reply Blair offered to Hume's attack on the book: "But what is to be done? Robertson and I have given our opinion already; we cannot retreat. You know too the nature of the author: not overmuch given to submit" (quoted in Mossner, *op. cit.,* p. 542).

Adam Smith presents a distinct problem. He became enraged at the book because he believed that some crucial points had been plagiarized from his own work. According to Carlyle, "This Ferguson denied, but owned he derived many notions from a French author [i.e., Montesquieu], and that Smith had been there before him" (Carlyle, *op. cit.,* p. 231). A German critic has attempted to adjudicate this controversy and has argued quite convincingly that Smith was in the right. In his view, the ideas at issue must have been common to both Smith and Ferguson, but missing in Montesquieu. The only important idea which fits this qualification is the emphasis both men place on the division of labor. Although Smith did not publish his findings until 1776, the student notes of his *Lectures on Justice, Police, Revenue, and Arms* prove that he developed his ideas concerning the division of labor in the public lectures he presented in Edinburgh in 1748–51 (A. Oncken, "Adam Smith und Adam Ferguson," *Zeitschrift für Sozialwissenschaft,* XII (1909), 129. In as close-knit a group as the Scottish philosophers' was, the question of priorities is even more unanswerable than otherwise. They shared so many problems and ideas that, except for a really individual thinker like Hume, the skein of mutual influence cannot be untangled—and the reward of even a successful attempt does not repay the effort required.

36. Greig, *op. cit.*, II, 11–12. Characteristically, Hume excused his harshness by a sincere concern for Ferguson's welfare. The letter continues: ". . . This is a very serious Matter: any Failure of Success in this particular, besides the Mortification attending it, operates backwards, and discredits his Class, which is at present in so flourishing a Situation."

37. *Ibid.*, p. 133.

38. *Ibid.*, p. 12.

39. Mossner, *op. cit.*, p. 543.

40. Small, *op. cit.*, p. 610. Ferguson's biographer maintains that "Hume had heard an opinion expressed, by the French philosophers Helvetius and Saurin with which he at the time concurred, that the fame of Montesquieu's 'Esprit des Lois' would not be lasting. As Ferguson's Essay may be regarded to a certain extent as a commentary on Montesquieu, Hume, perhaps, hastily adopted the same opinion with regard to the work of his friend."

41. In a letter to Rousseau, for example, Hume wrote: "I will use the Freedom of telling you bluntly, without affecting the Finesse of a well-turned Compliment, that, of all men of letters in Europe, since the death of President Montesquieu, you are the person whom I most revere, both for the Force of your Genius and the Greatness of your Mind" (cited in Mossner, *op. cit.*, pp. 428–29).

42. In addition to the tribute incorporated in the letter quoted above, Hume concluded the very letter on which Small relied for his interpretation by saying, ". . . tho' the 'Esprit des Lois' be considerably sunk in vogue, & will probably sink still farther, it maintains a high reputation, and probably will never be totally neglected. It had considerable Merit, notwithstanding the Glare of its pointed Wit, and notwithstanding its false Refinements and its rash and crude Positions" (Greig, *op. cit.*, II, 133).

43. Hume's report of a conversation about the book with Mrs. Montague (a noted hostess and amateur writer of London who had many friends among the Edinburgh intelligensia) reveals his concern with Ferguson's style. He wrote: "A few days ago I saw Mrs. Montague, who had just finished it with great pleasure; I mean she was sorry to finish it, but had read it with great Pleasure. I asked her, whether she was satisfied with the style? Whether it did not savour somewhat of the country? Oh yes, said she, a great deal; it seems almost impossible that anyone could write such a style except a Scotsman" (Greig, *op. cit.*, II, 131–32). Further evidence is provided by the fact that, in the comments on Montesquieu quoted above, Hume lists two objections to his style before arriving at a substantive criticism.

44. On the assumption that Ferguson learned of Hume's judgment at some time in his life, a passage in one of Ferguson's unpublished essays gives some indirect support to this explanation. The essay, cast in the form of a discussion among Smith, Hume, and General Clerk (Ferguson's spokesman), is also the one in which Ferguson nastily settled accounts with Smith (see note 35 *supra*). In the text, "Clerk" attacks "Hume" for refusing to help men see the real harmony of the world-system and for refusing to "discard all paradox and take to the investigation of useful truths." "Hume" answers: "I don't know what a man of letters is to get by that. To be writing what every body knows or may hear from every Coffee House acquaintance" (Edinburgh University Library, Unpublished Essays of Adam Ferguson, "Of the Principles of Moral Estimation," p. 3, hereinafter cited as Unpublished Essays).

45. Greig, *op. cit.*, II, 120–21, and 136. In his most glowing account, he wrote to Ferguson, "I may safely say, that I have met with no body, that has not read it, and these are the People, who by their Reputation and Rank commonly give the Tone on these Occasions" (*ibid.*, p. 126). An impressive illustration of Hume's eagerness to help his friend is presented by his action in writing to Blair an exact duplicate of the first flattering news he had already sent to Ferguson, explaining, "I have wrote [*sic*] the same article of Intelligence to Ferguson himself; but as he is the likeliest Person in the World to suppress it, I thought it safest to put it into your hands, in order to circulate it" (*ibid.*, p. 121).

46. The author is indebted to C. P. Finlayson, keeper of manuscripts in the library of the University of Edinburgh, for a detailed bibliography of Ferguson editions. In the catalogue of the Bibliotheque Nationale, there appears a book ascribed to Adam Ferguson and entitled *Essays on the Intellectual powers, moral sentiment, happiness & national felicity* (Paris, 1805), which probably represents the compliment of a pirated edition of selections from the *Essay on the History of Civil Society*.

47. For the widespread use of Ferguson's book in American universities, see Gladys Bryson, "Sociology Considered as Moral Philosophy," *Sociological Review*, XXIV (1932), 26–36.

48. Small, *op. cit.*, pp. 614 ff. This was the occasion on which Hume asked Smith to come to Edinburgh as Ferguson's temporary replacement (compare *supra*). Pessimistic about a successful outcome of the controversy, he analyzed the situation as follows: "The Settlement to be made on Ferguson is a very narrow Compensation for his Class, if he must lose it: He wishes to keep it, and to serve by a Deputy in his Absence. But besides that this Scheme will appear invidious and is really scarce admissible, those in the Town Council, who aim at filling the Vacancy with a Friend, will strenuously object to it; and he himself cannot think of one who will make a proper substitute. I fancy, that the chief Difficulty wou'd be remov'd, if you wou'd offer to supply his class, either as his Substitute, or his Successor, with a

Purpose of resigning upon his return. This notion is entirely my own, and shall never be known to Ferguson, if it appears to you improper. I shall only say that he deserves this friendly treatment, by his friendly Conduct, of a similar kind, towards Poor Russel's Family" (Greig, *op. cit.*, II, 285–86). The last sentence refers to Ferguson's having taken over without remuneration the natural philosophy class when Russel died, in order to provide the bereaved family with the salary.

49. Describing his visit, Ferguson wrote to his friend Alexander Carlyle: "[Voltaire] saluted me with a compliment to a gentleman of my family who had civilized the Russians [an apparent reference to the success of Ferguson's *Institutes of Moral Philosophy* in Russia]. I owned this relation and at this and every successive visit encouraged every attempt at conversation even jokes against Moses, Adam & Eve & the rest of the prophets till I began to be considered as a person tho' true to my own faith had no ill humour for the freedom of fancy in others" ("Letter to Alexander Carlyle, April 29, 1775, Edinburgh University Library).

50. Richard Price, *Observations on the Nature of Civil Liberty, the Principles of Government, and the Justice and Policy of the War with America, &c.* (8th ed.; Dublin: W. Kidd, 1776). Its popularity can be gauged by its issuance in eight editions within the year of its publication and its receiving at least twenty published replies.

51. Adam Ferguson, *Remarks on a Pamphlet lately Published by Dr. Price, Intitled Observations on the Nature of Civil Liberty, the Principles of Government, and the Justice and Policy of the War with America, &c. in a Letter from a Gentleman in the Country to a Member of Parliament* (London: printed for T. Cadell, 1776). The bibliographer Joseph Sabin ascribes another anonymous pamphlet, entitled *Remarks on Dr. Price's Observations on the Nature of Civil Liberty, etc.* (London: printed for C. Kearsley, 1776), to Ferguson as well (Joseph Sabin, *Dictionary of Books relating to America* [New York, 1783], VI, 389). The absence of any available confirmatory evidence and the difference between the style and substance of this pamphlet and Ferguson's known works lead to the conclusion that this is an erroneous ascription, engendered by the similarity between the titles. The last-named pamphlet can, in fact, provide illustrations of the sort of offensive dicta which Ferguson avoided: the author rejects Price's appeal to Lockian principles by observing that governments are derived from necessity, not "the whim of the frantic multitude"; in praise of aristocratic government, the author claims that "few are the instances of licentiousness in the highest orders of a state: their knowledge & experience will dictate to them its pernicious consequences" (*Remarks on Dr. Price's Observations*, p. 2). Ferguson, in contrast, rested his argument solely on the primacy of the rule of law.

52. Two of the commissioners, William Eden (later Lord Auckland) and George Johnstone, were long-time admirers of Ferguson.

53. Edinburgh University Letters, Nos. 11 and 12 to John Macpherson (datelined Delaware River and New York and dated June 19,

1778, and August 28, 1778, respectively). The University of Edinburgh collection also contains the letter from George Washington refusing a passport to Ferguson.

54. A younger contemporary of Ferguson and friend of his son wrote of these later years: "I never heard of his dining out except at his relation Dr. Joseph Black's where his son Sir Adam . . . used to say it was delightful to see the two philosophers rioting over a boiled turnip" (Henry Thomas Cockburn, *Memorials of His Time* [Edinburgh and London: T. N. Foulis, 1910], p. 45).

55. Small, *op. cit.*, p. 642.

56. For a useful list of editions and translations, see Bryson, *op. cit.*, p. 87. An abridged edition was published in New York as late as 1873. About the Edinburgh reception of the history, Carlyle reported: "The time came when those who were overawed by Ferguson repaid him for his haughtiness; for when his Roman History was published, at a time when he had lost his health, and had not been able to correct it dilligently, by a certain propensity they had, unknown to themselves, acquired, to disparage everything that came from Ferguson, they did his book more hurt than they could have done by open criticism. It was provoking to hear those who were so ready to give loud praises to very shallow and imperfect English productions—to curry favour, as we supposed, with the booksellers and authors concerned—taking every opportunity to undermine the reputation of Ferguson's book. 'It was not a Roman history,' said they (which it did not say it was). 'This delineation of the constitution of the republic is well sketched; but for the rest, it is anything but history, and then it is so incorrect that it is a perfect shame.' All his other [later?] books met with the same treatment, while at the same time, there were a few of us who could not refrain from saying that Ferguson's was the best history of Rome . . ." (Carlyle, *op. cit.*, p. 231).

The extent to which Hume was the sun which kept the Edinburgh constellation in orbit can be gauged from Carlyle's plaintive conclusion: "David Hume did not live to see Ferguson's History, otherwise his candid praise would have prevented all the subtle remarks of the jealous or resentful" (*ibid*). Hume's death in 1776 marked the beginning of the disintegration of the group's glory (i.e., its glory as a group—such individual members as Smith, of course, continued to enjoy the highest positions).

An anonymous Edinburgh man of letters presented the following judgment (in a private letter) of Ferguson's history: "Ferguson has given the world lately an important Work, a History of the Rise and Fall of the Roman Republic. Of this there are different opinions; but the most prevalent is rather not so high as the former character of the author would have led people to form. He has treated his subject rather in a Narrative than in a reflective way, & has been sparing of those general & philosophic views of the subject which is the great distinction between Modern History, since the time of Montesquieu & the ancient" (National Library MSS, No. 646).

57. This was John Playfair, noted for promoting Hutton's *Theory of the Earth.*

58. The MS collection at the University of Edinburgh contains Ferguson's lecture notes, revealing the constant and substantive revisions he made over the years.

59. Carlyle, *loc. cit.*, recounts the disappointing reception accorded the book in Edinburgh. Carlyle himself, and the other intimate members of the circle, of course, remained completely loyal.

60. The following is a list of the titles of the Unpublished Essays:

1. "Of Perfection and Happiness"
2. "What May be affirmed or apprehended of the Supreme Creative Being"
3. "Of History and its appropriate Style"
4. "Of Statesmen and Warriors"
5. "An Excursion into the Highland. Discourse on Various Subjects"
6. "Of Happiness and Merit"
7. "Distinction of Value and its source in Existence"
8. "Of the Comparative Forms of Being"
9. "Reputed Pleasures of Imagination"
10. "On Wisdom"
11. "Of the Categories or Constituents of Discourse and Fabrick [sic] of Thought. Language"
12. "Of the Distinctions which mankind experience or apprehend in the nature of things, to direct them in what they pursue or avoid"
13. "Of Cause and Effect, Ends and Means, order, combination and design"
14. "Of the French Revolution with its actual and still impending consequences in Europe"
15. "Of the Separation of Departments, Professions and Tasks resulting from the progress of Arts in Society"
16. "Of the freedom of Wit and Humour and their value as a test of Rectitude & Truth"
17. "Waking Dreams"
18. "Of the Distinctions on which we Act in Human Life"
19. "Of the Categories"
20. "Of the Distinctions on which it is the Lot of Man to deliberate"
21. "Of the Intellectual System"
22. "Of the Sciences of which the subject is Mind"

23. "Of Good and Evil Perfection & Defect"
24. "Of the first Law of Living Nature: Preserve Thyself"
25. "Of the Principle of Moral Estimation"
26. "Of Liberty and Necessity"
27. "Of the things that are or may be"
28. "Of Nature and Art"
29. "Of the different Aspects of Moral Science"
30. "Of Laws of Nature in the Department of Active Man"
31. "Of the Intellectual or Conscious Powers: Conceptive, cognitive and Spontaneous"
32. "Characteristics of Man's Nature"

The essays are hand-written in a ledger and average about twenty half-pages each. That at least most of the manuscripts were written after 1792 can be ascertained from Ferguson's reference to Napoleon's Egyptian campaign in No. 14.

61. According to Cockburn, Ferguson's friends referred to his home as "Kamchatka," both because of its remoteness from the center of town and because, apparently as part of his medical regimen, he kept it unheated. Ferguson dressed himself in fur-lined hat, greatcoat, and boots at all times; Cockburn, with greater metaphorical truth than geographical consistency, said that "he looked like a philosopher from Lapland" (Cockburn, *Memorials*, p. 119).

62. Ferguson gave a running report of his Neidpath negotiations and troubles to John Macpherson (Edinburgh University Letters, Nos. 23–35 *passim*). In these, as well as in the later letters from Hallyards, he also displayed his enthusiasm for the rural life and hinted at his attempts at farming (*ibid.*, No. 23 ff.). In a letter dated July 3rd, 1798, in which Ferguson devised two Greek epitaphs for himself, the second was intended to reveal his "verve for agriculture" (*ibid.*, No. 54).

63. His letters to Macpherson are filled with comments which reveal his continuing interest in international political events, particularly the development of the French Revolutionary War and the rise of Napoleon. The following excerpts—one from a letter written in 1797, the other from an 1802 letter—illustrate the range of his information and the liveliness of his analyses: "And here is a new and most interesting crisis. An assembly of the Batavian People met on the first of March to supersede all former Governments and deliberate on a new one. The result is uncertain: but probably the democratical leaven admitted into the Batch will never be clear'd away so as to restore the former self-electing aristocracy. It is also probable that the impulse given to that supposed but mistaken [*sic*—mistakenly supposed (?)] phlegmatic mass on the prospect of Democracy or what is now called Liberty will produce in that country a new scene of energy or national exertion. What are we to do in this case? Are we to brave the hostility of this rising Power & press it down into the Scale of France so as to have no

chance of counterpoise in the rest of Europe? May God who has prospered us hitherto forbid. We have nursed the French Republic in its cradle & we have sended [sic] it to school & brought it for ought I know to a state of confirmed vigour in the issue dangerous if not fatal to the other nations of Europe: or which certainly the half rotten or slumbering monarchs cannot resist. If the new republic of Batavia is to have a separate existence from that of Gaul I would willing nurse it as a young Hercules who may one day be our Friend and assistant against this Hydra of France. Their own jealousy may naturally enough take this turn against the power that is most likely to keep them in bondage & certainly some direction may be taken even in the conduct of our present war with the seven provinces or in our declaration and policy with respect to them that may facilitate their coming into our scale at last . . ." (ibid., No. 52).

"Then what sense do you put upon this soi disant new Constitution of France [i.e., the Constitution of the Year XII]. I understand that the Premier Consul is a great sovereign, supreme and absolute, standing upon the pinnacle of military merit and force. That apart from subsistence and self-preservation there is no principle of action in the state but military preferment. If there is any other pray tell me of it. But don't put me off with saying that the publick [sic] good is a great object. I own it: but I never knew the hundredth part of mankind actuated by that alone. Men are like planets; they must have at least two forces to make them go in their orbits: one a projectile by which they would fly, God knows where, another a control whose pressure in every moment is only nascent but continues & keeps them from flying off. Men's projectile force is directed to some personal advantage: but there is a control force that keeps him more or less correctly in a track of innocence or beneficence to those around him. Take the projectile force away from him, he might not go wrong: but for the most part would fall into the heap and not move at all. I must repeat there are individuals who would be inactive if it were not for a principle of good will to fellow creatures which does not allow them to be idle. This principle however I do not believe is yet the ruling passion in France. If you want me therefore to believe that this new constitution of France is anything more than a projected country dance in which couples are made to stand up without a fiddle to put things in motion, you must tell me what is to bring the constitutional assemblies, etc., together. In short what is the power of emolument to be got by running the career of communes, cantons, districts, & departments; of Senates, Tribunates, Legislatures, & so forth to the very pinnacle of Chief Consul. Even if there be emoluments as well as title in civil preferment & office, if such be the gift of the Chief Consul alone the way will be to pay court to him & not to run the career of an active political life" (ibid., No. 65).

64. The letter in which he informed Macpherson of his deteriorating eyesight also revealed that the "boundless vein of humour" which Carlyle ascribed to him (Carlyle, op. cit., p. 229) had not been

bound off by approaching decrepitude. He wrote, "I sit down in darkness or in a state approaching to blindness. . . ." Noting that he had by mistake enclosed a letter addressed to himself in the last envelope, he wonders, "I hope it was not a Billet Doux from any of the Octogenaire Nymphs of the Neighborhood; If so I can only beg of you to be discreet. . . ." (Edinburgh University Letters, No. 68 [dated February 12, 1803]).

65. *Ibid.,* No. 54; the text of the epitaph composed by Scott and engraved on Ferguson's tombstone is printed in Small, *op. cit.,* p. 665.

CHAPTER IV

Adam Ferguson: Political Opinion aud Political Practice

IT IS CLEAR, then, that as an intellectual Ferguson was not truly content to "behold" and "rejoice": he wanted to take an active part in shaping his world. Even in the letter which, according to available evidence, was the last he ever wrote to his lifelong friend, John Macpherson, this striving is movingly portrayed. Then aged eighty-three, he wrote:

> You may have heard of old age & its numberless defects: but indifference is none of them; it magnifies care and every anxiety: but has no energy to relieve them. I believe it is the intention of nature to wean from this scene of things and reconcile to its continuance & take the consolation of one of [the] Revolutionary Leaders of France had in her imprisonment viz., that she had nothing to do. But to have nothing to do because we can do nothing is but indifferent comfort.[1]

As Ferguson's comparison of his own helplessness with that
of one of the "Revolutionary Leaders of France" makes
clear, he was not bemoaning only his inability to attend to
personal affairs. His final message, despite its stress on de-
bilities of old age, recapitulates a theme dominant throughout his life: a fervent desire to participate in great events
—particularly in political events—always partially restrained by duties he assigned himself and ultimately
thwarted by the situation in which he was placed.[2]

Ferguson's political program contained, essentially, two
points: first, the necessity of maintaining and strengthening
the existent structure of law and order; and second, the
desirability of infusing that structure with a vigorous sense
of purpose and *elan.* Since he believed that, at least in the
short run, the second of these objectives presupposed the
achievement of the first, he was prepared to give way whenever he feared that insistence on it might jeopardize stability.
Therefore, although he was convinced that the most invigo-
rating force available to any society was widespread participation in active political conflict, he frequently counseled
against political agitation lest it upset the "system of subordination" upon which, in his view, the secure legal order
rested. In an important sense, then, even Ferguson's decisions to stay out of political controversy were political acts.

He did find some occasions, however, when he feared no
conflict, and on these occasions he did not hesitate to commit
himself to manifest action. The least complicated of these
were the instances when he could help to fend off some
challenge to the socio-political status quo as such. As the
argument presented in his theater pamphlet makes clear, he
considered the *Douglas* controversy to be, at least in part,
such an instance.[3] He maintained that the attack on the
theatre constituted, in effect, an attack on the prerogatives

of the wealthy and that it thereby posed a threat to the entire social order. He wrote:

> It has pleased Providence for wise purposes, to place men in different stations, and to bestow upon them different degrees of wealth. Without this circumstance there could be no subordination, no government, no order, no industry. Every person does good, and promotes the happiness of society, by living agreeable to the rank in which providence has placed him . . . Whilst from humanity we indulge the poor in their station, we ought from justice to indulge the wealthy in theirs, and to expect that they are to go on agreeable to the habits of living which belong to their station, and which, in effect, are necessary to the order and good of society, and to the maintenance of the poor.[4]

While the political meaning of the *Douglas* controversy was diluted by other elements, there was no such confusion in Ferguson's pamphlet against the apologists for the American Revolution. He was prepared to urge consideration for every legitimate request for redress of grievances; he maintained, in fact, that the colonists had a rightful grievance against the restrictive mercantilist policies of Parliament; but he insisted that no grievance could justify unconstitutional procedures. Even an adjustment in the constitution to meet changed conditions might be desirable, he conceded, but any such change would have to be made by the duly constituted authorities through proper legal channels. Any attempt to coerce these authorities and to bypass these channels had, in his view, to be suppressed by force. Ferguson rejected appeals to the "spirit and principles of the British constitution against the letter and the fact." The British constitution, in his view, was what the courts and Parliament had in the past said it was, until such time as they

decided to change it.[5] That Ferguson's argument was
addressed as much to the maintenance of the constitutional
order within the British Isles as to the refutation of colonial
claims is indicated by his comment in the following
year—that, because it would be impossible to retain control
over the American colonies for any extended time, it would
be best to "beat the colonies and leave them in contempt" in
order to establish the principle of right without incurring
the cost of trying to keep them in submission.[6]

Ferguson remained aloof from the reform movement at
home as well, even when it became quite fashionable in
Scotland, around 1783, to support the drive for expansion of
county and burgh franchises. His initial reaction to the
Yorkshire Association, in fact, was quite sharply hostile.
Early in 1780, he wrote to Macpherson:

> This cloud that is gathering in Yorkshire alarms
> me. . . . That county seems to be forming itself into a
> Republic. . . . It should in appearance be taken very
> lightly by government; but it is already or may be a very
> serious matter. Country gentlemen tasting of the Impor-
> tance they get in Public Assemblies by making Speeches,
> tasting of Party Applause, & receiving the enthusiasm of
> Party Enthusiasm rise above all considerations of Reason,
> of Private Interest or of Public Order. Direct Opposition is
> like a Bellows to blow up the Fire.[7]

There is evidence that, at about the same time, he wrote in a
similar vein to William Eden (later Lord Auckland), whom
North had given the task of watching the growth of the
association. Ferguson, expressing the fear of an antiparlia-
ment shared by so many, warned against the machinations
of the "new species of government forming in some of the
countys of England."[8]

A few years later when he was directly approached by
Christopher Wyvill, his reaction was less vehement but still

firmly unfavorable. He was courteous and sympathetic to some of the reforms but opposed to the reform movement. Because there has been some confusion about this, it might be best to quote his letter to Wyvill in full: [9]

You have done me a great deal of honour in making me the conveyance of a *proposal from the Committee of Association in the County of York for a Reformation of Parliament, and for the extension and better regulation of the Right of Election to Parliament throughout the Kingdom.* I took the first opportunity my health would allow to communicate the contents of your packet to Mr. Ilay Campbell, a gentleman of the first character in this country, who, I understood, was employed in preparing the draft of a Bill relating to the Right of Election in Scotland, and am desired to return his thanks to you and the other Gentlemen of the Yorkshire Committee. This matter is under consideration here, chiefly with a view to reform a supposed abuse which has recently crept into the manner of constituting qualifications to vote at County Elections. Persons having extensive superiorities in this part of the kingdom parcel them out to their retainers and friends in such manner as to multiply Voters without increasing the number of Votes, the person who confers these qualifications being understood to dispose of the Votes as he pleases. Of those concerned in this Reform, many, no doubt, are willing to reduce the qualifications of Votes so as to increase their number; but this, like many other Reformations, I am told, must be the work of time and some caution. My own earnest wish has long been, that we had the same Law of Parliament with you as far as relates to County Elections; but I confess that I do not hope ever to obtain it.

I am very happy that my writings make me be considered as a sincere friend of the Constitution: being so little able to serve it in practice, the least I can do is to pay it all due respect in my speculations. One of its beauties is, that it can withstand many evils without being overthrown. I know nothing so likely to be fatal to it as the weakness and

cowardice of those on whom its preservation depends; and
I sincerely believe, that to preserve the Rights of the
People, the vigour of the Crown is not less necessary than
their own. To make us as happy as our Constitution would
admit of, requires indeed many other conditions, which I
hope we shall long improve or retain.[10]

On most questions, then, Ferguson's primary commitment to stability overrode any sympathy he might have felt
for such energetic groups as the American revolutionaries or
the Yorkshire reformers and led him to a course of action
intended merely to defend the status quo. He felt free to
take the offensive on only one issue, but that one was his
most constant political concern. He was convinced that the
nation could renew its vital energies and forge new links of
comradeship among its citizens through military exertions.
Moreover, this invigoration of the national spirit, he believed, would in no way threaten the social order; it would,
rather, directly strengthen it. In the first pamphlet he ever
published, he launched his lifelong campaign in support of
these contentions. Arguing that the progress of commerce,
the establishment of public order, and the spread of cultured
gentility—while highly desirable in themselves—had deprived men of the spirit, solidarity, and courage fostered in
earlier days by the armed unity necessary for subsistence and
survival, Ferguson asserted that the institution of a universal
militia would counteract the evil consequences of progress
without hampering the progress itself.[11] Military duties, according to his scheme, would only occupy a small portion of
a man's time, but they would instil a high degree of pride
and patriotism. To quiet any fears that the arming of the
lower classes might threaten a violent disruption of established authority, he further proposed that "[the] law
. . . may provide that the nomination of Officers, in the
different ranks, should follow, as nearly as possible, that

subordination in point of dignity and wealth already subsisting in this nation." "By this means," he argued, "we take the
benefit of an authority which is already established, and we
give it some new addition *which will bring it still nearer to
military subordination.*" [12] Failure to adopt such a program,
he maintained, would therefore not only deprive the nation
of an opportunity to restore moral health to its population
and to provide a means of defense more reliable then professional mercenaries, but it would also forego an important
strengthening of the social order.[13]

Ferguson's convictions about this issue were even
sufficiently strong to lead him into veiled public opposition
to official policy when, in 1761, the House of Commons,
with the concurrence of Lord Advocate Dundas, rejected a
Scottish Militia Bill intended to extend to Scotland the
militia program which had been enacted in 1756 but restricted to England. Scottish nationalism intensified his ardor for the militia, and he wrote a pamphlet which, through
an elaborate and somewhat tortured allegorical satire, bitterly attacked the narrow-minded cowardice of the administration and the truckling subserviency of the Scottish delegation in Parliament.[14] He did not, of course, extend his
antagonism into organized political opposition; when he
took the lead in the formation of the Poker Club to keep
the issue alive, he carefully avoided any suggestion of
challenge to the political leaders of Scotland. Except for
the more general advocacy incorporated into his theoretical
works, he restricted the communication of his militarist
enthusiasm, after these two ventures into pamphleteering,
to the circle of his friends. But in his letters to them, he
repeatedly sounded the theme. During the American Revolutionary War, he welcomed the rumors of invasion stirred
up by John Paul Jones's forays to the British coast, and
he even expressed a wish for a little invasion, provided that

all respectable elements were armed, so that the national spirit might be roused.[15] He believed that the wars of the French Revolution, requiring a more thorough mobilization of British energies than any earlier one, closely approached the achievement of his objectives, and in 1799 he wrote:

> I really think them [i.e., "the times that are"] better than any we have formerly had. The Madness of France has made us understand and relish the sobriety of our own forms. The Multitude and insolence of so near an enemy has roused everyone in Britain to Politics and War as well as Trade. Women & Children can listen to talk about matters of consequence to mankind. The evils and follies of one quarter become lessons of wisdom to another and so the world is guided. Storms and Tempests have produced architecture and the manufacture of cloth.[16]

As the following letter, which also goes further in rejecting commerce than most of Ferguson's statements, makes clear, Ferguson's devotion to martial exertions did not lead him to advocate an aggressive foreign policy. He wrote to Macpherson:

> [You] will find that I, tho' a warlike philosopher, am far from being against your system of property & National Independence, altho' I do not know of any way to preserve it among thieves, highwaymen & conquering nations but force alone & to this we must look for safety & even not rely on ordinary means of defence so long as there is such an Army & such a directory in France. As the combination of Kings served the Jacobin cause in France, the threats of the Directory serve the National cause in this island. They will teach and drive us I trust to assume a just military posture which no efforts of theirs will reverse. And if they persist will I trust not be for a moment or a single generation but for ages to come. For this purpose I wish only in addition to what we are doing that the current of Estima-

tion and Honour should be turned as much as possible into this Channel. What is to become of Trade? My answer still is let so much of it as is inconsistent with national safety go elsewhere. A valiant people and independent state cannot want for resources. My only difficulty is to fit the just mean between the danger of subjugation & the danger of wishing to subjugate others, for men are such idiots as to think that conquest is prosperity for themselves & would set no limits to either. We complain that the French would be a conquering & great nation by Land: but our publick [sic] Scribblers at least are as offensive in their turn by Sea. Is not rule Brittania o'er the Waves as bad as Ca ira. The best of us should have a bridle in our mouths and a hook in our noses or at least have our tongues pulled out. . . . It is piteous to hear fools talk of the sovereignty of the land beyond his own territory. If vainglory had effect to raise or preserve a just national spirit it might be indured; but I distrust the effect—it is provoking to others & fraught with inefficient confidence to those who entertain it. So much for moralizations which if it does not correct the world may at least tell us what to think of it.[17]

Despite Ferguson's reference to the "evils and follies" of Revolutionary France, he never pictures the war as an ideological crusade against enemies of mankind. The purpose of the war was, for him, the defeat of France's expansionist designs, not the restoration of France's former rulers or the punishment of criminals and regicides. Because he believed that a republic in a country as large as France could only be sustained by a high state of military fervor, he did see an interdependence between French republicanism and French military adventurism. But he thought that the best strategy to be pursued was a policy like that of "containment," in the expectation that a France denied opportunity for expansion but not goaded to attack would soon return to a less dynamic, monarchical system. To attempt to force this

result or to insist that the new monarchy reinstate the old
royal family and nobility (as the Continental Legitimist
powers sought to do) he considered self-defeating as well as
useless. He argued that the more pressures the allies put on
France the greater would be the verve of the republic. In
any case, he was confident that the talented men permitted
to rise in the social scale by the Revolution could never be
forced back into their old positions: he expected that they
would fight to the death against any attempt to deprive them
of their new ranks.

Ferguson's analysis of the French Revolution and the
ensuing war is contained in a number of letters written to
Macpherson at the time and in an unpublished essay apparently written during the temporary peace of Amiens.
The reliance of the republic on war he describes in the
following words:

> The Republick of France has no chance to exist but in
> the turmoil of War & if its Leaders should have no
> pretence for War with Europe in General they will try to
> keep up the *delenda est Carthago* against this country.[18]

He set forth the policy of containment in a fanciful letter,
detailing what he would prescribe "if there were such a
profession as physician of state" after he had called "a con-
sultation to prescribe for the Patient whose life is at Stake."
The policy is expressed metaphorically as building a large
wall around France and losing the key.[19]

That the policy being pursued in 1797 was erroneous and
rested on a failure to understand the dynamics of the French
situation, he asserted in the following words:

> . . . I am sure that no conduct will be right where the case
> is not understood & hence the whole series of our conduct
> hitherto or the Coalition of Europe by which we roused,
> exercised & confirmed the democracy of France.[20]

He specified the error of the Continental powers thus:

All Europe stood aghast at this enormous scene [viz., the French Revolution] & not knowing how fruitless or dangerous it is to meddle with a people that is roused to any great act of Revolution in the prospect of some glorious change in favour of the People. In such Paroxisms they operate with irresistible effect whenever they move in a Body. . . . [Having argued that they should have been left alone in the hope that the power would crumble in internal division, Ferguson continued.] This was too profound a secret for German heads.[21]

In the following letter, he set forth his objections to restoration:

Our Project of restoring Monarchy with Priviledged Nobility in France has many difficulties. Property again to change hands. Low born men both in Civil and Military stations to lay their heads in the dust from which they arose. It was much easier to lay the frivolous corrupted pretenders to aristocracy in the dust than it will be to bring their rascally successors. The former exclusive pretension of birth to consideration and preferment will never be restored as long as any shred of the low born republican army subsists. I have been saying so for many years tho' nobody seems to mind it. Every army would prefer the monarchy of a favourite leader to any other government. And the whole French nation soldiers and all may be ashamed or disgusted with their tryal of Democracy if they are only allowed to suppose that want of birth for the future is not to stifle merit of any condition.[22]

In short, Ferguson's animosity toward the French Revolution rested primarily on the threat which he believed it posed to the security of England and to the peace of Europe. Apart from this consideration, he was an interested and not unsympathetic observer of French developments. There is no evidence to show that he ever shared the moral hysteria widespread among many Englishmen and good reason to believe that he did not.

In the first place, he can be expected to have been intrigued by the Roman fabrics which were woven into the texture of the Revolution. Like many of his contemporaries and like many of the revolutionists themselves, Ferguson saw the French events as a parallel to the rise of the Roman Republic, and Ferguson, the historian of the Republic, deeply loved it. Ferguson explicitly welcomed the early stages of the Revolution, and—unlike most English commentators—he did not base his approval on the mistaken assumption that the revolutionaries were aiming at a constitutional monarchy like that of England. Throughout, he assigned to the Revolution the republican goal of equality. In a letter to an influential acquaintance, he wrote (on January 19, 1790): "The Noblesse of France have had a greater fall than the King. It is resolved that for the future there shall be no distinction of persons in that Country, whether they can keep to their resolution is a doubtful question. The experiment is a matter of expectation to us for a twelve-month or two to come. . . . I think that what they are engaged in will make them better neighbours both in Europe & Asia than they have been heretofore." [23] Although he soon abandoned his sanguine expectations about the international ramifications of the Revolution, he never ceased to express his regard for the amazing spirit given to the French army by its egalitarian republicanism.[24] Only his conviction that a republic in modern times could exist only by virtue of aggressive militarism and his belief that in Napoleon that French Republic had already found its Caesar must have restrained him from becoming an outright supporter of the regime.

In the second place, Ferguson was demonstrably attracted

by the vigor and fervor of the French: here was that very outburst of patriotic heroism for which he had longed. But, unfortunately, the heroes threatened England; Ferguson's own patriotism dictated opposition to their designs. Unlike Burke's, however, Ferguson's opposition to the French Revolution was without venom, respectful, and even, perhaps, tinged with regret.

In the mildness of his reaction to the French Revolution, as in the fervor of his advocacy of the militia, Ferguson departed from his customary program of lending every support to official policy in order to sustain the firm authority he considered requisite to a civilized society. Although the intensity of his opposition to the French differed only in degree from that manifested by official spokesmen and implicit in official policy, the difference in quantity actually involved an important deviation from his normal political course. The violent diatribes uttered in Britain against the Revolution and all its works were not intended solely—or even primarily—to whip up enthusiasm for the war: they were intended to forestall the spread of subversive "French opinions" within Britain itself, just as the sedition prosecutions were intended to root them out wherever they had already taken hold.[25]

If Ferguson scrupled to equate a revolution against "frivolous corrupted pretenders to aristocracy" with a devastation of all morality and virtue, if he declined to join the crusade against the "vile levelling Jacobins," it was not because he rejected British institutions in favor of French ones.[26] His reluctance was rather due to the same reason which had led him to excoriate the Scottish political leaders when, in his view, they had betrayed the militia for the silver of continued government support of Scottish commercial interest. He would not glorify the rule of a class he judged unfit any more than he would condone the abandonment of a vital moral principle he believed unopposed to any other more vital principle. Ferguson conditioned his support of the status quo on the extent to which that order served principles he considered morally defensible.

In general he found that it did so to a high degree. When it did not, he opposed it whenever he believed that the terms of his opposition would not jeopardize that social stability he considered indispensable on moral grounds. Thus, he wrote the militia pamphlets in the conviction that the injection of moral energy therein advocated would promote order as well. But he could see no viable alternative to the existing structure. Whenever he feared that his opposition to the policies of the established authorities might upset the social equilibrium and thus pave the way to tyranny and chaos, he confined his murmuring to private conversations or correspondence. At times, in fact, the existence of internal conflict can only be inferred from ambiguous pronouncements or surprising silences.

A case in point is the whole file of Ferguson's letters to Macpherson from 1793 to 1805—totaling more than fifty letters, with often two or three a month during 1795 and 1796—which remarkably contains not one reference to the sedition trials or a single imprecation against the domestic "Jacobins."

Ferguson, then, agreed completely with the dominant groups in Scottish society about the form and distribution of socio-political power. He was an ardent defender of the constitution and of the prevailing pattern of social subordination. But to the extent that his energies were not fully absorbed by struggles against all threats to stability, he did express some misgivings about existing conditions. The object of his uneasiness was the "spirit" animating society: he was troubled by the absence of the kind of *elan* and patriotism characteristic of a community with a sense of high moral purpose. Most of his fellow-citizens, he observed, were quite prepared to obey the law and their superiors, but they did so without enthusiasm, driven by fear or interest rather than public spirit. Accordingly, he defined the basic problem of his time as a problem of spiritual regeneration. Many of his opinions about political questions and his ventures into political practice were directed at solving this problem. But the problem was transformed into a dilemma whenever it appeared as though the solution conflicted with the maintenance of that very social order which Ferguson sought to imbue with new moral authority.

Both the problem which preoccupied Ferguson and the dilemma which stymied him reflect his circumstances—the social setting in general and his own particular role in society. It has been shown that the radical transformation of Scottish economic life entailed significant disruptions of traditional habits and customary relationships. The architects of these changes, in most cases the same men who had been accorded social supremacy by tradition and custom, purchased progress at the cost of the established bases of their authority. This constituted a genuine problem for them, but, as noted above, it was a *political* and *practical* problem. They were prepared to shore up their authority by means of all the techniques placed at their disposal by political influence and wealth. Relying on economic inducements, santification by clergy and law, and—as a last resort—coercion, they were able to retain power throughout the period here under study. Regardless of their efficacy, however, these techniques of rule left unsatisfied the clergymen, lawyers, professors, and writers who composed the Scottish intelligentsia. Ferguson and his associates had, after all, been trained in a cultural tradition which demanded some moral justification for power and which assumed that, in general, the moral claims of legiti-

mate rulers would be recognized by the community. For
them the spectacle of an authority seemingly sustained
by indifference, selfishness, and arcana posed a serious
moral and *theoretical* problem. A genuine reconciliation to the existing order required, first, the formulation of
an acceptable principle of moral justification, and second,
the conviction that the society was in fact integrated by this
principle. The problem which Ferguson considered most
urgent, in short, was defined by his role as an intellectual at
a time when traditional modes of justifying power had
broken down.

But it is important to note that these intellectuals (with
very few exceptions) struggled to devise justification, not
criticism: they sought reconciliation, not revolution. Seeing
no alternative to rule by the enlightened aristocracy except
rule by ignorant preachers and reactionary masses, and
bound to the ruling group by ties of friendship and depend-
ency, they were in no way prepared to jeopardize stability in
the name of explosive and subversive principles. The formulations they devised had to conform at one and the same
time to the dictates of the humanistic tradition in which
they gloried and to the demands of the reality they respected. Their political activity had to aim at permeating the
ranks of men with a high moral tone without altering the
structure of ranks itself. Insofar as Ferguson's engagement
in politics was halting, it reveals the extent to which the
problem presented itself as a dilemma, the extent to which
historical circumstances made it, perhaps, insoluble.

His literary activity, too, manifests the full range of the
problem and the dilemma. From his conviction that the
existing order had to be maintained arose a propagandistic
and apologetic strain in his writings; from his belief that the
decisive problem had to be solved by moral rather than social
or political reform stemmed a constant endeavor to endow

his writings with exhortative values; and, finally, from his honest perplexity came the attempt to bring into harmony his understanding of moral principle and of social reality—an attempt which involved some revision of the received moral doctrine he sought to perpetuate and some reinterpretation of the reality he sought to comprehend and transvalue. His first literary role, that of ideologist, he filled with considerable success, as measured by the acclaim accorded his writings by the authorities. The assessment of his performance in the second role, that of moral teacher, must be more reserved: although Ferguson and others like him certainly helped to inculcate the fervid moral rhetoric which pervaded British public life for the succeeding century (and which can still be heard in England and America), there is no evidence to show that they produced the kind of community spirit towards which they aspired. The evaluation of Ferguson's writings in the light of their third and most important function, that of providing intellectual clarification of decisive problems and of offering viable solutions, requires more careful examination of the texts.

1. Edinburgh University Letters, No. 72 to John Macpherson.

2. The theme runs through his correspondence with Macpherson: "I suspect you are too much agitated with the winds that blow from so many different quarters of this Political Horizon. We who are not entrusted with either sail or rudder ought to take our station as Passengers & not accountable even if the ship go down. Such is my Preaching if not my Practice" (ibid., No. 71 to John Macpherson).

3. The Morality of Stage Plays Seriously Considered (Edinburgh, 1757). For details of the Douglas controversy, see supra, pp. 26 f.

4. Ibid., p. 24.

5. Remarks on a Pamphlet . . . , op. cit., p. 39 and pp. 39–50 passim.

6. Edinburgh University Letters, No. 7 to John Macpherson (dated October 27, 1777); already at the time of the Stamp Act crisis,

Ferguson had cautioned that British policies were threatening, not only the profitable colonial trade, but also the very existence of England. See *ibid.*, No. 1 to John Macpherson.

7. Edinburgh University Letters, No. 17 to John Macpherson (dated January 10, 1780).

8. British Museum, Additional MSS, 34417, fols. 36–37, cited in H. Butterfield, *op. cit.* Ferguson's quasi-official activities are not easy to trace. That he maintained constant connection with leading ministerialists at this time and later is clear; that he also performed some minor political services for them is probable. In October, 1783, Sir Thomas Dundas, acting political manager of Scotland, wrote to Lord North urging him to act on some matter on the advice of a Mr. Ferguson as "he and Mr. Robertson are the two persons who have undertaken the Burthen and Management of Kirk politics in this Country, and to whose activity Government is greatly indebted" (Meikle, *op. cit.*, p. 30). Without the titles for both professor and principal it cannot be established that they are meant, but it is quite likely.

9. For some reason, Black, *op. cit.*, p. 372, and Christie, *op. cit.*, p. 173 n., both suggest that Ferguson sided with Wyvill. But compare Meikle, *op. cit.*, p. 9.

10. Wyvill, *op. cit.*, IV, 215–16. Wyvill had no doubt that Ferguson's letter opposed the work of his committee. In a long footnote appended to his reproduction of the letter, Wyvill begins by explaining why he feels called upon to publish (ten years after the event) an "opinion . . . not comformable with the sentiments of the Yorkshire Committee. It would be ungenerous to suppress," he writes, "what has been briefly said, with the greatest appearance of Wisdom, by such a man, to dissuade their attempt of Reformation . . ."; then follows a long defense of the Committee's position (*ibid*).

11. *Reflections Previous to the Establishment of a Militia* (London, 1756), pp. 1–12 *passim;* Ferguson summed up this crucial stage of the argument in the following words: "But when I impute the decline of our martial dispositions to those very circumstances which we must value the most, I shall perhaps be understood to speak unfavourably for the Institution which I have professed to recommend. The happy form of our Government; the sacred Authority with which our laws execute themselves; the Perfection to which Arts are arrived; the Extent of our commerce, and Increase of our People; the Degrees of Taste and Literature which we possess; the Probity and Humanity which prevail in our manners; are circumstances of which a Nation may be allowed to boast of. Such is the height to which every improving Nation aspires, and at which but a few have arrived. We are, however, to blame for having suffered these halcyon days to lull us so entirely asleep. It may be allowed that the Perfection now attained in every Art, and the Attention required to furnish what is demanded in every branch of Business, have led away from the

military profession great Numbers of our People; and that Applications are becoming frequent which seem to disqualify men in a great degree for the Use of Arms. But self-defence is the Business of all: and we have already gone too far, in the opinion that Trade and Manufacture are the only Requisites in our Country. In Pursuit of such an Idea, we labour to acquire Wealth; but neglect the means of defending it. We would turn this nation into a Company of Manufacturers, which each is confined to a particular branch and sunk into the Habits and Peculiarities of his Trade. In this we consult the success of good Work; but slight the Honours of human nature: We furnish good Work; but educate men, gross, sordid, void of sentiment and Manners, who may be pillaged, insulted, and trod upon by the enemies of their Country" (*ibid.*, pp. 11–12). The theoretical implications and presuppositions of the criticism of excessive specialization running through the passage will be discussed in a later section.

12. *Ibid.*, p. 32 (emphasis supplied). Ferguson's endeavor to counter any fear that the militia schemes might upset existing class relations was called forth by the arguments offered by the opponents of the scheme, as well as by Ferguson's own preoccupation with the possibility. Speaking for the Whig aristocracy, Lord Chancellor Hardwicke reportedly said during the debate in the House of Lords: "I am afraid of carrying it [i.e., the militia service] down to the very lowermost rank of the people, because it might produce two very dangerous effects. In the first place it would take their minds very much off from industry or labour, and in the next, it would incline them to be mutinous and riotous. . . . Our men of property are our only freemen, according to the meaning of the word among the old Grecians and Romans: their servants were all slaves; and they never put arms into the hands of their slaves . . ." (*Hansard's Parliamentary History* [London, 1813], XV, 743–44).

In his attack on Pitt's Militia Bill of 1756–57, Lord Chancellor Hardwicke also contrasted the ideal of a commercial and civilized society to all militarism: ". . . I was never more convinced of any proposition in my life than of this, that a nation of merchants, manufacturers, artisans and husbandmen, defended by an army is vastly preferable to a nation of soldiers. . . . I repeat it again, that it is to this progressive change in your people from arms to industry, that your commerce, your colonies, and consequently your riches, are owing.

"What is the object of the present war? The preservation of that commerce and of those colonies. If you turn the bulk of your common people into soldiers, what will become of all these? You may indeed stand upon your guard with arms in your hands; but, in the course of years, I fear you will have little of value left worth guarding; an untrading, unmanufacturing, unimproving, impoverished country" (quoted from Hardwicke's version of his statement as printed in a footnote to the report in *Hansard's Parliamentary History*, XV, 734–36 n.).

13. Ferguson advocated a scheme basically similar to that in force for England since the Restoration. The King appointed a Lord Lieutenant in each county and "the subordinate offices were appointed by the Lord Lieutenant who selected them from among the local landowners, their rank in the militia being dependent on the income they derived from their real estate" (Leon Radzinowicz, *A History of English Criminal Law and Its Administration from 1750* [New York: Macmillan, 1957], III, 98–99). In its fear of the standing army, Ferguson's argument coincides with contemporary discussions in England, but his primary sources appear to be classical and republican because he neglects internal police questions altogether and rejects a morality-enforcing task for the militia. In this he breaks with the general tone of English proposals (Radzinowicz, *op. cit.*).

14. *Proceedings in the Case of Margaret* . . . , This rather labored production is largely given over to derisive gibes at the frantic scurryings of "Hubble-Bubble" (Duke of Newcastle) and the fumbling sycophancy of "Bumbo" (Robert Dundas). Carlyle and others regarded it as a masterpiece of wit.

15. Edinburgh University Letters, Nos. 14 and 16 to John Macpherson.

16. *Ibid.*, No. 62.

17. *Ibid.*, No. 53.

18. *Ibid.*, No. 52.

19. *Ibid.*, No. 56 (dated December 21, 1798).
The resemblance between Ferguson's reaction to the French Revolution and Winston Churchill's attitude towards Russia is striking. Not only is there the same idea of a *cordon sanitaire*, but also there is the same fear of rousing the spirit of a power which would become a dangerous foe if united. Anastas Mikoyan has reported that, during one of the wartime conferences, Churchill replied to a teasing reminder of his anti-Soviet role after World War I by claiming an Order of Lenin for his part in forging the strength of the Red Army. Ferguson would have said the same.

20. *Ibid.*, No. 51 (dated September 26, 1797).

21. Unpublished Essays, "Of the French Revolution with its actual and still impending Consequence in Europe," pp. 7–8.

22. Edinburgh University Letters, No. 61 (July 15, 1799).

23. National Library MSS, No. 1809.

24. *Ibid.*, No. 3464 (letters to Carlyle dated October 2, 1797, and February 10, 1800).

25. John Millar, Ferguson's contemporary and the radical professor of law at the University of Glasgow, analyzed these dynamics in a brilliant pamphlet—although he was prepared to go so far as to suggest that the whole war against Revolutionary France was motivated by domestic considerations. He wrote: "The intention of our

ministers in attempting the conquest of France was to stop the progress of what are called French opinions. The crusades, for the purpose of redeeming the holy sepulchre from the hands of the infidels, were not half so absurd; for those expeditions had really some tendency to procure the ridiculous end which was proposed. But the cudgelling twenty-five millions of people out of a system of opinions which they had most deliberately adopted and which they considered as essential to the security of their lives and their property, is evidently beyond the reach of human strength. Had we marched our victorious armies from one corner of France to the other, had we subverted all the new institutions, and restored the old government in France, had we broiled ten thousand Jacobins at a British *auto da fé,* we should probably have been as far as ever from our purpose, either of extinguishing republican tenets in that country, or of persuading the people in this island, that a reform of parliamentary representation is not indispensably requisite for the preservation of our liberties" (John Millar, *Letters of Crito on the Causes, Objects, and Consequences of the Present War* [Edinburgh: J. Johnstone, 1796], pp. 80–81). Although Ferguson, for reasons that will become clear in the examination of his analysis of modern society, never shared Millar's enthusiasm for radical reform, the type of analysis Millar employed in the pamphlet was identical with Ferguson's in the *Douglas* and American-Revolution pamphlets. In all three, the issues of the controversy are translated into their meaning for the domestic social arrangements. It is, therefore, not unlikely that Ferguson saw the implications of the anti-French crusade in a similar light.

But it is really unnecessary to depend on such speculations. The whole campaign against the "seditionists" in Scotland and England proceeded on the assumption that they were Jacobins, scourges of mankind as vile as their comrades across the Channel. See Henry Thomas Cockburn, *An Examination of the Trials for Sedition in Scotland* (Edinburgh: David Douglas, 1888); and, of course, Burke's *Reflections.*

Christopher Wyvill wrote in defense of the Yorkshire Association movement: "In a few years after those unsuccessful efforts to restore the Representation, a new system of Terror and Undue Influence was introduced by the Minister of Reform [i.e., Pitt] himself; and combining it with the miseries of a most calamitous war, he nearly drove the Nation into the gulph of Revolution. . . . But for what purpose was this complicated system of domestic crimes and miseries adopted? Doubtless, that a scheme of internal coercion might check the spirit of innovation, and guard the Constitution against the possible excesses of Reformers! And among other avowed objects of the war with France, this was the principal and the least chimerical" (Wyvill, *loc. cit.*).

26. The first phrase in quotation marks appears in the letter cited in note 22 above. That Ferguson went on to speak of their "rascally successors" does not affect the main lines of the present argument. The

term "rascal" carries far more the connotation of upstart impudence than of moral depravity.

The second quoted phrase appeared in a letter by Alexander Carlyle to John Macpherson, cited in Carlyle, *op. cit.*, p. 447. "Jupiter" (as Carlyle was nicknamed by his friends) wrote: "I wish that I were the Bold Thunderer for a week or two against the vile levelling Jacobins whom I abhor."

PART II

ADAM FERGUSON'S MORAL
PHILOSOPHY

By Philosophy, is understood the Knowledge acquired by Reasoning, from the Manner of the Generation of any thing, to the Properties; or from the Properties, to some possible Way of Generation of the same; to the end to bee able to produce, as far as matter, and humane force permit, such Effects, as humane life requireth.

—*Thomas Hobbes*

CHAPTER V

The Possibility of Knowledge

FERGUSON, like most of his Scottish contemporaries, was convinced that the epistemological speculations of Hume and his predecessors represented a dangerous threat to the certainty of knowledge and that this threat had to be repelled for the sake of morality and the public good. Before presenting his ideas on moral and social questions, therefore, he felt compelled to defend knowledge against skeptical doubts. In some ways, this might appear as a curiously unreasonable conviction, since Hume, in any case, had repeatedly and sincerely disavowed any intention of questioning the practical integrity of useful, empirically founded knowledge. No one rejected "excessive skepticism" or Pyrrhonism with greater vigor than Hume, and no one scoffed more heartily at any attempt to suspend action or judgment because of abstruse epistemological considerations. Hume claimed only two practical consequences for his philosophical speculations: first, that the skepticism of "academi-

#1

ag'st
Metaprs

cal philosophy" produces tolerance and eliminates dogma-
tism; and, second, that it leads to the "limitation of our
enquiries to such subjects as are best adopted to the narrow
capacity of human understanding"—that is, to "a correct
judgment . . . , avoiding all distant and high enquiries
[which] confines itself to common life and to such subjects
as fall under daily practice and experience." [1] On the face of
it, such a proposition might be expected to have appeared
completely unexceptionable to a man like Ferguson, who
prided himself on his disdain for useless knowledge. Yet he
and his friends refused to be comforted by Hume's assur-
ances and persisted in considering Hume's epistemology as a
source of serious, socially relevant concern.

Although for many this concern derived primarily from a
determined misunderstanding sustained by a sense of out-
raged theological dignity, this was not true in Ferguson's
case. He never joined the hysterical outcry against Hume as
a devilish subverter of all religion and morality because he
was aware of the distinction which Hume had drawn between "demonstrative reasoning," [2] subject to skeptical
doubts and addressed to speculation alone, and "moral reasoning," firmly drawn from experience and directed to action. But he refused to allow Hume this distinction; he
wrote:

> The sceptic sometimes affects to distinguish the prov-
> inces of speculation and action. While, in speculation, he
> questions the evidence of sense; in practice, he admits it
> with the most perfect confidence: But speculations in
> science are surely of little account if they have not any
> relation to subjects of actual choice and pursuit; and if they
> do not prepare the mind for the discernment of matters,
> relating to which there is actual occasion to decide, and to
> act, in the conduct of human life. [3]

This argument itself differs from that often advanced by Hume only in denying the legitimacy of a division between speculative and practical knowledge. Ferguson was determined to assert the unity and certainty of all knowledge. Knowledge, he insisted, is all based primarily on consciousness and sense perception, all relevant to human action, and all true, in the only possible sense of the word. In an important way, then, Ferguson's dispute with Hume was a dispute over words: viz., whether man's non-mathematical and non-tautological knowledge is simply vindicated by the "mighty authority of experience" [4] or whether it is "real" or true knowledge—whether man "believes" or "knows" the principles necessary for a decent life.

And, like most such disputes when they are contested, it touched on a point of honor, or pride. For Ferguson, Hume's speculations—despite all the concessions they make to common-sense practicality (and perhaps even because of them)—represented an affront to man's dignity. "[There] is a principle," he wrote, "in respect to which man differs from the other animals, not only in measure or degree, but totally, and in kind. This principle we term his intelligence or mind, intimately conscious of itself, as it exists in thought, discernment, and will." [5] Man's "dominion in nature" is based on "the authority of a mind over-ruling and wise," his government over his own mind rests on "a godlike form of understanding and of will." [6] Against such majestic claims for the human mind as those advanced by Ferguson, Hume asserted, "the experimental reasoning itself, which we possess in common with the beasts, and on which the whole conduct of life depends, is nothing but a species of instinct or mechanical power, that acts in us unknown to ourselves." [7] Ferguson's insistence on dispelling the doubts raised by Hume appears ultimately actuated by a desire to protect the "lofty pretensions" of the human mind and of the human species.[8]

This is not to say that Ferguson recognized no limitations on human knowledge. One of the crucial arguments he borrowed from Thomas Reid to counter Hume, in fact, revolves precisely about the constant reiteration that human reason is incapable of explaining such "ultimate facts" as consciousness, perception, and knowledge.[9] But for Ferguson as for Reid, the limitations of knowledge do not in any way render uncertain the truth of that which can be known; they guarantee, rather, that there can be no standpoint from which to question the knowledge which man does possess. The main point, then, which Ferguson sought to establish against Hume is that man is not only an animal capable of accumulating from experience the knowledge he needs to conduct his life affairs wisely, but a being of superior dignity capable of obtaining some real knowledge of the world. Although he made a few references to Reid's arguments in defense of this point, he relied above all on repeated assertions that the evidence of consciousness and perception is simply incontrovertible and that the questions of how men come to believe the most basic ideas and how one can validate these beliefs are meaningless. He capped his presentation by observing:

> Whatever we are conscious of, or whatever we perceive has an evidence prior to argument or testimony; and it is indeed from premises so known, that we are enabled in the construction of argument, to infer the most certain conclusions. But, as testimony has usurped the name of evidence in the courts of law, argument or inference has usurped it no less in the discussion of science. And the maxim, that no proposition is to be received without evidence, is supposed to imply the necessity of argument in support of every truth.[10]

This statement makes it clear that Ferguson cared little
for engaging in abstruse disputes with Hume; the issue
between them was moral and political far more than epistemological. Following Reid, Ferguson was prepared to concede to Hume that man cannot demonstrate the logical
necessity of inductive generalizations, that he cannot conceive of power apart from its effects; but he would not allow
these concessions to lead to any imputations against the
intrinsic and absolute reliability of man's thought processes
where they are based on facts of consciousness or of perception. He feared that the admission of doubt on this score
might sap man's vitality and self-respect; and, for Ferguson,
the assurance bred of firm conviction is an integral part of
personally upright and socially righteous behavior.

For similar reasons, Ferguson insisted on the possibility of
acquiring real knowledge, not only about the physical laws
which govern natural phenomena, but also about the moral
laws which ought to govern human conduct. Furthermore,
he was again not placated by the concessions which Hume
had made to the practical certainty and physical necessity of
traditionally-sanctioned civilized moral standards. In this
Ferguson differed from most of his contemporaries as well as
from Hume. Most of the others, like Hume himself, were
content to defend the psychological reality of benevolent
impulses against the attacks of Hobbesian hedonism which,
they insisted, had been viciously put forward by Mandeville. Hutcheson, Hume, and Smith had addressed themselves to the problem of accounting for the psychological
mechanisms of moral judgment and had, in general, defined
virtue as that which these mechanisms lead man to approve.
Thus having established (through a principle of beneficent
moral sense, benevolent sentiment, or sympathy) the psychological possibility and necessity of unselfish moral judgments, their moral theory goes on to explicate the

"qualit[ies] of the mind agreeable to or approved of by everyone who considers or contemplates [them]."[11] But Ferguson asserted that "the important and genuine question of moral philosophy [is] *de finibus* or what is the end"[12] and that explaining the phenomenon of moral approbation is at most only a preparation for genuine moral theory, which has to set forth the true nature of human excellence.

Moreover, he denied that Hutcheson, Hume, and Smith had adequately solved even the problem they had set themselves. Although he considered the term "moral sense," which Hutcheson had borrowed from Shaftesbury, a perfectly acceptable name for the process of correct moral judgment, he maintained that it is quite useless as an explanation of that process. He was even prepared, he said, to accept "moral sense" as an "ultimate fact" and to abandon the search for an explanation. But he was not willing to consider this tautology as itself a moral theory, and he feared that Hutcheson's formulation might lead to such a false conclusion. In other words, he was afraid that it might lead to a failure to recognize that the operation of the "moral sense" can only be identified by someone who has some real knowledge of the criteria for correctness in moral judgments. At most, he believed, the term can be properly used to indicate that, for some inexplicable reason, men "are by nature well qualified to perceive [the distinction of moral excellence]."[13]

In discussing Hume's treatment of this problem, Ferguson mistakenly insisted that Hume had built his whole theory around the principle of utility expanded by sympathy. Although, in the *Treatise,* Hume had given adequate grounds for such an interpretation, he had sought to clarify his position in the *Enquiries* so as to rest his explanation of moral approbation on a direct sentiment of agreeableness as well as on utility. This amplification or revision obviates those of Ferguson's criticisms which attack Hume's theory as even inadequate to account for the phenomena it set out to explain. Perhaps because he had not read the later book or even because it served his polemical purposes, Ferguson focused attention exclusively on the earlier version of Hume's theory. He charged that it cannot account for the approbation bestowed on actions which are well intentioned but unsuccessful, and he rejected the contention that men approve the concern which others display for their own self-preservation. His constant complaint against Hume is that he explains only the approbation of useful consequences, not the praise men bestow on benevolent intentions. This emphasis on the externals of morality, he believed, disregards the decisive internal qualities which properly constitute virtue.[14]

Ferguson's most violent attacks, however, were directed against Adam Smith's theory of sympathy.[15] He argued, in short, that it rests on an abuse of language. In normal usage, according to Ferguson, men often speak of sympathizing with others although they do not grant moral approval to their actions; they never speak of sympathizing with themselves. Ferguson believed that the theory is saved from patent absurdity only by giving the word a "sense [that] is generally unknown," and he insisted that, therefore, "to explain moral sentiments by sympathy is to explain the known by the unknown."[16] Furthermore—and most importantly—Ferguson asserted that Smith's theory escapes complete relativism only through the introduction of a *petitio principii*. Denying that the criterion of genuine sympathy, in his sense, is the subjective feeling of every man or the opinion of the masses, Smith ultimately relied on a "well informed and impartial observer"; but this person, according to Ferguson, can only be discovered by one able to discern

extra
Sultan.

the man "well informed" about virtue—and this cannot be discovered without some standard outside sympathy. "Here then," wrote Ferguson, "ends your [i.e., Smith's] system after beating round a circle of objections and answers." [17]

These criticisms remain within the limits of Hutcheson's, Hume's, and Smith's definition of the key problem in moral theory, but Ferguson's main objection is addressed to that definition itself. He wrote:

> To substitute theory, even of mind, for moral science would be an error and an abuse. This abuse, indeed, has been incurred by many, who take the distinction of physical and moral science from the subjects to which they relate, not from the objects to which they are directed. Physical science they suppose to be a knowledge of subjects material; moral science a knowledge of mind, or of subjects intellectual: And they accordingly place theoretical speculations on the subject of mind, among the discussions of moral philosophy. In their apprehension, moral approbation and disapprobation are mere phenomena to be explained; and in such explanations their science of morals actually terminated. The phenomena of moral approbation have been supposed no more than a diversified appearance of the consideration that is paid to private interest, to public utility, to the reason of things: or they have been supposed to result from the sympathy of one man with another.
>
> But if moral sentiment could be thus explained into any thing different from itself, whether interest, utility, reason or sympathy, this could amount to no more than a theory. And it were difficult to say to what effect knowledge is improved, by resolving a first act of mind into a second, no better known than the first. The effect of a theory so applied, for the most part, has been to render the distinction of good and evil more faint than it commonly appears under the ordinary expressions of esteem and love, or of indignation and scorn.[18]

For these philosophical and morally pragmatic reasons, then, he demanded that attention be redirected to the really important problem of defining "the greatest good of which human nature is susceptible"; [19] he insisted that this problem cannot be approached by equating the criteria of goodness with theories accounting for actual psychological happenings.

But if it is correct to characterize Ferguson as primarily an intellectual who engaged in philosophizing in order to accumulate ideas which would enable him to articulate his orientation to practical life, then it might still appear strange that he refused to accept theoretical formulations which, despite some speculative difficulties, offered intellectually respectable support for his practical point of view. The moral teachings endorsed by Hutcheson, Hume, and Smith closely approximate his own; why then did he demand a certain knowledge of ends distinct from the generalizations about the actual standards of moral judgment which his contemporaries had combined with a demonstration that these principles necessarily inhere in human nature?

If he were only concerned with a proud assertion of the mind's capacity for certain knowledge, as in his opposition to Hume's epistemology, he could have rested content with the moral theories of Hutcheson or Smith, who eschewed skeptical doubts. But his claims in behalf of the unique dignity of mind were not restricted to its cognitive powers: he also sought to celebrate its capacity for choice. If correct judgment were allowed to be the consequence of irresistible natural laws, then, in his view, the mind would be denied its special, godlike power of self-determination. As the following passage makes clear, he was prepared to support this power by drawing on religiously heterodox arguments from Hume as well as on the usual principles from Reid:

The power of choice is a fact of which the mind is conscious: It is therefore supported by the highest evidence of
which any fact is susceptible. Attempts to support it by
argument are nugatory, and attempts to overthrow it by
argument are absurd.

The axiom that every effect must have a cause cannot
bring any new light on this subject. The axiom itself is not
better known than the fact, that will is free, and truths are
certainly consistent one with the other. The consciousness
of freedom hath been termed a deceitful feeling; but why
not the axiom, that every effect must have a cause, a
deception also? If we say the axiom is a necessary truth; it
may be so when well understood. Effect is correlative to
cause, and they are inseparable; but there may be existence
without any cause external to itself, as there may be will
without any cause but the mind that is willing.

Every rational action, indeed, has a motive; for the very
purpose which constitutes rationality is itself a motive: But
may not the mind determine itself; and amidst the consideration or objects which are presented to its choice, be the
cause of its own determination? [20]

The implication of universal prescience in the perfect
intelligence of God, from which we would infer, that every
future event is no less certainly future, than that every past
event is certainly past, is an argument of the same kind.
We would reject a fact that is perfectly within our cognizance, on the credit of an argument taken from a subject
that is beyond our reach. We know not the nature of
divine omniscience; and if the Almighty hath opened a
source of contingence in nature, we may suppose that
contingence itself is a perfection in his works. Who can
doubt that intelligence is a quality of the highest order in
the scale of created being; and that discernment and freedom of choice are essential to intelligent beings. [21]

Since intelligent volition must, in his view, be free, the
ultimate standards of virtuous judgment must be distinct
from deductions drawn from the necessary fundamental
attributes of actual human nature.

Nor was Ferguson prepared to accept moral standards derived from generalizations about actual practice, even if the process of generalizing entailed a purifying elimination of contradictory principles. He was unwilling to consign man to normal or average standards of behavior: the striving for a perfection never to be completely attained he regarded as the culminating glory of mankind. A true moral theory, accordingly, has to set goals which only a hero or a saint can approach. No such theory can be developed by mere abstraction from practice; Ferguson urged the following distinctions:

> A physical law of nature is a general statement of what is uniform or common in the order of things, and is addressed to the powers of perception and sagacity. A moral law of nature is equally general, though an expression not of a fact but of what is good; and is addressed to the powers of estimation and choice.
>
> Respecting the subjects of moral law, whatever may be their actual condition, the law does not state what is, but enjoins what ought to be done or avoided.
>
> Physical law is applied to the formations of theory, or the explanation of phenomena; and is the foundation of power. Moral law is applied to determine the choice of voluntary agents, and suggest the purpose to which their power is or ought to be employed.
>
> As, in physical science, our object is to investigate and comprehend the actual state of things, no mere hypothesis or supposition can be admitted among the laws of nature: and in moral science, our object being to determine a choice of what is best, no mere fact can be adduced to preclude our endeavours to obtain, in any subject, what is better than its actual state.[22]

Although the distinction between physical and moral law is thus laid down as a fundamental principle of Ferguson's writings, he did not adhere rigidly to its dictates.[23] His moral

arguments frequently rely—in "moral-sense" fashion—on
the claim that certain principles of judgment are irresistibly
present in all men or—in a manner common even to Epicurean philosophers—on the assertion that other principles of
judgment only seem to lead to a feeling of happiness but
really lead to ultimate misery. In addition, his "perfectionist"
and "heroic" moral teachings differ remarkably little from
the "normal" and "natural" principles inculcated by Hume
and other contemporaries. But these very inconsistencies
serve to illuminate the main point of the present discussion:
Ferguson's insistence on a separate but certain theory of
ends is important, first of all, as the act of a moral teacher,
and secondly, as a moral act—a public statement of principle. It seems intended—like his excursion into epistemology—to assert a specific conception of human dignity,
because failure to make the assertion is, in Ferguson's view,
itself a socially irresponsible act. Any aspersions on the
unique qualities which he considered as cause, symbol, and
authority for man's superiority over non-mindful nature
confuses man's moral judgment and destroys his self-confi-
dence. Ferguson's forays against Hume's epistemology and
his strictures against his contemporaries' approaches to
moral theory do not mean that he was prepared to dispense
with the ideas and analytical tools these might provide:
they indicate his determination to preserve entire an ideal
of man—rational, free, and reaching for the stars.

But the common determination underlying Ferguson's
attack on skepticism and his disagreement with his colleagues about the proper procedure in moral theory must not
obscure important differences between the two situations.
To dismiss the doubts raised by Hume, he could simply call
on the authority of Reid, rehearse a few of Reid's arguments,
and assert with conviction that the knowledge acquired
from self-consciousness and observation is objectively true.

He could, in short, simply proclaim his adherence to the popular trinity of Bacon, Newton, and Reid. But his venture into a moral theory not limited by facts brought him to more treacherous domains. The very theory of knowledge which provided him with security in the first situation here created serious difficulties. If "all knowledge is either of particular facts or general rules," if "the knowledge of facts is prior to that of rules," and if "general rules, and their applications, to regulate or to explain particulars, constitute science," [24] then how can there be a science in which "no mere fact can be adduced . . ."? [25] It was precisely this difficulty which led his colleagues, who were no less morally earnest than he, to attempt the construction of an empirically founded moral science which could replace the Aristotelian structures demolished by the scientific revolution. Since Ferguson, for the reasons enumerated above, rejected such a solution, he was confronted with a gravely perplexing problem.

The simplest way out of such perplexity is to ignore it, and he often did just that. He argued that virtue is that which produces "true" or "higher" happiness and that the distinction between such happiness and mere pleasure is familiar to any uncorrupted mind and has, in any case, frequently been illuminated by the sage moral teachers of antiquity. He relied, in short, on the tradition of moral teachings endowed with the authority of the classics. Furthermore, he insisted that it is best not to push the analysis of this matter too far: there are some areas which science ought to avoid. It is quite true, in his view, that true happiness as well as bestial enjoyments may logically be subsumed under the category of pleasure, because, after all, "in every act of the human will there is some propensity to be gratified and as gratification is but another name for pleasure this in every instance is to be pronounced the object of the will." [26] But it is dangerous to extend the scientific task of generalization to these topics: "After having in this term of pleasure levelled all matters of choice we may endeavour to distinguish them [as either?] dignified or mean," he wrote, "but we shall never perhaps be able to repair the breach in the wall of separation between them." [27] From this point of view, then, Ferguson fought off the whole enterprise of moral science and insisted that the main need was to retain the distinct "*names* of Pleasure and Virtue," [28] on the assumption that the literary associations of the latter term and its reverberations in conscience would be enough to guide moral behavior. Virtue, he maintained, is the same thing as happiness and perfection; wise men have revealed its true constituents; and only a fool can refuse to pursue it.

This traditionalist escape from his philosophical dilemma also provides a quasi-solution for the problem of motivation. Everybody seeks happiness and everybody admires perfection. The wise man will, according to Ferguson, encourage those of his propensities which lead to the true form of these universal ends and will subjugate those which threaten to mislead him. This charming solution, then, cut all the knots of moral theory and prepared the way for a glowing account of the traditional catalogue of virtues unadulterated by philosophical complexities. This approach is an important constituent of Ferguson's writings throughout (and particularly in the *Institutes*), [29] and it served most of his purposes as popularizer and moral teacher.

But as an intellectual, it may be surmised, he must have been made a little uncomfortable by such a blatant evasion of all the issues which formed the heart of informed ethical discussions and which he had himself raised in his critique of the moral-sense school. Accordingly, he sought—in the *Principles of Moral and Political Science* as well as in some of the later unpublished essays—to discover a formulation which would make possible the knowledge of moral principles without ignoring completely the difficulties raised by his commitment to Baconian empiricism and by his awareness of the limited control man's rational wisdom has over his will. While it was all right for him, in some contexts, to give way to his impatience over the difficulties of philosophical reasoning and profess to be "puzzled to guess how this question [of the grounds on which conscience proceeded] came to be started in modern times. Or how it came to hold such a place in Modern Philosophy," [30] this was not a pose suitable to all situations. Ferguson knew very well that it was not "in great measure accidental," [31] but rather due to the very considerations he himself raised against the moral philosophy of Clarke in the following passage:

> Doctor Clarke, and some others, considering virtue as the fitness of man's character and practice to his own frame, and to his place in the system of nature; and, considering reason or understanding itself as competent to observe the fitness of things, have assumed human reason as the principle of moral discernment.
>
> . . . .
>
> But these systems have been rejected, as unfit to explain the phenomenon of moral approbation; which, being itself an affectation or sentiment of the mind, must be derived from a principle to be sought for among the considerations that influence the will, not among the perceptions of mere intelligence, which go no farther than to remark the existence of things.[32]

It took more than a play on the word "happiness" to produce a tenable orientation to the related problems of the possibility and relevance of knowing moral principles. And since Ferguson did not disavow, or in some basic way modify, the characteristically modern rejection of the Platonic hierarchy or of the Aristotelian teleology, his citations of classical authors in support of "true" happiness is simply an evasion.

The approach to a reasoned theory of ends most familiar to Ferguson was, of course, a teleological one, and it is some variant of this which he applied whenever he attempted to establish his position by argument rather than by authoritative fiat. He had ample precedent for such a course: not only was teleology the stock in trade of all the theologians and popular moralists of his time, but it was also invoked by Newton and most of the other naturalists. They were convinced that the logical structure they discerned in the nature of things evinced a divinely purposed harmony, and it was their custom to conclude scientific studies with paeans to the divine craftsman who had made it all. Ferguson's work frequently echoes such hymns of praise. He rarely resisted the temptation of pointing out how wings fit birds for the sky, how gills fit fish for the sea, and so forth. But such an assertion of teleology could serve Ferguson's present theoretical purpose only if it could, somehow, overcome two difficulties, both most clearly presented in Hume's criticism of a teleological viewpoint.

Hume denied the possibility of discerning a divine purpose in the universe itself, and—although his position was somewhat ambiguous—he refused even to concede the attempt to do so the kind of practical justification he accorded to causality. While the custom of assuming causal relations, in his view, can be explained as a natural result of observing the repeated sequence of events encountered in human experience, no such repetition can be experienced with regard to the unique universe. The notion of a universal purpose derives, he maintained, from an unjustified extension to God of man's subjective experience of purposing. Furthermore, he argued, while the assumption of causality is indispensable for practical life, the assumption of divine purpose is completely barren of useful consequences for a reasonable individual. In an argument which he prudently placed in the mouth of a hypothetical friend hypothetically posing as an "Epicurean"—but which he never challenged on its merits—he stated:

> When we argue from the course of nature, and infer a particular intelligent cause, which first bestowed, and still preserves order in the universe, we embrace a principle which is both uncertain and useless. It is uncertain; because the subject lies entirely beyond the reach of human experience. It is useless; because our knowledge of this cause being derived entirely from the course of nature, we can never, according to the rules of just reasoning, return back from the cause with any new inference, or making additions to the common and experienced course of nature, establish any new principles of conduct and behaviour.[33]

At most, Hume was willing to grant the argument the value of a "superstition" socially useful for maintaining order among the uneducated men who erroneously believe that moral teachings can in fact be inferred from teleology; "and those, who attempt to disabuse them of such prejudices, may," he wrote, "for aught I know, be good reasoners, but I cannot allow them to be good citizens and politicians; since they free men from one restraint upon their passions, and make the infringement of the laws of society, in one respect, more easy and secure."[34]

In summary, then, Hume contended, first, that the assumption of teleology rests on a faulty inference from experience, and secondly, that it can, in any case, never provide man with a rational standard for judging any existing phenomenon or practice. The first of these objections Ferguson answered quite easily to his own satisfaction by recourse to Reid. He asserted that the discernment of purpose, like the discernment of cause, is an unassailable "ultimate fact" of consciousness irresistibly "suggested" to man by the things he sees about him. But no such argument meets Hume's second objection. A teleological approach which ascribes harmonious purposiveness to the actual pattern of natural events can function as the basis of theodicy; it can also support a naturalistic moral theory by endowing actual moral impulses with a cosmic sanctity. It can, in other words, justify the kind of moral theory Ferguson had set out to avoid; it cannot define goals which transcend common practices and demand a constant struggle towards perfection.

Insofar as Ferguson failed or did not care to realize that the Newtonian type of teleology which Reid's argument defended was only a prop for the kind of moral theory advanced by Hutcheson and Smith, he developed arguments which were, in fact, indistinguishable from theirs.[35] Thus, he violated his own dictum that moral science ought to be radically separated from physical science: he merely made explicit the metaphysical rationale which tacitly underlies their speculations. Much of Ferguson's moral argument, accordingly, is the kind of generalization from men's actual judgments and from the inborn necessities of human nature which he had condemned in principle. But this kind of confusion can come as no surprise.

As was noted above, Ferguson insisted on the principle of separation primarily because the declaration of insistence itself served an important purpose. Once that purpose had been served, he often felt free to call on almost any kind of theoretical argument to support the moral dictates he considered desirable. It is precisely this eclectic and opportunistic character which precludes considering Ferguson as primarily a serious philosopher. But Ferguson was not totally oblivious to the problem: first, because he really did want to provide a foundation for a few doctrines which the course of empirical generalization—no matter how freely interpreted—could not support; and secondly, because ideas inserted into a body of thought, regardless of the limited purposes for which they are introduced, will germinate and may produce offspring. He therefore repeatedly returned to the question, and his writings reveal two more approaches to the knowledge of true moral theory, both modifications of teleology.

The first of these is more or less a return to premodern formulations, although the continuing tradition of the "great chain of being" provided Ferguson with contemporary models. From this point of view, the divine purpose manifests itself in the creation of a world which is not only harmonious, but also hierarchically ordered. By cataloguing all species according to their unique attributes and ordering them according to a natural criterion of excellence, the philosopher can ascertain the special function(s) assigned to each in the divine economy and distinguish between its "higher" and "lower" characteristics. This was the approach which Ferguson did, in fact, apply to the organization of the first part of the *Principles of Moral and Political Science*. Utilizing the classical technique of divisions, he began with the distinction between dead and living natures; subdivided the latter into inactive (vegetable) and active (animal); further divided the latter into solitary and gregarious; and then carried on the familiar process until he arrived at a definition of men as not merely gregarious but "in the translation of an elegant title bestowed upon them by Aristotle . . . gregarious and political," [36] and, as the culminating quality, endowed with intelligence. Ferguson's identification of intelligence as the highest point in the scale of life rests simply on unquestioned traditional authority.

As it had done for most moral theorists since Plato, this approach enabled Ferguson to expound principles of moral excellence which were not limited by the actual achievements of man but which called on him to employ his highest faculties and capacities. It had two shortcomings for Ferguson, however. In the first place, its traditional formulations culminated in a contemplative ideal in conflict with the eager commitment to social practice which was Ferguson's most characteristic attribute and which he sought to inculcate into his students. But both the Aristotelian and Stoic versions are sufficiently ambiguous on this point to have served Ferguson's purpose if it were not for the presence of a second major difficulty: Ferguson's return to the classical mode of thought left him unprotected against the second horn of a basic dilemma.

It will be recalled that this whole venture into abstruse philosophizing began with the following problem: Ferguson sought to defend the possibility of a scientific moral theory unbounded by mere facts while insisting that all scientific knowledge rests on the perception and consciousness of facts. Even the extension of the term "fact" to such "ultimate facts of consciousness" as causality and teleology supports only a Newtonian type of teleology. The classical type, with its "higher" potentialities and unique essences, requires the kind of epistemology and metaphysics which Aristotle had devised and whose elaboration had been the primary task of scholastic philosophy. But Ferguson, the professed disciple of Bacon, Newton, and Reid, could not accept these preconditions. It would smack of that "infinite deal of dust and rubbish collected in the ages of scholastic sophistry" [37] for whose elimination his master, Reid, had profusely thanked even Descartes, Malebranche, and Locke; it would also call into question his own frequently reiterated claims as a strict empiricist. As can be expected, Ferguson frequently ignored these difficulties and freely used Aristotelian and Stoic arguments with little regard for philosophical niceties.

But he also devised a fourth scheme which really was for him the most generally satisfactory and congenial one. Rather than view all things in nature as possessed of essences which are striving for self-realization, he limited this characteristic to mind. In the following passage, he distinguished between "progressive" and "stationary" subjects:

> To be stationary, it is not necessary that a subject should be incapable of change, even from any external cause. It is sufficient that it have not any principle of change in its own nature. To be progressive, on the contrary, does not consist in any variation or change which an external cause may produce; but in those transitions, from one state to another, which proceed from a principle of advancement in the subject itself.[38]

For progressive natures, accordingly, he held it possible to define the ends they ought to seek on the basis of empirical facts without having those ends limited by the actual facts themselves. He wrote:

> In determining the course which man ought to run, we must observe the steps he is qualified to make, and guess at the termination of his progress, from the beginning of it, or from the direction in which he sets out.[2]
>
> As the study of human nature may refer to the actual state, or to the improveable [sic] capacity of man, it is evident, that, the subjects being connected, we cannot proceed in the second, but upon the foundations which are laid in the first. Our knowledge of what any nature ought to be, must be derived from our knowledge of its faculties and powers; and the attainment to be aimed at must be of the kind which these faculties and powers are fitted to produce.[39]

Since, according to Ferguson, the study of man's actual state proceeds according to the "plain historical" method of Bacon and Reid, this represents, in effect, an attempt to translate the Aristotelian teleology into concrete, historical terms.

Clearly such a formulation raises enormous difficulties of which Ferguson was only dimly aware. Nor, it must be reiterated, was he concerned to eliminate such difficulties in themselves. The present analysis can be viewed as uncovering the philosophical artifacts produced, largely without Ferguson's being aware of their full implications, by a process of thought intended to make bearable certain largely practical conflicts. The notion of limiting progress toward higher ends to mindful subjects enabled Ferguson to avoid admitting his full debt to the Aristotelian world view, provided a rationale for a transcendent scheme of human ends, and still gave at least the appearance of adherence to an empirical methodology.

A major difficulty implicit in Ferguson's fourth approach arises in determining the relationship between this progressive conception of human mind and the over-all view of a universe guided by divine purpose. Hume had already pointed out that, barring the evidence of supernatural revelation, man can ascribe to God future purposes not yet achieved only by identifying God's mind with his own. Even in his basic defense of a teleological view, Ferguson, following Reid, came close to accepting this challenge. The argument which Ferguson accepted was stated most clearly by Reid in the following words:

> I am not able to form any distinct conception of active power, but such as I find in myself. I can only exert my active power by will, which supposes thought. It seems to me, that if I was not conscious of activity in myself, I could never, from things I see about me, have had the conception of idea of active power. I see a succession of changes, but I

see not the power that is the efficient cause of them; but having got the notion of active power, from the consciousness of my own activity, and finding it a first principle, that every production requires active power, I can reason about an active power of that kind I am acquainted with, that is, such as supposes thought and choice, and is exercised by will. But if there is any thing in an unthinking inanimate being that can be called active power, I know not what it is, and cannot reason about it.[40]

The anthropocentrism implicit in this argument is reinforced by Ferguson's insistence that purpose is evidenced and revealed by progress. Although at times he maintained that "the best that can be said even of the universe itself or any created thing is that it is coming into order," [41] he usually described only the human mind as demonstrably progressive. This was done both because progress implies imperfection and thus cannot be reconciled with the traditional view of God as possessing the attribute of perfection and because only human mind and its productions can be subjected to empirical study. The world of matter, he wrote, "exists but for the sake of mind." But, while God is the creator of all, "his meaning is to be collected from the lot [of his creations] & as all is made for man, his lot alone can furnish information of the Creator's will and meaning." [42]

These considerations point up the decisive difference between the position which haltingly emerges in Ferguson's writings and the views of the classics, traditional Christian philosophy, and Newtonian naturalism. Ends implicit in nature (in either the ancient or modern sense) as well as ends implicit in the divine nature or commanded by divine will are all overshadowed by the ends alleged to be implicit in human nature that are suggested by the supposed tendency of its progress. When the distinction between "nature" as the subject matter of physical and of moral science which

Ferguson made in the following passage is combined with his insistence that no direct knowledge of God's mind is possible, the effect is clear:

> The sense in which the terms art and nature are employed when the critic tells us that nature is the standard of excellence in the works of art or the moral philosopher tells us that nature is the standard of felicity in the manners of men, is not nature in a partial view of its parts in their actual [sic] or Art in any change it may produce for the better or the worse: but existing things in the progress & attainments of which the specimens are realized with or without the interposition of human ingenuity and power which are in reality a part of the system of nature, and by their functions destined to contribute to the order of beings [which] gives things the aspect which they bear. In this sense the art, industry & skill of man has its place in nature. . . .[43]

Ferguson's progressive teleology eventuates in a thorough-going anthropocentrism.

Man, in short, is urged to govern his actions and judgments by the goal of realizing his own higher potentialities, and progress consists in giving ever greater play to his own faculties. To all intents and purposes, then, Ferguson's writings suggest that teleology is immanent in nature and, specifically, in human nature. As with the Greeks, it might be said, nature comes alive, resurrected from its mechanical death in Renaissance cosmology. But nature has been transfigured in the process: it lives only in the progressive, purposing, practicing mind of man.

But it must again be pointed out that Ferguson did not pursue these metaphysical speculations with any rigor. The present detailed analysis is justified primarily because, first, the emphasis on man's progressive nature as the source of empirical knowledge about the ends he ought to pursue is embodied in most of the methodological pronouncements contained in Ferguson's last, most comprehensive work; and secondly, it indicates several crucial characteristics of Ferguson's thought, viz., humanism, a tendency toward "historicism," and, finally, a deeply ingrained secularism despite its surface piety. Humanism is revealed by his emphasis on the development and exercise of human faculties. The term "historicism" is here applied in the loosest possible sense to refer merely to Ferguson's recurrent reliance on the concept of temporal development for the solution of problems. That Ferguson's thought was fundamentally secular—and certainly not Christian—can be more extensively documented than it has been so far; such documentation will be offered in another place.

In summary and in conclusion of the present survey of Ferguson's attempts to establish an approach to the knowledge of human ends, it can be noted that four distinguishable approaches are intermingled in Ferguson's writings. The basic problem is defined by his insistence, on the one hand, that moral science must not consist of generalizations derived from facts; on the other, by his equally firm acceptance of empiricism as the path to truth as well as by his recognition that moral truths would be irrelevant if they did not call into play some actual human sentiments capable of directing the will. The first approach to disposing of this problem may be identified as a traditionalist authoritative one. It disparages all complex philosophical disputation and focuses on the inculcation of wise maxims enunciated by ancient sages, disposing of the motivational problem through ambiguous references to man's search for "true" happiness. Although Ferguson found this approach often practically useful and constantly employed it to lend assurance to the conclusions of his more subtle arguments,

it is so clearly an evasion of all the intellectual issues of
his time that he could not rely on it alone.

The second strand of argument discernible in Ferguson's
writings has been called here the Newtonian type of teleology. Relying on Reid's assertions that the events of nature
necessarily suggest a purposive pattern to any intelligent
mind, this approach lends divine authority to the normal
processes of human judgment and thereby transforms the
question of motivation from a perplexing problem into the
major theoretical tool. But the result is precisely the sort of
naturalistic moral science produced by Hutcheson, Hume,
and Smith which Ferguson was presumably trying to avoid.
As is true of the first approach, Ferguson did not hesitate to
utilize arguments based on Newtonian teleology whenever
they did not explicitly impinge on the concerns which had
originally led him to reject such an approach in principle.

Ferguson's heavy debt to classical sources, however, and
his affinity for a conception of virtue more heroic than that
promulgated by his contemporaries (as well as the occasional intrusion of transparent theoretical difficulties), led
him to a third approach. This is closely patterned on the
model of Aristotelian—or, more generally, classical—teleology. Such an approach does provide a method for distinguishing "higher" ends from "lower" ones and for identifying man's essential attributes and excellences quite apart
from the actual choices made by the generality of unwise
men. At the same time, however, it implies a metaphysical
apparatus which Ferguson, in company with his fellows,
had gleefully cast off. Unwilling or unable to break decisively with the modern judgment of the classical world
view and deeply imbued with the belief that "an extension
of knowledge is an extension of power," [44] he could not
rest quietly with an approach which ultimately depended

on "explaining the primary facts of which nature has given us the use but not the theory." [45] The third approach, too, was used by Ferguson in constructing his arguments, but it could not be explicitly avowed as a methodological principle.

It was the fourth approach (here termed the progressive teleological), then, which he espoused in programmatic passages and which best meets the formal theoretical requirements of his endeavors. This formulation of teleology limits the aspiration towards perfection to such beings as can, in fact, be said to display it. By virtue of his mind and on the evidence of his practice, in this view, man can be cited as the clearest exemplar of such a progressive being. Accordingly, it is said, man's destined goal can be inferred from the actual tendency of his progress. Since this approach presumably bases itself on facts without being limited by them, it offers at least a formal solution to Ferguson's dilemma. Furthermore, by claiming to discover an instinctive propensity to seek perfection in all men—although they may err in their definition of perfection—Ferguson also believed that he had solved the problem of the psychological mechanisms underlying moral approbation. Although Ferguson valued this approach above all the others, he did not use it alone.

The reasons for this failure are both theoretical and practical. In the first place, Ferguson's progressive teleology is not sufficiently thought through to stand alone. For the distinction between "progressive" and "degrading" tendencies, it still relies primarily on aids provided by tradition, moral sense, and/or Aristotelian essences. This fundamental weakness is manifest in Ferguson's definitional discussion of the approach: he wrote, "we . . . *guess* at the termination of [man's] progress." [46] He never devised an immanent logic of development which could have enabled him

to transform this "guess" into knowledge. But such lofty
speculative flights were probably beyond his capabilities and
certainly outside the range of his interest.

A second, more specifically practical, explanation for Ferguson's failure to stress consistently even a patched-up version of his progressive teleology can here be suggested, although a detailed exposition of this point must await the
introduction of additional materials. The progressive viewpoint, with its stress on perfection, is inherently critical of all
existing practices and conduct. No matter how Ferguson
might define "perfection," this approach to moral theory
precludes the bestowing of absolute approbation on any
human institution or action. Despite his admiration for heroic striving, Ferguson was not prepared to handle such an
explosive notion under all circumstances. His commitment
to the status quo, as expressed in his role as ideologist, alone
made certain of that. But this line of explanation must be
further explored in another place.

For the present, it is necessary to gather together all the
strands of Ferguson's metaphysical and epistemological speculations. His views of reality and knowledge eventuate in a
conception of man as a being capable of knowing as much
about nature as he needs to know and capable of guiding his
genuinely free decisions by clear principles of moral excellence. This being, in Ferguson's view, is consequently endowed with a grandeur and dignity second only to that of
God—about whom, however, nothing can be said. In the
process of establishing such a picture—or, better, in defending it against all challenges—Ferguson felt constrained to
fight off the threats he believed posed by excessive refinement of critical philosophy and by the extension of mechanistic science to the determination of moral excellence. For
the former task, he sought the assistance of Reid's writings;
for the latter, he relied on a variety of intellectual weapons.

Throughout can be detected the leaven of classical ideas, but Ferguson was never prepared to give up, in principle, the advances in knowledge which he believed had been achieved through the ideas of Bacon, Newton, and even of Hume. Constantly tempted to avoid difficulties by recourse to authoritative truisms, he nevertheless constantly returned to the attempt to set matters aright through some plausible combination of ideas. This intermingling of influences and characteristics—classical and modern scientific, truistic common sense and speculative ideas, pious and secular, practical and "idealistic"—permeates all of Ferguson's writings. And the result sought is always intellectually respectable support for an orientation predicated on a view of man as at home in a world of noble actions.

1. David Hume, *Enquiries Concerning the Human Understanding and Concerning the Principles of Morals,* ed. L. A. Selby-Bigge (2nd ed.; Oxford: Oxford University Press, 1902), p. 162.

2. *Ibid.,* p. 35.

3. Adam Ferguson, *Principles of Moral and Political Science* (London: printed for A. Strahan and T. Cadell; Edinburgh: printed for W. Creech, 1792), I, 91.

4. Hume, *Enquiries,* p. 36.

5. Ferguson, *Principles,* I, 48.

6. *Ibid.,* pp. 2, 3.

7. Hume, *Enquiries,* p. 108.

8. *Ibid.,* p. 41.

9. Ferguson, *Principles,* I, 75.

10. *Ibid.,* pp. 89–90.

11. Hume, *Enquiries,* p. 261.

12. Unpublished Essays, "Of the Principle of Moral Estimation," p. 31; compare Hume, *Enquiries,* pp. 25–27. This essay gives forceful expression to Ferguson's conviction that both Hume and Smith had paid inadequate attention to this problem, although they both were aware of it.

13. Ferguson, *Principles,* II, 127.

14. *Ibid.*, p. 120.

15. Unpublished Essays, "Of the Principle of Moral Estimation," p. 13.

16. *Ibid.*, p. 19.

17. *Ibid.*, p. 13.

18. Ferguson, *Principles*, I, 160–61.

19. *Ibid.*, II, 121.

20. *Ibid.*, I, 152–53.

21. *Ibid.*, p. 154; compare Hume, *Enquiries*, p. 142.

22. Ferguson, *Principles*, I, 159.

23. It is important to note that Ferguson introduced a radical separation between "physical" and "moral" laws as an aid to acquiring true knowledge of moral ends, not as an admission of human incapacity to know such ends. Hume had already defended a similar distinction and, however different his reasons for introducing it, his aim was similar to Ferguson's. Although it is sometimes asserted that Hume distinguished between judgments of fact and judgments of value in order to maintain a "non-cognitivist" theory of values like that advanced by Weberian and logical-positivist ethical philosophy, this assertion is directly contrary to fact. Hume made the distinction precisely in order to found a moral theory which would have as high a degree of probable truth as any other scientific theory. He believed that an analysis of the structure and tendency of the sentiments employed by all men, by virtue of their common humanity, would enable him to point out with greater accuracy than is possible for common sense the implications of man's basic preferences. To the resulting body of moral principles he ascribed prescriptive validity as well as descriptive accuracy. In Hume's view, only a man with a diseased or otherwise unnatural mind could, or would even want to, evade the obligations of these moral teachings. On this point Ferguson and Hume agree. The difference between them stems rather from Ferguson's attempt to devise a true moral theory apart from the facts of human nature, in Hume's sense. Paradoxically enough, then, the separation between "facts" and "values" is given a much more radical formulation by Ferguson, whose moral theory most modern adherents of the "scientific" viewpoint would scorn as hopelessly absolutist and antique, than by Hume, whom they welcome as a fellow.

24. Adam Ferguson, *Institutes of Moral Philosophy* (Edinburgh: printed for A. Kincaid and J. Bell, 1769), pp. 1, 3.

25. Ferguson, *Principles*, I, 159.

26. Unpublished Essays, "On Wisdom," p. 11.

27. *Ibid.*, p. 5.

28. *Ibid.*, p. 17 (emphasis supplied).

29. Ferguson, *Institutes*, p. 139.

30. Unpublished Essays, "Of the Principle of Moral Estimation," p. 26.

31. *Ibid.*

32. Ferguson, *Principles*, II, 117.

33. Hume, *Enquiries*, p. 142.

34. *Ibid.*, p. 147.

35. Since Hume expressly disclaimed all ontological validity for moral principles, it would not be fair to charge him with a contradiction with regard to this problem of teleology. At most, it can be said that his presumption that principles which are necessary and satisfactory by nature are also morally binding has the same form as those arguments which rest on a Newtonian view.

36. Ferguson, *Principles*, I, 21.

37. Reid, *op. cit.*, pp. 20–21.

38. Ferguson, *Principles*, I, 190.

39. *Ibid.*, p. 5.

40. "Letter from Thomas Reid to Lord Kames," quoted in Tytler, *op. cit.*, III, 25; compare Ferguson, *Principles*, I, 116–17, and Unpublished Essays, "Of Cause and Effect, Ends and Means, order, combination and design."

41. Edinburgh University Letters, No. 29 to John Macpherson.

42. Unpublished Essays, "Distinction of Value and Its source in Existence," pp. 2–3.

43. Unpublished Essays, "Of Nature and Art," pp. 2–3.

44. Ferguson, *Principles*, I, 2.

45. *Ibid.*, p. 76.

46. *Ibid.*, p. 5.

CHAPTER VI

The Virtuous Man

ALTHOUGH Ferguson dealt with a number of different topics in his writings and although many of his most interesting observations concern the nature of social life—particularly in its political aspects—the focal point about which almost all of his thinking revolved was the nature of individual virtue. Above all else, he sought to set forth the criteria by which each man ought to govern his own behavior. The extent to which this preoccupation over-shadows all other factors in Ferguson's venture into episte-mology and metaphysics has already been shown; the domi-nant role it plays in his social and political theorizing will be demonstrated in a later place. The task of the present dis-cussion is to consider Ferguson's explicit moral teachings, as he formulated them in maxims addressed to his students, the public, and himself.

Viewed in his professional and professed capacity as moral teacher, Ferguson could be expected to place personal

morality at the center of his attention as a matter of course.
But it is essential to realize that his other roles, too, impelled
him to such an emphasis. Certainly one of the hallmarks of
all ideologists is their endeavor to persuade men to adopt
certain clear-cut and practically relevant standards of judgment and action. While the problem of political obligation,
for example, has been discussed by all political philosophers,
many have been content to assign it a position secondary to
such other problems as the definition of justice or to deny
that the solution of this problem can dictate the course of
desirable action in any specific instance. Some, moreover,
display little interest in deducing any specific programs from
their theories at all. But ideologist doctrines, in contrast, are
always programmatic: they are always intended to mold
action through molding opinion. For ideologists, ideas are
weapons to subdue and command men's choices. Ferguson's
eagerness, therefore, to preserve the political status quo,
displayed in his political pamphlets and in the pattern of his
political action, also led him to formulate guides for individual action.

Nor did Ferguson's role as intellectual draw him from a
primary concern with such formulations. Always implicit in
the intellectual's search for an orientation expressed in ideas
is the supposition that he can freely guide his own conduct
and that he will only act in any specified way if he can
explain and defend his choice as appropriate to the achievement of some desirable end. All intellectuals are, therefore,
moralists—even if their personal morality takes the form of
scorning "mere" individual morality for the sake of some
higher good or necessity. Although it is not correct to equate
intellectualism with "individualism" if the latter is considered as a special doctrine with particular teachings, it is
correct to point out that all intellectuals are convinced—
whether they acknowledge it or not—that at least one

individual can and ought to decide for himself what course is best. Ferguson's desire for clarification, accordingly, was always at least in part a desire for clarification about the proper conduct of his own life. In one of his very last writings, an unpublished essay, he wrote:

> This branch of science [i.e., the "history and conduct of the power cognitive"] however important it is is but the avenue to a mansion in which the intelligent being is to fix his habitation and his throne: to command his perfections & his enjoyments; to correct his defects and to avoid his suffering.
>
> Such is the end of the power selective, whose the history and conduct is to man in a special degree the knowledge of himself & his way to improvement, felicity & safety.
>
> Armed with this definition I think that no source of enjoyment or suffering should escape my notice. Perfection & defects should be justly estimated. Enjoyments that mislead should be detected & suffering that promote to conduct to superior enjoyment I should acknowledge and chearfully endure and that institution & manner of human life could be justly estimated and turned to advantage. I should then not only know but be master of myself & arbiter of my fortune.[1]

The "mansion," then, which Ferguson sought to approach in his role as intellectual comprised the principles which ought to govern the choices of virtuous men.

But the convergence of all three situational influences on the same crucial question does not mean that they all called forth the same answers. Ferguson's conception of individual virtue, like his approach to the discovery of such a conception, is plagued by contradictions and ambiguities. Precisely because the definition of virtue occupied such a prominent place in his thought, the definition he evolved reveals most of the conflicts among and within his several roles.

In broadest outline, the conflicting elements may be grouped under the two headings of "passiveness" and "activism." The first of these includes those moral teachings which counsel acquiescence in the existing order, primarily in the sense of willing submission to the wisdom of a benevolent providence. Under "activism" may be collected the principles which prod man to plunge actively into a struggle for perfection and, thereby, in effect urge discontent with any existing situation. Still speaking very generally, it can be said that Ferguson's recourse to the first pattern corresponds to his roles as ideologist and transmitter of socially respectable moral standards to the young and that the second emerged from his position as intellectual, which implies a certain measure of criticism by the very fact that it treats standards of conduct as problematical. The crudity of these categories and of these explanations will soon become apparent, but as very rough approximations they can guide the discussion.

Of all the non-theological Western schools of moral philosophy, the one which has most systematically taught the duty of joyously acquiescing in the divinely established order is the Stoic; and as already indicated by his constant recurrence to Epictetus and Marcus Aurelius as final authorities on moral questions, Ferguson identified himself with this school above all others. He wrote:

> The Author, in some of the statements which follow, may be thought partial to the Stoic philosophy; but is not conscious of having warped the truth to suit with any system whatever. His notions were taken up, where certainly Truth might be learned, however little it were formed into system by those from whom it was collected.
>
> . . . If his enquiries led him to agree with the tenets that were held by a sect of philosophers about two thousand years ago, he is the more confirmed in his notion. . . .[2]

And, in fact, the substance of Ferguson's teachings frequently reveals many of the basic characteristics of the Stoic
view of virtue. The following passage suggests the extent of
the parallel:

> [The] highest point to which moral science conducts the
> mind of man, is that eminence of thought, from which he
> can view himself as but a part in the community of living
> natures; by which he is in some measure let into the design
> of God, to combine all the parts together for the common
> benefit of all; and can state himself as a willing instrument
> for this purpose, in what depends on his own will; and as a
> conscious instrument, at the disposal of providence, in
> matters which are out of his power.[3]

This avowal of Stoicism involves several related propositions. In the first place, it expresses a very high estimation of
contemplative wisdom. From a Stoic point of view, a man is
not virtuous because he desists from certain actions: he
becomes virtuous as he gains full understanding of the *logos*
which pervades the universe and as he consciously wills to
bring his own desire into harmony with it.[4] The exercise of
reason, therefore, and the conquest of all passions by reason
are seen as the apex of human activity. Secondly, the Stoic
view limits the range of human power to the control of the
will. Since, for the Stoic teachers, man can be held morally
responsible for only the choices which he has made in
freedom, the area of virtue is necessarily confined to the
matters which are completely within the command of the
individual. The external consequences of human actions,
they believed, are governed by a beneficent necessity; only
the "will to get" and the "will to avoid" are within man's
power. Finally, because the harmonious order of things
places man in the society of his fellows, it is the duty of the
virtuous man to accept his social obligations and to perform

the tasks appropriate to the position he occupies in society. To characterize the Stoic view, therefore, as passive does not mean that it counsels inactivity. It does mean that, from the Stoic point of view, neither the ends sought through action nor the action itself has any moral value or should in any sense command the serious concern of the actor: what counts is the willingness to perform whatever duties fall to a man's lot. The "philosopher," who is the Stoic man of virtue, gains his merit and his freedom through his wise indifference to all external conditions and consequences.[5]

In many places, Ferguson was prepared to endorse all of these Stoic propositions. He asserted, in the passage already quoted, the superiority of wise contemplation and acceptance of the universal harmony.[6] Many times he insisted that "to man there is a subject of study, and a material of art, of more immediate concern than the soil from which he raises his food, or the mechanical resistance which he may wish to overcome: His own mind is a province of more importance, and more entirely subjected to his own government."[7] Moreover, citing Epictetus directly, he wrote:

> Epictetus seems to rest the foundations of virtue and happiness on the proper discernment and choice of objects, which are in our own power, in contradistinction to things which are not in our power. Among the things in our power, he reckons "our opinions, our pursuits, our desires, and aversions; and in a word, whatever are our own actions." Among the things not in our power, he reckons "body, property, reputation, command, and, in a word, whatever are not our own actions." Attachment to the first, and indifference to the second, are, according to him, the essence of wisdom and happiness.
>
> It is surely happy for anyone to be conscious that the best things are in his own power.[8]

The obligation to perform the duties assigned to one's station, too, is given a central place in Ferguson's moral teach-

ings. So, for example, he listed the following opinion as a
major cause of misery and, because virtue and happiness are
one, a major source of vice. "It is unhappy," he stated, "to
entertain an opinion, that anything can amuse us better
than the duties of our station, or than that which we are in
the present moment called upon to do." [9] There can be no
question that a Stoic type of passiveness constitutes an important element in Ferguson's conception of virtue.

But, as has already been indicated, Ferguson also
espoused principles difficult to reconcile with Stoicism.
With regard to the primacy of wisdom, the limitations of
human power, as well as the duty of heeding one's social
obligations, he introduced qualifications and extensions
which significantly clash with a conception of virtue as
comprising above all a loving resignation to an irresistible
but beneficent world order. The general tone communicated
by this second set of principles is brought out most strikingly
in the following passage from his *Essay on the History of
Civil Society*:

> Men are to be estimated, not from what they know, but
> from what they are able to perform; from their skill in
> adapting materials to the several purposes of life; from
> their vigour and conduct in pursuing the objects of policy,
> and finding the expedients of war and national de-
> fence.[10]

To see the tendency and structure of the activist principles, it is best to show in some detail their relationship to
the three basic Stoic tenets. First of all, Ferguson was frequently prepared to deprecate the value of knowledge not
directly applicable to action and to deny the desirability of
contemplation. Some instances of this attitude have already
been cited in discussing the possibility of knowledge, but the
most important points are revealed in passages like the two
following:

We may be satisfied, from the example of many ages, that liberal endowments bestowed on learned societies, and the leisure with which they were furnished for study, are not the likeliest means to excite the exertions of genius: even science itself, the supposed offspring of leisure, pined in the shade of monastic retirement. Men at a distance from the objects of useful knowledge, untouched by the motives that animate an active and vigorous mind, could produce only the jargon of a technical language, and accumulate the impertinence of academic forms.[11]

Providence has fitted mankind for the higher engagements which they are sometimes obliged to fulfill; and it is in the midst of such engagements that they are most likely to acquire or preserve their virtues. The habits of a vigorous mind are formed in contending with difficulties, not in enjoying the repose of a pacific station; penetration and wisdom are the fruits of experience, not the lessons of retirement and leisure; ardour and generosity are the qualities of a mind aroused and animated in the conduct of scenes that engage the heart, not the gifts of reflection and knowledge.[12]

In effect, these directly contradict the decisive distinction made by Epictetus when he wrote:

You must be one man, good or bad: you must develop either your rational soul, or your outward endowments, you must be busy either with your inner man, or with things outside, that is, you must choose between the position of a philosopher and that of an ordinary man.[13]

Ferguson repeatedly substituted a distinction between leader and follower for that between "philosopher" and "ordinary man." For him, the difference between virtue and vice only rarely depends on the presence or absence of knowledge about the universal scheme of things and almost never involves the practice of contemplation.[14]

Ferguson did not, as a rule, regard wisdom as the culmina-

tion of virtue: he considered it, rather, as primarily an
instrument for the achievement of virtuous objectives. He
defended the inclusion of wisdom among the cardinal virtues by urging, in one place, that "good intentions have no
effect if not properly conducted." [15] Another passage, although cautiously phrased in the conditional tense, is
sufficiently clear to reinforce the impression that wisdom as
such, in the sense of knowledge, is often subordinated in
Ferguson's writings to other constituents of a virtuous mind.
Ferguson wrote:

> were we to state wisdom as the fundamental principle of
> morality, we should be thought to substitute a prudential
> choice of our interests for what ought to be a matter of
> affection, and the effusion of a benevolent heart. Mere
> prudence is an excellence of the understanding only; but
> virtue includes, as a preferable consideration, the energy
> and direction of an amiable and happy disposition. [16]

Although the reservations Ferguson expressed about the
relevance of speculation to virtue do, in themselves, distinguish him from the Stoics, they would not alone lead to
consequences significantly different from those sought by
Stoic morality. Epictetus, too, after all, urged his students to
depart from a life devoted to pure contemplation and to re-
enter the life of action demanded by their duties. Furthermore, he, too, restricted the search for knowledge to matters
relevant to a true description of man's place in the world and
to the mastery of man's will. Ferguson's insistence that
genuine wisdom must be useful, then, does not necessarily
indicate a significant departure from his Stoic authorities.

The cleavage between them, however, is seen as more
marked when it is noted that Ferguson often considered
useful a range of knowledge far broader than that valued by
Epictetus. Ferguson ascribed to man considerable power

over other men and over external nature, as well as complete power over his own will. Even in his most thoroughly Stoic pronouncements, Ferguson carefully wrote that man's own mind was a "subject of study and a material of art" "of *more* immediate concern," "of *more* importance," and "*more* entirely subjected to his will" than external nature; he did not say that it was the *only* important object of human power. Arrian, the pupil of Epictetus, had written:

> What matters it whether the world is composed of atoms or of infinite parts of fire and earth? Is it not enough to know the true nature of good and evil, and the limits of the will to avoid, and again, of impulses for action and against it, and using these as rules so as to order our life and dismiss those things that are beyond us. It may be that the human mind cannot comprehend them, and even if one should assume that it can, of what use is it to comprehend them? Should we not say that those who lay down that these things are necessary for the philosopher trouble themselves in vain? [17]

Although Ferguson could have accepted this insofar as it is simply a rejection of a metaphysics of nature, he did not share the conviction that all study of nature is basically useless. He was too strongly impressed by the achievements of modern science for such a view. As an admirer of Bacon and Newton, he believed that "knowledge is power" and that knowledge about many natural phenomena is accessible to the human mind. He was not limiting the range of knowledge to the inner workings of the mind when he wrote:

> Knowledge of the laws of nature, and the application of such laws to explain their phenomena, are not merely, like method in the details of descriptive history, a form of arrangement, for the purposes of comprehension and mem-

ory. They lead to the possession of power, or the command
of events. For in proportion as men become acquainted
with the circumstances required to the production of any
natural effect, or know the law according to which any
natural operation proceeds, if the subject be within their
reach, or the circumstances under their command, they are
thereby enabled to repeat the operation, and obtain its
effect.[18]

Implicit in this positive valuation of science and of the
expanding scope of human power which it entails is a
conception of virtue as the exercise and expansion of all
distinctly human faculties. This also underlies Ferguson's
occasional deprecation of mere speculation. Prepared to
concede—even to insist on—the importance of man's rational faculty, he was not willing to foster its development
at the cost of all others. In addition, he denied that even
reason can be developed apart from the other human capabilities. As the passages quoted above show, he believed
that intelligence, as well as all other human faculties, re-
ceives its major stimulation through an active engagement
in social life.

Ferguson's most significant departure from Stoicism appears in the special sense he often gave to the Stoic notion
that each man ought to play his assigned role in society. For
the Stoics, such activity is the command of a duty which the
virtuous man accepts. A man becomes virtuous when he
brings his will into harmony with the universal *logos*. Then,
knowing that the success or failure of his venture is beyond
his control, he purges himself of all passionate concern with
such external things and pursues the task assigned to him
simply because reason commands his will to do that which
must be done. For Ferguson, in contrast, passionate involvement in social life is at once the path to virtue and the
manifestation of its highest realization. Far from urging

virtuous men to eliminate the "motives that animate an active and vigorous mind," he wrote:

> So long as the passions retain . . . [some] measure of propriety, and are effectual to animate the mind to its proper exertions, it is unnecessary to observe that they are no more than the purpose of nature seems to require; for, even if a person could, without any emotion, ward off the dangers of his country or his friend, we think it becoming, that the energy of his affection should be in due proportion with the occasion on which it is felt. It is no more than the force of a spring wound up to give the engine the movement required; and when that force keeps pace with the resistance to be overcome its variations constitute a beauty in the structure of which it is a part.[19]

The passion which Ferguson identified most closely with virtue is love of man: "The first law of morality," he stated, "requires the love of mankind as the greatest good to which human nature is competent." [20] The truly virtuous man, from this point of view, commits himself lovingly and with passion to the affairs of his fellow men, because such a commitment itself displays a high development of his capacity for fellow-feeling and because activity carried on in fulfillment of his commitment will bring into play all of his other human faculties. Since Ferguson believed that faculties improve with exercise, such a course also represented for him the fullest employment of man's unique ability to progress, both as an individual and in the species.

The active benevolence for the sake of perfection advanced on this side of Ferguson's teachings is far removed from the dispassionate attention to duty taught by Epictetus and from the abstract philanthropy urged in Stoic texts. His activism led him to disavow two of the most characteristic tenets of his Stoic teachers. First, he departed from their firm opposition to all conflict among men. "To the sociable nature of man," he wrote, "the joint exertions or struggles of numbers in the same cause together, brings into actual exertion, the highest powers of enjoyment as well as of actions." [21] The virtuous man must not, as a rule, remain aloof. Ferguson asserted, "They are not always to be reckoned of the most sociable disposition who equally fawn on all. Indifference, more than candour, is likely to produce the appearance of impartiality, when the cause of our friend, or our country is at stake." [22] Love of mankind thus does not take the form of a cosmopolitan *humanitas* for Ferguson: it must normally be expressed in commitment to some particular society, in sharing its aims and struggles.

Moreover—and this constitutes Ferguson's second and most decisive break with crucial Stoic principles—man can continue to act with the vigor characteristic of virtue only if he is continually striving to improve his situation, as well as himself. In a striking passage, Ferguson epitomized this non-Stoic phase of his thought when he wrote:

> Man is not formed to acquiesce in any precise situation. In the best, he finds something to do; and, in the worst, is then only unhappy, when he suffers his courage and powers of exertion to be overwhelmed. While he exerts himself to remove an inconvenience, he ought to be so far patient under it, as, in his endeavours, to procure relief, fully to possess himself and his faculties. [23]

The elevation of feeling and action to a position at least equal to reason and contemplation; the celebration of man's power over external nature and over the destinies of his fellow men, as well as his powers of self-discipline; the directing of man to social action under the promptings of loving concern, not duty; and finally, the endorsement of discord and discontent—all of these characterize Ferguson's activist conception of virtue. Over against this stands the passive conception which he took over from the Stoics: teaching the wise contemplation of the universal order; the acceptance of, and reliance on, the limitation of human power to the control of the will; and the patient acquiescence in the demand of any assigned station in society. Throughout Ferguson's writings (sometimes even within the same sentence) these two strands are interwoven, and it is very difficult to ascertain which of the two is more important to the texture of the whole.

As was stated above, Ferguson himself believed that his moral teachings tended more towards Stoicism than towards any other body of doctrine. This judgment is, of course, justified by much in his performance. But it also required some self-deception for Ferguson not to note the extent to which he had enunciated principles at variance with Stoicism. The evasion proceeded through the use of Stoic phrases to encompass a new and different content. This is illustrated by the passage which reads, "the character of goodness, applicable to man, . . . consists in pious resignation to the will of God; or, at most, in perfect good will to mankind, in every instance in which the active powers of the individual can apply." [24] Although at first glance this may look like an unexceptionably Stoic pronouncement, further study discovers a significant difficulty. If "perfect good will to mankind" was intended to mean nothing more than it meant for the Stoics, it need not have been introduced by the expression "at most," or qualified by "in every instance to which the active powers of the individual can apply." From a Stoic point of view, "perfect good will to mankind" is one concomitant of "pious resignation to the will of God"—it is not a new and more far-reaching duty. Furthermore, the direction of the will is always within man's power; it is, in fact, the only thing that is. Only if "perfect good will to mankind" is seen to include a concept of "effective beneficent action" does the treatment accorded the phrase in this sentence make sense. But if this conception of goodness requires actions, however limited in scope, it has broken much more sharply with the Stoic view than this sentence makes clear on its face.

Sentence after sentence could be subjected to this type of analysis, but it would never be possible to decide with any assurance about the general direction of the argument or even about the logic of its inconsistency. Certainly the progressive teleology has clear affinities with the activist stand; but, to the extent that Ferguson followed Epictetus in equating "progress" with increasing mastery over the will, the progressive teleology was applied to the justification of the passive conception of virtue as well. In view of these and other similar considerations, it is best to abandon the attempt to offer an internal explanation of the amalgam and to recall the functions which these moral writings performed for Ferguson. Here as elsewhere the most helpful perspective for examining Ferguson's work is viewing it as a social act.

In his capacity as moral teacher, Ferguson wrote as he lectured—in order to propagate the useful and respectable maxims generally considered proper for the indoctrination of the young. Although his writings never explicitly address themselves to one or the other of the distinct functions ascribed to them here, it is possible to discern the different patterns with some measure of reliability. The major aid, with regard to their homiletic purpose, is the discrepancy between the *Essay on the History of Civil Society*, which was written before Ferguson became professor of moral philosophy, and the *Institutes of Moral Philosophy*, which was designed almost exclusively as a textbook for his classes. A comparison between the preoccupations stressed in each of these can help to isolate the expressly pedagogical aspects from the others. Since the *Principles of Moral and Political*

Philosophy encompasses the main points of both earlier works, it can be stated with considerable certainty that Ferguson never changed the general tendency of his opinions and that the contrasts revealed by a comparison between the earlier works can guide the interpretation of the later.

One point becomes clear immediately. The inculcation of religious orthodoxy, to the extent that Ferguson attempted it at all, is relevant only from a pedagogical point of view. Ferguson made this explicit when, in the introduction of the *Principles,* he wrote:

> [The author] conceived that what is intended for a book submitted to public inspection, might require the suppression of some things not improper in the first introduction of youth to the study of a subject. He has therefore omitted some titles that were entered in his notes and in the Institutes.[25]

An examination of the Tables of Contents of the two books reveals that the "titles" omitted in the later one are the chapters, "Of the being of God" and "Of the attributes of God," which, in the *Institutes,* occupy a distinct section entitled "Of the Knowledge of God." Although a few injunctions to formal piety occur in the *Principles,* the topic is never raised at all in the *Essay.*

A second clue provided by the comparison between the *Essay* and the *Institutes* is the absence of lessons on the "cardinal virtues" and similar homiletic exhortations in the former. This is not due simply to the difference in subject matter; it follows from the conviction frequently expressed in the *Essay* that "proper occasions alone operating on a raised and happy disposition, may produce this admirable effect [i.e., virtue in man], whilst mere instruction may always find mankind at a loss to comprehend its meaning, or

insensible to its dictates." [26] The exhortations voiced in the
first book are primarily directed to the problem of creating
"proper occasions," although considerable space is allotted
to pleas for considering all occasions equally "proper." In
any case, it can safely be said that the *Institutes* as a whole
and the treatment of the "virtues" in the *Principles* are the
clearest manifestations of Ferguson's role as transmitter of
conventional morality.

As has been suggested above and as might be expected,
the dominant tendency in this aspect of Ferguson's writings
is towards the passive conception of virtue. Certainly the
result sought was the creation of upstanding, decent citizens
who would dutifully adopt the prevailing mores of civilized
society, play their parts in the ongoing scheme of things, and
develop attitudes proper to the sober conduct of affairs. Even
some of the terms which Ferguson employed in his catalogue of virtues testify to this tendency: he considered "wisdom" synonymous with "prudence," and "goodness" the
equivalent of "justice."

The definition of the terms and the list of their constituent elements further strengthens the impression that, as
moral teacher, Ferguson sought to foster among his charges
a wholesome acquiescence in the status quo. Such an aim is
apparent in the passage which states:

> Wisdom, stated as one of the cardinal virtues, refers chiefly
> to those duties which result from reflection, and which
> terminate in preserving the state and character of the
> individual unimpaired. Such are decency, property, mod-
> esty, economy, decision, and caution.[27]

Propriety, which Ferguson considered the most important
component of wisdom, he defined in the following
manner:

Propriety is the suitableness of action to the person who
acts; to the occasion; and to the place. . . . Impropriety
may be incurred by a person when alone, as often as he
neglects what is due to himself or to his fellow creatures, or
as often as he incurs what is unsuitable to the part he has
to sustain, either in respect to rank, profession, or
age. . . . Among the proprieties of high rank, we may
reckon the conditions which are peculiarly requisite to
preserve respect. . . . The genuine expression or effects
of respect constitute the proprieties of inferior station, in its
relation to that which is superior.[28]

Similar overtones occur in the following definition of justice
or goodness:

In referring to the offices of goodness, as they may be
separately comprised under the titles of Innocence and
Beneficence, we may consider Fidelity, Veracity, Candour,
and Civility as modifications of the first; Piety, Personal
Attachments, Gratitude, Liberality, Charity, and Politeness as modifications of the second.[29]

Furthermore, goodness is in no way seen to conflict with
personal prudence; Ferguson wrote:

Under every form of society, the individual does a real
service to the public by the reasonable and proper care of
his own preservation, by attention to the welfare of his
family, and by a diligent observation of what belongs to his
own rank, his profession, or condition of life. An immediate view of the public is unequally required under different constitutions of government; most under democratical
governments, and least under absolute monarchies, where
public determinations are limited to the councils of the
Prince. But wherever just precautions are taken in the
national establishment for the safety and welfare of the
people, it is happy for every individual to know and enjoy
the advantages of his own situation, without giving way to
that restless spirit, which in the absence of any real griev-

ance would aim at fanciful refinements of Law and
State.[30]

Temperance and fortitude, which round out Ferguson's
adaptation of the traditional catalogue, are viewed as subordinate qualities serving to protect and strengthen the major
attributes of a virtuous mind.[31]

Although the maxims here presented can clearly be characterized as tending to engender an accommodating frame of
mind and therefore assimilated to the passive conception of
virtue, it must be noted that Ferguson's role as conventional
moral teacher also called forth responses subversive of the
kind of Stoicism he sought to model after that of Epictetus.
Stoicism alone was an inadequate prop for the morality
socially respectable in his time. If such Stoicism is viewed as
the core of the passive element in his teachings and if the
whole is considered as an interplay between passive and
activist elements, it can be seen that the homiletic function
itself can help to account for the presence of non-Stoic
principles in Ferguson's books.

Ferguson himself testified to the dubious respectability of
the Stoic teachings among the educated men of his time. He
concluded his avowal of affinity to Stoicism quoted above on
the following defensive note: "notwithstanding that the
name of this sect has become, in the gentility of modern
times, proverbial for stupidity." For an understanding of the
animus against the Stoics which Ferguson found prevalent
among his contemporaries, it is useful to turn to David
Hume's *Enquiries concerning the Principles of Morals*.
This is not only the work of the most genteel and urbane
moralist among Ferguson's contemporaries but also, by explicit intention, a work which seeks to set forth the moral
principles actually professed by most civilized modern men.
An examination of Hume's objections to Stoicism will reveal

some important sources of conflict between the conventional morality of the time and Stoic morality; therefore, it suggests the pressures exerted upon Stoic passiveness by Ferguson's attempt to inculcate conformity to convention.

If additional justification were needed for relying on Hume as the spokesman for conventionalism in this instance, it would be provided by the grounds upon which he offered his two major objections to Stoicism. The first is addressed to its heroic character, and the second, to its unconcern with warm social feelings; both are based principally on the contention that such teachings are not suited to "modern times." The following statement gives a preliminary view of Hume's position:

> Among the ancients, the heroes in philosophy, as well as those in war and patriotism, have a grandeur and force of sentiment, which astonishes our narrow souls, and is rashly rejected as extravagant and supernatural. They, in their turn, I allow, would have had equal reason to consider as romantic and incredible, the degree of humanity, clemency, order, tranquillity, and other social virtues, to which, in the administration of government, we have attained in modern times, had any one been then able to have made a fair representation of them. Such is the compensation which nature, or rather education, has made in the distribution of excellencies and virtues, in these different ages.[32]

But this is only a very mild manifestation of the abhorrence Hume felt for the Stoic conception of virtue, as well as for any moral doctrine which demanded a heroic effort of self-discipline. Grouping them all as "virtues" bred of "superstition," he asked, "for what reason are they everywhere rejected by men of sense, but because they serve to no manner of purpose; neither advance a man's fortune in the world, nor render him a more valuable member of society;

neither qualify him for the entertainment of company, nor
increase his power of self-enjoyment?" He answered his own
question by saying, "We observe, on the contrary, that they
cross all these desirable ends. . . . We justly therefore,
place them in the catalogue of vices." He was prepared to
grant courage and "philosophical tranquillity" a minor place
among the virtues, but he believed that the former is considered the "predominant excellence" only "among all uncultivated nations, who have not as yet had full experience of the
advantages attending beneficence, justice, and the social
virtues" and that the "pretensions" to the latter "when
stretched to the utmost, are by far too magnificent for human nature." [33] In addition to its anachronistic character,
then, Hume's castigation of the heroic type of morality
exemplified by Stoicism cites its conflict with human nature.
When his opponent in the *Dialogue* attempted to controvert
Hume's assertions about a universal morality based on a
common human nature by pointing to the absolute opposition between the principles of Diogenes and those of Pascal,
Hume answered:

> An experiment . . . which succeeds in the air, will not
> always succeed in a vacuum. When men depart from the
> maxims of common reason, and affect these artificial lives,
> as you call them, no one can answer for what will please or
> displease them. They are in a different element from the
> rest of mankind; and the natural principles of their mind
> play not with the same regularity, as if left to themselves,
> free from the illusions of religious superstition or philo-
> sophical enthusiasm. [34]

These passages illustrate Hume's scorn for any conception of virtue which demands an unusual degree of self-
discipline and "enthusiasm" and which can therefore apply
at most to a few outstanding individuals. He considered it

unnatural and presumptuous. Moreover, as already indicated by the distinction he drew between "ancient" and "modern" conceptions in the passage quoted above, he believed that such a view militates against the prime virtues of beneficence and social feeling.[35] Disdainfully he referred to Stoicism as "only . . . [a] more refined system of selfishness";[36] and, with evident disapproval, he pointed out that "Epictetus has scarcely ever mentioned the sentiment of humanity and compassion, but in order to put his disciples on their guard against it. The virtue of the Stoics seems to consist chiefly in a firm temper and a sound understanding."[37]

This examination of Hume's response to Stoicism—which, incidentally, also serves as a reminder that Ferguson, for all his objections to Hume's method, never departed very widely from Hume's conclusions[38]—helps to explain the ways in which Ferguson's role as a transmitter of conventional morality led him away from the Stoic conception of passiveness. The abandonment of the heroic ideal took the form, in Ferguson's thought, of reducing wisdom to an instrument for successful living and of transforming courage into the minor virtue of a "forcible or resolute mind." Such virtues are accessible to all: they are not restricted to heroes of philosophy.[39] In response to the second objection, Ferguson was led to replace the Stoic ideal of the virtuous man who retains his inner independence although he is by duty compelled to enmesh himself in social relationships with a call for "civility," "personal attachments," and so forth. To some extent, therefore, the introduction of a few principles characteristic of the activist strand in his thought derived from the conventions which, as moral teacher, Ferguson was eager to inculcate into his students. This role, then, although essentially conducive to a passive conception of virtue, helped to foster and to sustain the amalgam which comprised an intermingling of both.

Much the same can be said of Ferguson's role as ideologist. Discovering the manifestations of this role is a more uncertain task than was the isolation of the homiletic elements, and, therefore, it is more subject to the risk of arbitrarily seeking confirmation for preconceptions. It is nevertheless possible to distinguish, with some degree of confidence, those of Ferguson's admonitions to virtue which sought to influence attitudes of the general public towards the socio-political system as a whole from, on the one hand, the maxims of personal conduct addressed primarily to his students, and on the other, from the principles of action evolved in an attempt to clarify his own relationship to life and society. The examination of Ferguson's political opinions and activities presented in an earlier chapter helps, as does a view of the relationship between the political context of his writings and the socio-political situation also sketched out above. Despite difficulties, in short, the impact of Ferguson's role as ideologist on the interplay between the passive and active constituents in his conception of virtue can usefully be assessed. A full assessment must await the analysis of all his social and political ideas; but his moral principles themselves reveal that the ideological function, like the homiletic one, inclined Ferguson towards the passive view while it also induced him to accept some notions alien to the Stoic version of passiveness.

It has been repeatedly noted here—and illustrated even in the passages addressed primarily to his students—that Ferguson was a strong supporter of the social status quo. As might therefore be expected, Ferguson taught that personal virtue requires accommodation to prevailing structures of law and order, full obedience to established authority, and, in general, a spirit of co-operation with the forces constituting his society. The following passage illustrates the general tone of Ferguson's injunctions to political acquiescence:

> On the part of the subject, and under the title of Allegiance, are included Fidelity, Deference, and Submission to the will of the Sovereign or Magistrate. This is the head of the society, and is therefore an ostensible or principal object of that affection we bear to the society itself; his virtues are the securities and blessings; his authority is the source of peace and good order to the whole.
>
> Unhappy is the subject, who can mistake for Liberty, a disrespect to the person of the magistrate; and who can perceive no beauty in the gradation of influence, or distinction of ranks, in which providence has made the order of society to consist.[40]

Ferguson also applied Stoic doctrines when, in urging each man to do his assigned duty, he wrote:

> We may conclude . . . that the love of amusement is unhappy, if it proceeds from a notion, that any thing can amuse us better than the duties of our station, or that any employment is more to be wished for than that precisely which in the present moment has fallen to our share. If any one have formed such a notion, he must be told to beware of it. It will disqualify him for his best enjoyments and embitter his life with peevishness and melancholy.[41]

At times extending the Stoic principle of accommodation to the benevolent plan of Providence beyond action even into the sphere of opinion, Ferguson urged:

> The authority of prevailing opinions makes at least one bond of society; and it is more fit that the people should move together, though not in the best way that might be devised for them, than that they should disband and separate into different ways, where no one might find, in the

way he had chosen for himself, anything to compensate his
separation from the rest of his kind.[42]

Finally, Ferguson advanced the following argument against
any misguided sentimental attempt to counteract the operation of necessary natural laws of society:

> Whenever property is established, it comes of course to be
> unequally distributed. It accumulates in the possession of
> some, and is entirely wanting to others. As this inequality
> may be traced to its origin in the unequal dispositions of
> men to frugality and industry, as well as more casual
> advantages, so it serves to maintain, in the most prosperous
> and wealthy societies, some remains of that necessity
> which nature has intended for the species as a spur to their
> industry and incentive to labour. If the wealthy are re-
> lieved from the necessity of toil, or may chuse the objects
> of their pursuits, the poor still remain subject to this
> necessity; and few are exempted from every application
> that may contribute to enlarge the stock or promote the
> welfare of their community.
>
> .   .   .   .
>
> As we may venture to assume that the wealth of nations
> consist in the labour of the poor, or in the industry and
> ingenuity of those who are desirous to make for themselves
> acquisitions of fortune; so to the poor, health, strength, and
> whatever else qualifies men for daily labour and successful
> pursuits, are the inheritance which nature has provided,
> and the use they make of that inheritance is the source of
> wealth and prosperity to the community of which they are
> members.
>
> If the use of industry or labour could be entirely super-
> seded in any society, or, in other words, if the poor could be
> supported gratuitously, this would be to frustrate the pur-
> pose of nature, in rendering toil and the exercises of
> ingenuity necessary to man; it would be to cut off the
> sources of wealth, and, under pretence of relieving the
> distressed, it would be to reject the condition upon which
> nature has provided that the wants of the species in general
> shall be relieved.

For these reasons, poverty alone is far from being a sufficient recommendation to charity, and the undistinguishing practice of this virtue would be highly pernicious; as by enabling the poor to subsist in idleness, it would deprive them of one great preservative of their innocence, and a principal constituent of happiness, the habit of regular industry; and deprive the community of its best resource, the labour of its members.[43]

All these aspects of virtue—"allegiance," attention to "the duties of our station," accommodation in the interest of stability, and restraining of humane impulses which threaten nature's harmony—are clearly consistent with Ferguson's avowals of Stoicism and clearly serve important ideological purposes. They inculcate the desirability of adjusting to the existing social order. But the social order which Ferguson, as ideologist, sought to bolster displayed some characteristics demanding attitudes not readily assimilable to the Stoic types of passiveness. It was, as Ferguson repeatedly observed, a commercial society, and a commercial society depends on a spirit of enterprise, ambition, and astute pursuit of personal interest. Furthermore, in Ferguson's view, such a society demands a system of government which will secure the fundamental property rights of each individual; such a system is possible only when all men are willing to fight in defense of their interests. Although the discussion of Ferguson's social and political ideas is reserved for a later chapter, these two major points must be grasped in order to comprehend the full impact of Ferguson's role as ideologist on his conception of virtue. The virtuous man, in brief, was urged by Ferguson to adopt some maxims incompatible with Stoicism in order to become an obedient and useful member of society.

Accordingly, Ferguson was led to incorporate certain distinctly bourgeois and liberal values into his scheme, and these served to sustain the activist rather than passive components of his moral teachings. In most general terms, these values may be described as pertaining to a sober concern for the protection and expansion of the individual's interest—particularly his economic interests. At times Ferguson was content to show that a man living in a commercial society was not thereby prevented from living a virtuous life, a view still close to his Stoic standpoint.[44] But, at other times, he argued that the pursuit of wealth as such serves to foster virtuous qualities like "industry, sobriety, and frugality." [45] In a few passages, moreover, Ferguson suggested that the striving after "new objects" was in itself a part of virtue. The following passages illustrate the extent to which Ferguson was prepared to move in the direction of adapting the notion of virtue he held to the requirements of a business society:

> [Man] is indeed able to subsist, or to drag a precarious life, even in his rudest state: But he is so far from being stationary in this or any other condition, that, after many ages of progress, he must either continue to advance, or is exposed to decline; And though relieved of much inconvenience, even after he has attained to what at a distance appeared to be the summit of his fortune, he is in reality only come to a point, at which new objects are presented to entice his pursuits, and towards which he is urged with the spurs of ambition, while those of necessity are no longer applied. Or, if the desire of any thing better than the present should at any time cease to operate in his mind, he becomes listless and negligent, loses the advantages he had gained, whether of possession or skill, and declines in his fortune, till a sense of his own defects and his sufferings restore his industry.[46]
>
> Nature has made the subsistence, the safety, and the accommodation of human life to depend upon certain external circumstances and possessions, to which men, accordingly, with good reason, direct their attention. They

are the objects of art and industry, and furnish the occasion of invention, and other trials of genius to the mind of man, which is ever busy, and which is at once gratified and improved by its active exertions.[47]

Although Ferguson's approval of industry can, perhaps, be reconciled with his Stoic notions, the positive valuation of ambition departs radically from any conception of virtue as a calm resignation to the eternal order. It does, however, accord well with Ferguson's identification with the groups which were rapidly transforming Scotland into a commercial and industrial country.

Similar considerations help to explain Ferguson's occasional abandonment of passive obedience as the prime political virtue. It must be borne in mind that, although the oligarchic structure of political power in Scotland was fairly clear, the dominant political rhetoric was Whig and, therefore, liberal. As an ideologist, Ferguson was committed to view the British constitution as a constitutional monarchy checked by representatives of the propertied classes and devoted to the preservation of individual rights. The full implications of this view will be examined later; for the present, it is enough to note that the ideological function of his writings involved the incorporation of a concern for personal liberty into the concept of virtue.[48] Ferguson wrote:

> Liberty is a right which every individual must be ready to vindicate for himself. . . . Even political institutions, though they appear to be independent of the will and arbitration of men, cannot be relied on for the preservation of freedom: they may nourish, but should not supersede that firm and resolute spirit, with which the liberal mind is always prepared to resist indignities, and to refer its safety to itself.[49]

While it would be erroneous to read such a passage only as ideology, its social impact is clear. Politically as well as socially, then, the ideologically suitable conception of virtue binds man to duties and interests which go beyond and, to some extent, contradict a policy of Stoic indifference to external goods.

The interplay between the activist and passive constituents of virtue, as it bears on social and political conduct, is well illustrated in the following passage:

> Inasmuch that, if any person looking forward to the future is unhappy for the present, we may venture to affirm, either that he has mistaken his object, and fixed his desires on that which does not admit of his taking any reasonable measures for the attainment of it; or, that if his object be reasonable, and such as he may pursue with advantage, he has certainly failed in the proper exercise of his faculties, in that course of industry and diligence, which his object prescribes; Insomuch that raillery and censure too are very properly applied to those who, ever intent on the future, are unable to enjoy the present.
>
> Whatever be the end, which persons of this description propose to themselves, their present sufferings imply sloth, ill temper, pusillanimity, either a want of proper exertion for the attainment of their end, or the wrong choice of an end which does not admit of any reasonable exertion.[50]

This also provides a clue to the way in which Ferguson managed to reconcile the two elements within the ideological context. Although, Ferguson suggested, the virtuous man ought to strive for betterment, his "object" must be "reasonable." In practical political terms, Ferguson invariably translated these words to mean that the poor must accept their lot in life. The most frequent and least ambiguous applications of Stoic principles in his moral writings are addressed to the laboring classes of society. Two examples indicate the pattern:

What is the lesson of reason, then, to the poor man, who
complains of his lot, or rather who enquires what, in the
situation which providence has assigned to him, is required
to be happy? He may be told, "Providence has given to
you, and to all other men, a set of wants; and it is the will
of providence that you proceed to supply them; Be dilli-
gent, industrious, and frugal. Do whatever the present
moment requires with benignity and fortitude. These are
the constituents of happiness, and not less in your power
than they are in the power of your richest neighbour." [51]

It is unhappy to depend for enjoyment on what we
cannot command, or to fix our desires on what is beyond
our reach. Thus, it were unhappy for the labouring man,
to long for exemption from labour. It were unhappy, in the
poor, to aim at appearing like the rich; to long for an equipage, a retinue, a palace, a table; and think himself excluded from happiness, in being deprived of these
things. [52]

It is only a slight overstatement to say that, for Ferguson, the
virtues of passive acquiescence were particularly appropriate
for the poor, that he transformed the heroic consolations of
the Stoic wise man into ideological sops for the servile class.
The full irony of this transformation will only become clear
later, in the light of an examination of Ferguson's conviction
that the poor had become so degraded that only habit,
prejudice, and superstition could govern their behavior. To
the extent that the problem of controlling the poor was
uppermost in Ferguson's definition of the ideologist's task,
the passive and active elements in Ferguson's view of virtue
took on a class character.

But this is perhaps too strong. Passivity is the predominant motif which sounds through the version of virtue
applied to ideological purposes, regardless of the class
addressed. In fact, as illustrated above, this perspective reveals more formulations which are purely Stoic than the
view of his writings in their homiletic role. The consistency

of the argument is only broken by the insistence that the
duties of many stations in a commercial society demand an
ambitious concern to protect and expand certain external
goods. In limiting this insistence more or less to the propertied classes of society and in hedging it about with many
safeguards against disruptive, future-oriented discontent,
Ferguson was simply following through the logic of his
essentially passive conservative ideological message. For Ferguson as ideologist, virtue was above all a willing accommodation to existing circumstances.

It has now been shown to what extent only oversimplifica-
tion could completely identify Ferguson's pedagogical and
ideological roles with the passive elements in his teachings.
The two roles which were primarily oriented toward passiveness have been seen to account, at least in part, for
certain principles here denominated activist: viz., the elevation of common human practice over esoteric philosophical
speculation, the displacement of an emotionally indifferent
pursuit of duty by an actively benevolent fellow-feeling,
and the transformation—at least for some men—of man's
resigned accommodation to his ordained station in society
into an animated interest in protecting and bettering his
own lot. Furthermore, it has become clear that the activist
element cannot be simply equated to an espousal of eter-
nally discontented striving for perfect human fulfillment.
As purveyor of conventional morality and of conservative
ideology, Ferguson was able to reconcile these non-Stoic
principles with a total absence of dissatisfaction with the
customs and practices prevailing in his time. It has, in fact,
been argued that precisely the need to forestall such dissatisfaction helps to explain the presence of these principles
in Ferguson's writings. Some of the broad distinctions offered above, therefore, have now been given a less sharply
contrasting formulation, although their ultimate integrity

can be seen to emerge intact from the process. The basic purpose has been to clarify the import of the two categories and to explain how Ferguson could—and why, in a sense, he had to—include within his conception of virtue elements which are, from a logical point of view, at least unconnected and often directly opposed to one another.

But several crucial gaps are left by the explanation so far presented. In the first place, neither as pedagogue nor as propagandist did Ferguson encourage men to aspire to a heroic detachment sustained by wise contemplation of the divinely created, necessary, and benevolent universal harmony. Yet Ferguson's Stoic sources place this element of virtue above all others, and, as indicated above, Ferguson followed them in at least a few places. Secondly, both of the roles discussed precluded his setting standards which would lead to active discontent with the moral norms actually professed by the majority of cultivated men or with the opportunities for progress towards virtue presented by the existing social and political order. Nevertheless, it has been shown that, to some extent, Ferguson's activist stress on perfection through active commitment did result in postulating just such standards. Both passive and active aspects, therefore, require further explanation. If a view of Ferguson's writings in the light of his role as intellectual can perform this dual task, it would indicate that in this capacity, as well as in the others, Ferguson was deeply enmeshed in both strands of his conception of virtue.

Unlike the portions of Ferguson's work oriented primarily towards his pedagogical and ideological roles, the sections particularly expressive of his status as intellectual do not bear readily identifiable external characteristics. The proposition that this role best defines the residual category is ultimately no more than a hypothesis which can only be supported, never irrefutably demonstrated. Little can be done beyond attempting to explain from this point of view the aspects of Ferguson's writings not yet accounted for and showing that the concerns and conflicts revealed by such a view correspond to those suggested by the earlier historical discussion of his position as intellectual. The identification of the "intellectualist" emphasis in his writings, in other words, can only be certain to the extent that the over-all interpretation is persuasive. And the assumption underlying the interpretation as a whole, it may be recalled, is that, as an intellectual, Ferguson sought to compile ideas which would "make sense" of the experience he encountered in his situation.

With regard to the definition of virtue, an experience directly relevant was, first, his exposure to the cultural tradition of his society, in its modern scientific aspects as well as in its classical components. It is his education, after all, which provides one of the basic justifications for attributing the role of intellectual to him at all. Secondly, the crucial point to be made about his relationship to the cultural heritage is his overwhelming desire to use it as an aid to practical decisions in practical life. This distinguishes his position from that of the "scholar" or philosopher as such, who is typically concerned—at least in profession—to defend or expand some body of knowledge doctrinally defined as truth.[53] To put this point in other words: The formal philosopher is primarily oriented to an audience of other philosophers, either members of his own school or members of rival schools; Ferguson, like other intellectuals, was oriented towards other men like himself who were seeking to make their peace with their positions as men of ideas in a world of activity. The third important characteristic of Ferguson's situation as intellectual is his relative powerlessness in a world where power depended much more on class position, practical skills, and—in general—usefulness to the execution of tasks set by the dominant tendencies of social

change than on the ability to manipulate ideas or to concep-
tualize distant and lofty goals. As moral teacher and ideologist, he could participate in power to some slight extent
because in those capacities, by definition, he accommodated himself to the dominant directions of power; as a
relatively independent intellectual, however, he was correspondingly estranged from power. Accordingly, from this
point of view, the relationship to existing power—whether
to accept its direction or to oppose it—emerged as a genuine
problem. These three facets of Ferguson's position as intellectual, then—exposure to culture, orientation to practice,
and estrangement from power—combine to provide the
most inclusive explanation for the ambiguities and unities in
his conception of individual virtue.

It has already been stated that the cultural tradition to
which Ferguson was exposed included both classical and
modern elements. To these must be added, as a distinct
factor, the teachings of Calvinist Christianity. This is true
despite the fact that nowhere in his published or unpublished writings did Ferguson rely on specifically Christian
dogmas and that, in fact, nothing in his writings endorses or
even leaves room for such uniquely Christian doctrines as
original sin, the reincarnation and atonement, divine grace,
or the Last Judgment. Ferguson never acknowledged the
extent to which his teachings appear to make superfluous
the basic tenets of orthodox Christianity. Perhaps his training in the lax "moderate" theology of his time really had left
him in genuine ignorance on this point; but it is hard to
believe that a writer whose theological education had been
in the Calvinist tradition—however attenuated—did not
realize the full implications of the following passage (particularly the last sentence):

> It may be asked, perhaps, why [the author] should restrict
> his argument, as he has done, to the topics of mere natural

religion and reason. This, being the foundation of every
superstructure whether in morality or religion, and therefore, to be separately treated, he considered as that part of
the work which was allotted to him. Farther institutions
may improve, but cannot supersede what the Almighty has
revealed in his works, and in the suggestions of reason to
man. . . . And what the Author of our nature has so
taught must be considered as the test of every subsequent
institution that is offered as coming from him.[54]

Even stronger evidence that Ferguson's disregard of formal
Christian principles was not accidental is furnished by his
discussion of the origin of religion, where he stated:

It is in search of a model, and of a patron of what is
previously known to be right, that we arrive at our best and
our highest conceptions of the Supreme Being.
  This conception, if we take it at a medium of what
nations in general have possessed is to be valued, rather as
indicating a capacity of further attainment, than as a
blessing already compleat. It is like other articles in the
progressive and variable nature of man, a foundation on
which he may build; a germ which, in the progress of his
nature, may wax to indefinite magnitude and strength; or,
if we may still vary the image, it may be considered as one
of the rude materials on which he himself is to exert his
talent for art and improvement.[55]

The heterodoxy of these statements, when combined with
the evidence presented in an earlier chapter, strongly suggests that Ferguson quite deliberately rejected many specific
teachings of historical Christianity as guides to action, even
though his rejection was prudently veiled and even though,
for a variety of reasons, he remained throughout his life an
active communicant in the Church of Scotland. In any case,
Christian elements which do appear in his writings appear
only in a form adapted to the classical and modern doctrines
which provide the main intellectual substance for his
thought.

The matter of Ferguson's relationship to Christianity is raised at this point only because his treatment of one traditional Christian topic, the question of immortality, provides some important clues to an understanding of his conception of virtue. Ferguson's general responsiveness to the many diverse components of Western culture resulted in this instance in his setting a higher value on the contemplative life than he was elsewhere prepared to do. It is certainly true that the question of immortality attracted the attention of non-Christian writers. But—especially in view of the cool, almost indifferent tone which Ferguson adopted towards the matter—it is very likely that Ferguson broached the issue at all only in an attempt to retain some surface harmony between his main teachings and his Christian professions. To judge from his letters, any genuine interest he may have had in Christian revelation was attracted solely by its promise of immortality. His own speculations, however, departed markedly from orthodox doctrine; they are interesting because they tend to equate virtue—if it is really virtue which merits immortality—with the highest possible development of man's purely rational faculties.

The main outline of Ferguson's conjectures concerning immortality is simple. Resting his argument on the assumption of design, he maintained that, since the will to create implies a will to preserve, those creations whose natures are suited for eternal existence may well be destined for such a fate. The rational soul—with its adaptability to an "infinite variety of situations," requiring no food save knowledge, and occupying no space—is, in his view, fit for unlimited existence. Furthermore Ferguson asked:

> In this condition of mere animal, for what purpose observe the heavens? or strive to penetrate appearances, with which the globe of the earth itself has no connection? What concern has any mere animal of this globe with the

ring of Saturn, or the belts of Jupiter? Whence this affecta-
tion of simplifying the complicated order of nature. . . ?
Why embarrass the faculties with mathematical and metaphysical abstractions, while the animal is to be gratified
only with the solid specimen of bodies, not with such ideal
conception. . . . May not such aberrations of thought
appear as little fitted to this present state of an animal, as
the provision of teeth, of stomach and intestines, might
have appeared to the foetus while, in the womb, he was
furnished not with food, but with an immediate supply of
blood by the umbilical cord. And may not appearances,
mysterious in the present scene be cleared up in a similar
way by apprehending a future state of existence, for which
faculties though superfluous in the life of an animal, are
yet wisely provided, for the remaining course of a rational
soul.[56]

From this ingenious argument, he concluded, "thus, *it appears no violent stretch of the imagination* to conceive the
human soul, in present state, as the embryo of a celestial
spirit. . . ." [57]

As the emphasized clause indicates, Ferguson was very
careful not to insist too strenuously on the possibility of
immortality: the very introduction to the topic sets the tone
of caution. Ferguson there characterized the issue as "a
question of conjecture which men have frequently agitated,
and on which they have for the most part fondly adopted
a decision in their own favor." [58] The reasons for this diffidence are not hard to discover. In the first place (as noted
above), Ferguson's thought was primarily anthropocentric;
above all, he rejected any maxims which would elevate
transmundane considerations over the demands of a socially
responsible human life. Man's obligation is to "attend to his
present task and not suffer himself to be diverted from it by
prospects of futurity, toward which he can contribute
nothing, besides the faithful and diligent performance of
the part which is now assigned to him." [59]

Moreover, his argument for immortality must have made him uneasy because it conflicts so strongly with principles to which he was drawn by his other roles as well as by the intellectual's concern for practice. The argument places the highest value on "useless" contemplation and accepts the classical distinction between "philosophers" and "ordinary men." Ferguson wrote:

> This argument [for immortality], however, may seem to halt with respect to those who have made no such use of their faculties: with respect to those who are cut short even in the progress of animal life; with respect to those who perish soon after their birth; or at an early period; or those who lived to employ their talents, as the instincts of a brute are employed, for mere animal purposes; and with respect to those especially, who become more brutish and selfish as they advance in years. In respect to such instances, there must be just apprehension of future punishment, not reward, and doubts of their being destined to raise a superstructure, of which they have not laid a foundation: These are not fitted to supply the stock of celestial spirits; nor is it contrary to the analogy of nature, in the course of things with which we are acquainted, to suppose that, while such as become qualified for higher scenes of existence are conducted thither, the unqualified will miscarry; and such as are debased, particularly may sink in the scale of being, or actually perish.[60]

Ferguson's reluctance to insist on his argument for immortality and his failure to apply the argument at any other place in his writings can be accounted for by all of the considerations which led him to qualify and even to negate the Stoic conception of full virtue as exclusively the attribute of a philosophically wise man.

But the main point of the present discussion is rather the opposite; viz., explaining the presence of this heroic elevation of philosophy in Ferguson's thought at all, both here

and in other portions of his writings. The fundamental
source would seem to be the cultural tradition itself, particularly its classical components. That Ferguson should have
adopted the classical view of virtue in connection with a
topic which, at least in Ferguson's mind, must have had
primarily Christian associations is only momentarily puz-
zling. Once he raised the question, he was compelled to
choose between a Christian and a pagan-humanistic definition of man's extraordinary position in the universe. Ferguson's general commitment to man's ultimate independence,
expressed in both his passive and activist formulations, dictated the rejection of the Christian alternative which—particularly in the Calvinist forms most familiar to
Ferguson—made man's salvation dependent on the grace of
God rather than on the free choice of man.[61] The heroic
theme, then, emerged in Ferguson's writings at least in part
as a defense against anti-heroic emphases of Calvinist
Christianity, a reaction explicable by Ferguson's ideological
opposition to the orthodox, "populist" divines as well as by
his role as intellectual.

The heroic dimension in Ferguson's thought is not restricted to the passive conception of virtue. When most critical of the existing order, Ferguson also relied on a perfectionist, grandiose conception of human potentialities. Man's
power, his capacity for love—his ability, in short, to
"perform"—are at times said to be capable of infinite progress. Moreover (as has been noted), Ferguson occasionally
insisted that the virtuous man ought at all times to struggle
for the expansion of his human faculties, disdaining the
comforts attained by any stage of his achievement. Many
activist passages advocate just the sort of striving which the
Stoics called *hybris,* Christians condemn as presumptuous
pride, and Hume scorned as an enthusiastic and futile manifestation of an unnatural mind. To explain the presence of

proud *hybris* in Ferguson's writings, it is necessary to view more closely the content of the cultural tradition from which he drew his ideas.

The intellectual equipment of an eighteenth-century cultured European man like Ferguson consisted primarily of some familiarity with the classical writings of antiquity, a more or less informed enthusiasm for modern science, and a lifelong contact with some version or other of Christianity. As has been pointed out, all three influences could converge on a passive orientation with the modern emphasis on necessary natural laws reinforcing the Stoic submission to the inscrutable but benevolent will of God. But all three constituents of the cultural tradition also embody moods subversive to such resignation to an assumed universal harmony. Classicism, of which Stoicism is only one manifestation, carries with it a notion of human excellence, of man rising far above his original animal nature; Christianity, which speaks also in voices other than Calvin's, conveys a sense of individual dignity, of the integrity of the human personality; and modern science stresses not only human subjection to natural law but also man's mastery over nature, the capacities of human power. The restless perfectionism which Ferguson frequently incorporated into his conception of virtue, the admonitions to bring into play and thereby develop all human faculties, the sanction given to relentlessly ambitious striving—these aspects of Ferguson's activism stem at least in significant part from the literary heritage. Unlike either a dilettante connoisseur of ideas or a dedicated philosophical scholar, Ferguson delved into this heritage in search of practical guidance and was, therefore, prone to emphasize those elements which provide a focus for defining action, rather than thought. The heroic—one might say Promethian—side of the cultural tradition elicited a response of recognition in Ferguson as a man craving action and proud of human achievements, disdainful of the cowering servility and ignorance he saw as the consequence of Calvinist orthodoxy and mechanistic materialism.[62]

In another way, too, the peculiarly intense relationship between ideas and practice characteristic of an intellectual like Ferguson helps to account for the critical overtones in Ferguson's activism. When a writer integrates his ideas by the doctrine of some philosophical school, he can set up some concept like "prudence" or "practical wisdom" to mediate between the self-constituting and autonomous body of his rational philosophical principles, on the one hand, and the day-to-day demands of the practical world, on the other. The speculative definition of virtue can then be viewed as absolute, while the practical maxims governing behavior can be given great flexibility relative to the customs and necessities of any specific situation. But Ferguson usually denied the distinction between truths of speculation and truths directly applicable to practice, just as, in general, he rejected the separation of "philosophers" from "ordinary men." His aim was to develop a conception of virtue which could direct his own practice and the practice of others like him, men engaged in ordinary pursuits but enlightened by ideas. "Society itself," he said, "is the school." Thus, he was occasionally forced to confront low achievements with high ideals in direct contrast, unmediated by relativistic principles of accommodation. He set the vision of man realizing his highest potentialities on the same level as the other components of his conception of virtue, and thereby incorporated into the same scheme of moral injunctions the exhortation to strive for goals never fully attainable and the demand for acquiescent recognition of necessity. The need to use ideas as explanation, justification, and guide for practice—a need engendered by Ferguson's position as intellectual—in sum, led him to apply at least some of his chosen ideas in a manner clashing with the passivity he sought to inculcate in his other roles.

The extent to which Ferguson's identification with the world of thought served to qualify his dedication to practice and, thereby, to round out the Stoic passive element in his conception of virtue has been discussed above. It remains to be seen that the very dedication to practice which most usually characterized his position also contributed to the retention of passive elements in his thought. As illustrated in the historical and biographical discussions above, Ferguson and the other members of the intelligentsia stood on the margin of the most powerful group in their society. Although they were connected to this group by many ties of cultural affinity, personal dependence, and common hostility to "populist" obscurantism, they also strove to establish a position of independence and insisted that their support of the status quo depended on the satisfaction of certain authoritative norms. But the measure of actual independence they achieved was also a measure of their divorce from power in society. For a variety of reasons, they were completely unable and largely unwilling to challenge the prevailing distribution of power. Since the sphere of activity best suited for virtuous practice, at least in Ferguson's view, was pre-empted, the possibilities for autonomous practice available to the intellectual were severely restricted. Ferguson's reiterated reminders that virtue requires attention only to the duties of one's own station was, at least in part, a response to this situational limitation. Although the discussion of Ferguson's role as ideologist quite properly stressed the important degree to which he advocated compliant acceptance of one's socially defined tasks simply in order to bolster the existing power structure, it must

now be noted that this same teaching also served to reconcile him as intellectual to the restrictions actually placed on
his own power.

Ferguson's role as intellectual, then, like his other two
roles, helped to forge together the two sides of his conception
of virtue. As was also true of the other perspectives, the
amalgam reveals a distinct and fairly coherent character
when viewed in the light of this role. It stresses the value of
activity for the sake of exercising and developing human
faculties; it stresses the motives engendered by commitment
to society as the proper dynamic for sustaining such activity.
While it does not dismiss the value of successful
achievement—especially when the objects of action will
enhance the welfare of society—it attempts to forestall the
feeling of bitterness consequent on the longing for totally
unapproachable goals and to avoid the morally destructive
effects of preoccupation with antisocial goods. The former
desire accounts for the insistence on recognizing the limitations placed on every individual's power by his position in a
specific society. From the second follows Ferguson's attack
on the "rage for comparative advantages," when "the success
of one is disappointment to another; and the industry of one
to better himself a scheme of hostility to those who must sink
under his elevation." [63] Despite the slight ambiguities introduced by a certain measure of pride in the life of the mind
and by daily reminders of severely circumscribed power,
Ferguson's role as intellectual impelled him towards an activist conception of virtue.

Leaving the social criticism implicit in this formulation
for later examination, it must now be noted that the most
important practical difference between the activist and the
Stoic passivist views lies in the attitude toward social action
which each seeks to inculcate. Both obliged a man to play
his part in society, but one argues that the duty is to be

carried on dispassionately—one might almost say in response to a "categorical imperative"—while the other advocates passionate involvement in society and intimate concern about those affected by actions. In other words, passiveness stresses the possibility of virtue above and even
despite man's social responsibilities; activism stresses the
attainment of virtue through and because of man's social
engagements. For the one, virtue is primarily a state of
mind; for the other, it is a way of life.

Whatever he may have believed or professed, Ferguson's
most characteristic role tied him more closely to the non-
Stoic element in his thought than to the other; several
important consequences follow immediately from this. Ferguson's attempt to guide himself and others to a life of self-
fulfillment sensitized him to the need for principles of action
which would rouse vigorous human responses without, at
the same time, leading to the isolation of the individual in a
competitive jungle where he would devour himself as well
as others. Secondly, his yearning for action was colored by
the desire for commitment and for opportunities to bring
into play a wide variety of emotions and faculties. Both of
these factors directed his attention to the study of society.
The ideas he found to clarify his eagerness for practical life
gave his study an intensity and direction which his situation
alone could not give it.

The ideas employed by an intellectual, then, are not
merely empty formulas to express his predispositions. A view
of his situation and of the inarticulate attitudes expressed by
his actions and alignments can account for the selection and
organization of his major ideas. But it can never *predict*
them. Similarly, as has been illustrated above, the systems of
thought embodied in a cultural tradition are not without
practical effect on those educated in that tradition. All that
can and must be said is that, unless the tradition is com-

pletely univocal and fully supported by the experiences of those exposed to it, the precise nature of its effects will vary from one social group to another and can be comprehended only through study of the various social positions. Ideas do have consequences; but the consequences result from the interplay between the content of the ideas and the demands of those who adopt them.

In Ferguson's case, the search for ideas capable of governing men's moral choices was dictated by his social role as an intellectual, as well as by his pedagogical and ideological roles. Ferguson found the teachings of the Stoics relevant to the tasks set by all three roles, although each also impelled him to adopt principles which diverged from those teachings. As teacher, he responded to the pressures of convention, and he qualified his Stoicism so as to equip his students with respectable and useful maxims. To adapt his writings to the task of inculcating co-operative obedience to the predominant forces in society, he again modified the counsels borrowed from Epictetus and Marcus Aurelius. Both these functions of his writing, despite the reservations they suggested, still enabled him to keep intact the main thrust of the Stoic ideas. Or rather, it may be said that, with respect to these roles, the sociological explanation exhausts the content of his writings and that the authoritative ideas he adduced were primarily manipulative tools, without effect on the meaning of his principles. Here, then, the ideas themselves were sterile.

Only in his capacity as an intellectual could he let the ideas he adopted bear some fruit: the situation with which he was trying to cope and his close ties to several systems of ideas combined to reduce decisively his reliance on Stoicism. Certainly some Stoic ideas still played a part. Moreover, it was probably his role as an intellectual which dictated the use of Stoicism as a support for his homiletic and propagan-

Stoicism Minor *Stoicism Major*
Activist Myr
G) *Intellect* as *know*

distic teachings. After all, the artifacts of analysis must not disguise that he was one man, not three, and that Stoicism was far more congenial to him than any of the alternatives available for the performance of his roles other than that of intellectual. But the mingling of social and cultural influences to which he was exposed led him to combine ideas into a pattern which, in turn, roused in him an awareness of issues he could not have seen either from a purely Stoic point of view or from a non-articulated, unmediated reaction to his circumstances. The emergence of the activist conception of human virtue, accordingly, can only be explained by the peculiar interplay between social conditions and cultural traditions which is the unique mark of the intellectual's position.

The moral imperatives most significant to Ferguson's orientation toward practice commanded him to foster the attitudes and to seek the opportunities which would best bring into play man's capabilities for effective understanding and strong social feeling. His expectation was that a way of life patterned on these injunctions would, at one and the same time, assure the progress of mankind and the full satisfaction of the individual—it would provide both virtue and happiness.

1. Unpublished Essays, "Of the Categories or Constituents of Discourse and Fabrick [sic] of Thought. Language," pp. 3–4.

2. Ferguson, *Principles*, I, 6–7.

3. *Ibid.,* p. 313.

4. Compare the following passage from the writings of Epictetus: "Where then is progress?

"If any one of you, dismissing things without, has brought his mind to bear on his own will, to work out its full development, that he may bring it into perfect harmony with nature—lofty, free, unhindered, untrammeled, trustworthy, self-respecting; if he has learnt that he that wills to get or to avoid what is not in his power cannot be trustworthy nor free, but must needs himself change as they change, fitful as the winds, and must needs have made himself subservient to others, who can procure or hinder such things" ("Arrian's Discourses of Epictetus," in Whitney J. Oates [ed.], *The Stoic and Epicurean Philosophers* [New York: Random House, 1940], p. 231).

5. Epictetus wrote: "[We] picture to ourselves the work of the philosopher to be something of this sort: he must bring his own will into harmony with events, in such a manner that nothing which happens should happen against our will and that we should not wish for anything to happen that does not happen. The result of this is that those who have thus ordered their life do not fail to get what they will, and do not fall into what they will to avoid: each man spends his own life free from pain, from fear, and from distraction, and maintains the natural and acquired relations which unite him to his fellows—the part of son, father, brother, citizen, husband, wife, neighbor, fellow traveller, ruler, subject" (*ibid.*, p. 308).

6. Compare Ferguson, *Principles*, II, 40.

7. *Ibid.*, I, 3.

8. *Ibid.*, II, 73; compare Ferguson, *Institutes*, pp. 165–76.

9. *Ibid.*, p. 166.

10. Ferguson, *Essay on Civil Society*, p. 44; compare *ibid.*, p. 305.

11. *Ibid.*, p. 274.

12. *Ibid.*, pp. 392–93.

13. Oates, *op. cit.*, p. 369.

14. Ferguson, *Principles*, II, 402.

15. Ferguson, *Institutes*, p. 74.

16. Ferguson, *Principles*, II, 109.

17. Oates, *op. cit.*, p. 458.

18. Ferguson, *Principles*, I, 280.

19. *Ibid.*, I, 77.

20. *Ibid.*, II, 143.

21. *Ibid.*, p. 17; see also Ferguson, *Essay on Civil Society*, pp. 36, 154.

22. Ferguson, *Principles*, I, 33.

23. *Ibid.*, II, 99; compare Ferguson, *Essay on Civil Society*, p. 64.

24. *Ibid.*, p. 35.

25. Ferguson, *Principles*, I, vi–vii; see *infra*.

26. Ferguson, *Essay on Civil Society*, p. 60.

27. Ferguson, *Principles*, II, 112.

28. *Ibid.*, pp. 336–37.

29. *Ibid.*, pp. 352–53.

30. *Ibid.*, p. 381.

31. *Ibid.*, pp. 382–91.

32. Hume, *Enquiries*, pp. 256–57.

33. *Ibid.*, pp. 270, 255, 256.

34. Hume, *Enquiries*, p. 343. Hume also wrote: "A gloomy, hair-brained enthusiast, after his death, may have a place in the calendar; but will scarcely ever be admitted, when alive, into intimacy and society, except by those who are as delirious and dismal as himself" (*ibid.*, p. 270).

35. Hume equated "beneficence" with such terms as "softness and tenderness of sentiment," "warm sentiment," "fondness and delicacy"; and he described its operations as follows: "The tear naturally starts in our eye on the apprehension of a warm sentiment of this nature; our breast heaves, our heart is agitated, and every humane tender principle of our frame is set in motion, and gives us the purest and most satisfactory enjoyment" (*ibid.*, p. 257).

36. *Ibid.*, p. 40.

37. *Ibid.*, p. 319.

38. Compare, for example, Ferguson's admonitions to public spiritedness with the following passage from Hume's writings: "[W]hile every man consults the good of his own community, we are sensible, that the general interest of mankind is better promoted, than by any loose indeterminate view to the good of the species, whence no beneficial action could ever result, for want of a duly limited object, on which they could exert themselves" (*ibid.*, 225 n.).

39. Compare Joseph Cropsey, *Polity and Economy: An Interpretation of the Principles of Adam Smith* (The Hague: Martinus Nijhoff, 1957), p. 55.

40. Ferguson, *Principles*, II, 379.

41. *Ibid.*, p. 90.

42. *Ibid.*, I, 218.

43. *Ibid.*, I, 371–72.

44. *Ibid.*, II, 328.

45. *Ibid.*, I, 255.

46. *Ibid.*, p. 56.

47. *Ibid.*, II, 60.

48. Ferguson defined liberty in the following manner: "[As] every one has a right to the condition in which, by the ordinary course of human nature, he is fairly placed, in which he is in no way injurious to his fellow creatures, it must follow that liberty, in every particular instance, must consist in securing the fairly acquired conditions of men, however unequal" (*ibid.*, II, 464).

49. Ferguson, *Essay on Civil Society*, p. 408.

50. Ferguson, *Principles*, II, 97–98.

51. *Ibid.*, p. 61.

52. *Ibid.*, pp. 93–94.

53. See F. Znaniecki, *The Social Role of the Man of Knowledge* (New York: Columbia University Press, 1940).

54. Ferguson, *Principles*, I, vii–viii.

55. *Ibid.*, p. 167.

56. *Ibid.*, pp. 327–30.

57. *Ibid.*, p. 330 (emphasis supplied).

58. *Ibid.*, pp. 315–16.

59. *Ibid.*, p. 318.

60. *Ibid.*, p. 332.

61. It is interesting to note that, if Ferguson's discussion of immortality is juxtaposed to his discussion of the division of labor, Calvinist predestinarianism reappears in a curious guise. In the latter discussion, which will be treated at length below, Ferguson ascribed to the lowest positions in society an irresistible effect of stifling man's rational capacities. Since immortality depends on the development of just those capacities, it would appear as though social law determined the "damnation" of those individuals condemned to be brutalized by the most menial occupations. Needless to say, Ferguson never explicitly avowed this harsh implication; he was probably quite unaware of it.

62. The following letter, although written bv Thomas Reid rather than Adam Ferguson, conveys a lively sense of the intellectuals' mood at the time: "I am not much surprised that your Lordship [i.e., Kames] has found little entertainment in a late French writer on human nature [i.e., Helvetius, *De l'Esprit*]. From what I learn, they are all become rank Epicureans. . . . I detest all systems that depreciate human nature. If it be a delusion, that there is something in the constitution of man that is venerable and worthy of its Author, let me live and die in that delusion, rather than have my eyes opened to see my species in a humiliating and disgusting light. . . . Were it not that we sometimes see extremes meet, I should think it very strange to see atheists and high-shod divines, contending as it were who should most blacken and degrade human nature. Yet I think the atheist acts the more consistent part of the two: for surely such views of human nature tend more to promote atheism than to promote religion and virtue" (Tytler, *op. cit.*, iii, 221–22).

63. Ferguson, *Principles*, II, 57; see also *ibid.*, p. 15.

CHAPTER VII

Virtue and Society

Society in General: The Promise

FERGUSON'S thoughts about society can be fully understood only in the light of his conception of virtue. Apart from the secondary, derivative, ideological and homiletic functions performed by Ferguson's attempt to define virtue, that definition constituted his definition of self. Information about who and what Ferguson was, is indispensable for the interpretation of his conception of virtue precisely because the conception was an ideal projection of his own role. On the basis of such an interpretation, it is now possible to examine those of his writings which address themselves to the explanation and evaluation of social institutions. However much these may reflect the relationship between Ferguson, his role, and his circumstances, their most prominent characteristics are dictated, rather, by the interplay between Ferguson's self-conception and the social reality which he confronted.

Two links, in Ferguson's view, bind the understanding of virtue to the understanding of society. First, virtuous men require knowledge about the truly good ends of society and about the means appropriate to achieving those ends because love of society manifested in active social benefaction is the main attribute of virtue. Secondly, promoters of virtue must learn about society because, he believed, human virtue can arise only in society and—more specifically—can as a rule arise only in the kind of society which provides it stimulation and encouragement. Ultimately, Ferguson reduced these two connecting links to one. Since the highest form of virtuous activity is activity directed towards the maintenance and/or creation of a society conducive to virtue, the two questions around which Ferguson can be said to have organized his study of society are served by the same answers. These converging questions may be restated as follows: "What contributions must the virtuous man make to his society?"; and "what contribution does the state of society make to human virtue?"

In a most general way, Ferguson could provide a clear and coherent answer. The virtuous man, he could say, manifests and furthers virtue when he acts to strengthen the social ties among men because a society of men bound together by close ties is an all-important aid to the emergence of virtue in men. Virtue, after all, is the perfection of human nature, and human nature is inconceivable without society. In his discussion of society, Ferguson first sought to refute every notion of inherent conflict between man's progressive nature and his universal role as a member of society. Against all who postulated a hypothetical presocial "state of nature" —whether such hypotheses were derived to justify or to criticize civil society—Ferguson opposed the repeated assertion that "mankind are to be taken in groupes, as they have always subsisted." [1] Society is man's state of nature. He argued that any attempt to study man apart from man's experience of sociality is useless:

> A wild man . . . caught in the woods, where he had always lived apart from his species is a singular instance, not a specimen of any general character. As the anatomy of . . . an ear which has never felt the impulse of sounds would probably exhibit defects in the very structure of the organs themselves, arising from their not being applied to their proper functions; so any particular case of this sort would only shew in what degree the powers of apprehension and sentiment could exist where they had not been employed, and what would be the defects and imbecilities of a heart in which the emotions that pertain to society had never been felt.[2]

At the very outset of his speculations, then, Ferguson affirmed the congruence between man's social and individual destinies.

Ferguson rested his case, not only on the empirical fact that no records exist of non-social men or on the a priori assertion that non-social man is not truly human, but also on a detailed deduction from man's "instinctive propensities" and faculties. Like all animals, he maintained, man has inborn motives impelling him to action.[3] Some, like hunger, he shares with other animals; but the most significant ones—the drives to self-preservation, society, and ambition—he possesses in a unique form. While animal instincts dictate both ends and means, human propensities do no more than to indicate a general direction, leaving it to man's faculties to devise the means most appropriate to his ends.[4] In Ferguson's view, each of these propensities contributes to the existence of society, and—conversely—society serves all the ends suggested to man by his nature.

Ferguson noted that even those writers like Hobbes, whom he considered antisocial, had seen the importance of society for the preservation of the individual. Ferguson cited Hobbes' contention that the pursuit of "interest"—if reasonably conducted—serves to attach men to society. Man's natural powers are so weak, according to Ferguson, and the gifts of nature so sparse that men can protect themselves against dangers and satisfy their bodily needs only through ingenuity and joint action, both possible only in society. To this extent, Ferguson was prepared to echo the arguments of the "Hobbesians." But moral and empirical considerations combined to lead him to deny that "interest" can properly "be thought to comprehend at once all the motives of human conduct."[5] His conception of virtue, the perfection of human nature, always demanded some natural impetus towards a life of disinterested benevolence; he opposed Hobbes and Mandeville because he believed that they undercut true morality by denying the efficacy of all motives except that of self-interest. Sometimes he reinterpreted self-interest in such a way as to make it wholly compatible with virtue,[6] but in the main his argument followed a different line. Ferguson claimed that actual social behavior cannot be accounted for by a psychology of interest alone. Jibingly he wrote:

> In accounting for actions we often forget that we ourselves have acted; and instead of the sentiments which stimulate the mind in the presence of its objects, we assign as the motives of conduct with men, those considerations which occur in the hours of retirement and cold reflection. In this mood frequently we can find nothing important, besides the deliberate prospects of interest; and a great work, like that of forming society, must in our apprehension arise from deep reflections, and be carried on with a view to the advantages which mankind derive from commerce and mutual support.[7]

Elsewhere he pointed to the evidence of malevolent disinterested passions which, he insisted, "will not be denied," even if "men be not allowed to have disinterested benevolence." [8]

Ferguson was not, of course, really prepared to concede the absence of a sociable disposition in man: the propensity to seek out other men was for him one of the dominant characteristics of all mankind. Drawn together by numerous necessities, sexual as well as economic, men are held together by emotional bonds derived from an instinctive longing for society. "What comes from a fellow-creature is received with particular attention," he urged, "and every language abounds with terms that express somewhat in the transactions of men different from success and disappointment." [9] Man's natural propensities do not determine the form to be taken by man's association with others, but they do dictate that social life in some form will be sought by all men and, consequently, that all societies will be integrated —at least in part—by the satisfaction which their mere existence provides to man. Ferguson believed that man's social propensity has a corollary which, at first sight, appears contradictory to it. Man, in his view, is "disposed to opposition" [10] as well as to unity. He found the contradiction easy to resolve: he argued that "separation itself has an effect in straitening the bands of society; for the members of each separate nation feel their connection the more, that the name of fellow-countryman stands in contradistinction to that of an alien." [11] The "rivalship of nations and the practice of war" are, in his view, an inevitable and invaluable aspect of man's sociality. [12] Ferguson held, in short, that combativeness and love together constitute man's social propensity.

Ferguson found it difficult to name the third natural propensity of man, but he sought to describe it in each of his books and always insisted that it, too, contributed to the maintenance of society. In the *Essay on the History of Civil*

Society, Ferguson talked about something underlying the
"moral sentiment"; in the *Institutes of Moral Philosophy,* he
encompassed the propensity within a "law of eminence";
and in the *Principles of Moral and Political Philosophy,* he
spoke of "ambition" as a universal human drive.[13] In all
cases, the third propensity is seen as a striving for perfection,
excellence, or simply "something higher than is possessed at
present." [14] The philosophical function performed by the
postulation of such a propensity has been scrutinized in an
earlier chapter; for the present, it is enough to describe
briefly the relationship between the "ambitious" propensity
and society. First, because it is the propensity underlying all
moral judgments, it will lead men to love society, provided
that they have a correct understanding of human excellence.
Secondly, regardless of men's judgments, their ambition will
keep them actively engaged in human pursuits even when
their original physical and emotional needs have been met.[15]
Such an engagement in itself normally serves, according to
Ferguson, to maintain society. Thus, society is a manifestation of all the natural sources of human motivation—
the propensities to self preservation, sociality and ambition
—and the experience of living in society provides satisfaction for all fundamental human needs.

Important as these arguments for the basic compatibility
between man's social state and his propensities were for
Ferguson, they could not by themselves complete the
justification of social life from the standpoint of virtue, or
point to all the aspects of society important to him. Man is
distinguished from the animals, Ferguson believed, by
unique faculties as well as by distinguishing propensities. As
noted above, man's propensities themselves differ fundamentally from animal instincts in being satisfied only
through the intervention of man's mind. Mind, in Ferguson's view, exercises two major powers: understanding and

will. Human action depends on the blending of intelligence and sentiments into opinion; propensities are given concrete expression only in a form mediated by opinion. As the following passage makes clear, Ferguson maintained that man's reasoning and judging capacities depend on society for their development. He wrote:

> The atmosphere of society, from the whole, we may conclude is the element in which the human mind must draw the first breath of intelligence itself: if not the vital air by which the celestial air of moral sentiment is kindled: we cannot doubt but it is of mighty effect in exciting the flame; and that the minds of men, to use a familiar example, may be compared to those blocks of fuel which taken apart are barely to be lighted; but if gathered into heaps are easily kindled into a flame.[16]

Not only is understanding dependent on the accumulation and comparison of individual experiences, but also—and this was decisive for Ferguson—it is impossible without language. Ferguson put the matter thus:

> Language is the instrument of society; and, we may presume, is not employed in any other matter but what the communications of society require; a consideration from which it should seem to follow, that man is indebted to society for every exercise of his faculties, of which language is formed to express the attainment or the use; a title under which we may fairly comprehend all the efforts of understanding or genius.[17]

It will be noted that in both of these passages Ferguson insisted more strongly on the debt of reason to society than on that of sentiment. In part, this was probably due to a desire to leave open the possibility of a natural moral sense which dictates correct feelings regardless of circumstances. A more important consideration, however, was the moralist's determination to preserve the area of feeling as a sphere for individual improvement. Nevertheless, Ferguson generally maintained that the passionate side of the mind's activity, too, is shaped by man's social state. The influence of society on the sentiments is both direct and indirect. Contacts among men and participation in societal affairs, in his view, provide direct stimuli to feelings and crystallize men's sentiments; they transform men's social propensities into benevolent opinions. Indirectly society affects the passions, according to Ferguson, through reason and habit. While powerless alone, understanding animated by some propensity can govern judgment and action, and understanding is a product of society. Another connection between society and sentiment—even more important in his view—arises from the power of habit.

Habit, which Ferguson considered to be the most important single factor determining most men's sentiments, opinions, and judgments, derives from men's experiences. It operates according to the following psychological law: "That whatever the living nature is able to perform without impairing its organs, if persisted in, will produce a habit." [18] Ferguson used the concept of habituation to account for many phenomena—the possibility of individual moral reform (by adopting new habits of thought through an initial effort), the increments of skill gained through practice, the presence of idiosyncratic and seemingly absurd opinions in individuals, and the variety of opinions within one society—and many of these applications will be examined below. For the present, however, it is sufficient to discuss Ferguson's contentions about the interconnections between habit and society in general.

Habit, first of all, reinforces social ties already established by propensities and stimulated feelings: "mere acquaintance and habitude," wrote Ferguson, "nourish affection, and the experience of society brings every passion of the human mind upon its side." [19] Secondly, Ferguson noted in every society a prevailing pattern of opinions which the individual adopts as a result of habit, not reason or personal emotional experiences. As the following passage makes clear, Ferguson regarded such habitual consensus of opinion as an important integrating factor in society. He stated:

> The authority of prevailing opinion makes at least one bond of society; and it is more fit that the people should move together, though not in the best way that might be devised for them, than that they should disband and separate into different ways, where no one might find, in the way he had chosen for himself, any thing to compensate his separation from the rest of his kind.[20]

Society, Ferguson believed, rests on man's instinctive urges towards self-preservation, society, and ambition; through stimulation and habituation it shapes man's intellectual and emotional capacities so as to maintain itself and—in turn—to make men happy. Putting the matter somewhat differently, he argued that, although nature gives man his capabilities, only society can provide the moral and physical strength to sustain a virtuous life. In loving society, then, a virtuous man at once expresses and strengthens his virtue. In fostering virtue, society at once justifies and maintains its existence:

> From society are derived not only the force, but the very existence of man's happiest emotions; not only the better part, but almost the whole of his rational character. Send him to the desert alone, he is a plant torn from its roots: the form indeed may remain, but every faculty droops and withers; the human personage and the human character cease to exist.[21]

Ferguson's discussion of the ties between society and human nature has been treated here at considerable length, not because it manifests great originality, but because it provides preliminary guidance to the functions and mechanism of society which Ferguson made the primary objects of his study. He interested himself in the ways in which society contributes to man's self-preservation, the outlets it provides for man's sociable and antagonistic feelings, and the opportunities it provides for exercising the striving towards perfection. Furthermore, he sought to identify the mechanisms whereby a mind is stimulated to gain knowledge and emotions are roused to moral sentiments. Finally, he addressed himself to the operations of habit as a constituent of society. Although—as will be seen—Ferguson's analysis became far more complex when his focus turned from society in general to concrete social phenomena in particular societies, the basic concerns and consequent framework remained.

With this framework defined, it is now possible to provide an "internal" explanation—complementing the "external" ones offered in earlier chapters—for the characteristic of Ferguson's social writings which has been remarked most often by commentators, viz., his constant preoccupation with political institutions.[22] Ferguson maintained "that political establishments are the most important articles in the external condition of men," [23] and he offered his reasons in the following passage:

> It appears from the history of mankind, that men have always acted in troops and companies; that they have apprehended a good of the community, as well as of the individual; that while they practice arts, each for his own preservation, they institute political forms, and unite their forces, for common safety.
> It may be proved that most of the opinions, habits, and pursuits of men result from the state of their society; that

men are happy in proportion that they love mankind; that their rights and their duties are relative to each other and, therefore, that their most important concerns are to be found in their mutual relations, and in the state of their communities.[24]

Political institutions, then, encompass almost every function and mechanism of society relevant to virtue. They protect men against internal and external enemies; they promote the common good and organize the struggle against outsiders; they provide a path for ambition; and—most importantly —they offer stimulation for the development of human faculties. "It is in conducting the affairs of civil society," wrote Ferguson, "that mankind find the exercise of their best affections." [25]

The conclusion to be drawn from these considerations about society in general was clear to Ferguson: the form of government appropriate to society, seen as an arena for virtue, is a moderate but democratic republic. Ferguson stated this conclusion in the following way:

> [The] history of mankind . . . has abundantly shewn, in the instance of republican governments, that the attainments of knowledge, ability, and public virtues are proportioned to the concern which numbers are permitted to take in the affairs of their community; and to the exertion of ingenuity and public spirit, which they have occasion to make in national counsels, in offices of state, or public services of any sort.[26]

The reference to history in this passage indicates something about the source and models of Ferguson's views about society and govenment. Ferguson sought, quite deliberately, to pattern his approach on those of classical writers, and he took as his model the highly idealized picture which Cicero had drawn of the Roman Republic. Throughout

Ferguson's published writings, especially in his history of
Rome, can be found statements like these: "If ever there was
a body of men fit to govern the world, it was the Roman
Senate. . . ."; and "A Roman citizen was not an artist, but
he was a man fit to command every artist." [27] The institutions and men of that time provided him with the cardinal
illustration of the ultimate harmony between the structure
of society and the demands of virtue.

Moreover, when Ferguson directed his attention to republican Rome, as when he spoke about society in general, he
could apply his conception of virtue without revealing its
ambivalence. For the citizen, the "passive" obedience to the
dictates of his place in society demanded "active" participation in the struggle for the common good. Discontent and
conflict, Ferguson believed, are the very essence of order in a
free society like that at Rome. Although he could not fit in
the more purely contemplative aspects of his Stoic passivism,
his Stoic sources themselves were sufficiently unclear about
this and sufficiently unanimous in their praises of the non-
contemplative man of action, Cato, so that Ferguson experienced no difficulty in ascribing every virtue to the Romans
and their society. The conflict between activist and passivist
elements in Ferguson's conception of virtue arose, as explained in the preceding chapters, from factors in Ferguson's
own situation; it made itself felt in his study of society only
when he applied his general views to concrete cases,
specifically to the case of Britain.

But Roman history itself contained matter to disturb the
optimism displayed in Ferguson's depiction of society as a
school for virtue and of the Roman Republic as a model of
society. The history of the Roman Republic was, as he well
knew, a history of "termination," as well as of "progress." If
Roman institutions could decline into absolutist tyranny and
Roman citizens become abject slaves, gravest doubt is

thrown on the harmony between social institutions and individual virtue. Ferguson's study of Roman history represents his attempt to resolve that doubt. In that work, he pointed out that the quality of Roman society and the virtues of its citizens depended on certain specific conditions, that when those conditions changed Rome could no longer be the same, and that under the new conditions social institutions emerged which were in every way hostile to virtue. From these considerations, he concluded (as had his Stoic predecessors) that virtue need not be manifested and strengthened through acts of public benevolence: it could be a private, internal affair of discipline, duty, and submission to circumstance.

In the context of his Roman studies, however, he could never do more than to view this second, passive type of virtue as a "consolation and support"—as a second-best. The crisis in Ferguson's conception of virtue may, in a sense, be said to coincide with the crisis of the Roman Republic. Departing from his avowed intention "to avoid expressions of mere praise and blame," [28] Ferguson interrupted his description of the republic's last agonies to assess the moral praise or blame due to Cato, Cicero, Brutus, Caesar, Pompey, and Octavius. He brushed aside the contention that the defenders of popular rule should have assented to the inevitable, that they were blameworthy for pursuing an impracticable and inexpedient policy. "The virtuous who resign their freedom," he wrote, "at the same time resign their virtue, or at least yield up that condition which is required to preserve it." [29] Corresponding to the high praise he heaped on the senatorial group was his scorn for those who, in his view, had maliciously destroyed the republic. For Ferguson, no arguments based on the timeliness of their action or on "our predilection for monarchy in general" could justify the self-seeking course of the revolutionaries. [30] Not without

bitterness—and even incredulity—he pointed out again and
again that these men were "born to inherit" freedom and
were, therefore, obligated to abstain from any activity inimical to republicanism. This very condemnation does imply an
important qualification which opened Ferguson's way to an
assertion of compatibility between non-republican states and
virtue: Men born in other times, presumably, can act vir-
tuously without following the principles appropriate to the
free-born; they need not struggle to create a social situation
conducive to general virtue. Ferguson could, thus, praise
those who maintained free minds and "manly indifference"
in the midst of despotism. Yet he never suggested this possibility without a tone of regret, and he always insisted that
mankind in general cannot be truly happy or virtuous under
such conditions.[31] Fundamentally, then, Ferguson's book on
Roman history reveals an adherence to the passive view of
virtue granted only as a grudging and wavering concession
to factors he considered irresistibly compelling. Moreover,
it illustrates the kind of problems which led Ferguson to
develop his analysis of society beyond a satisfying demonstration of congruence between virtuous human nature and
society in general.

Societies in Particular: The Threat

The two basic problems which emerge are: first, how to
reconcile himself to the fact that republics have failed to
survive although they have provided the greatest happiness
to mankind; and secondly, how to cope with the fact that, in
the form of despotisms, there have existed examples of societies which "crush [man's] spirit, that debase his sentiments,
and disqualify his mind for affairs." For Ferguson, these
were not problems of mere antiquarian interest: he believed
that both confronted his own society. In an essay entitled

"Of History and its appropriate Style," Ferguson wrote: "History we say is instructive but we do not specify the respect in which it is properly and peculiarly so. It is a narration of past actions and by informing us of what has been in particular instances tends to reveal the actual course of things in which we are engaged and which we may lay our account with in the future as in the past, and so to become prudent in guarding against one event & in taking measures to obtain another." Ferguson's preoccupation with Roman history arose from his concern about the conditions of his own time.[32] Just as he could not examine the Roman Republic—the historical embodiment of all the promise he saw in society—without encountering the phenomena of decline and corruption, so could he not look about him from the vantage point of that promise without noting perplexing symptoms of a similar fate. In both cases, his response entailed the substitution of complex schemes of social analysis for an initially simple hymn of praise and the transformation of a simple criterion for evaluating society into one which was at least more complex and occasionally even self-contradictory.

But before the refinements and modifications in Ferguson's social theory can be examined, it is necessary to show that Ferguson did indeed uncover serious signs of trouble when he tried to judge his own society simply according to a standard derived from the contribution society in general can make to human virtue. Most of this evidence Ferguson considered in the *Essay on the History of Civil Society*. It was in this work that he developed the essential elements of his orientation to society. The later books reflect, in their greater emphases on passive virtue and a correspondingly reassuring evaluation of society, the extent to which he managed to meet the challenge of the major problems he had discovered. Because, as has already been shown in the case of individual virtue, Ferguson's orientation was never free of ambivalence and a certain measure of perplexity, he did nevertheless strive even in his later books for further clarification and more persuasive justification of the social situation in which he found himself.

Measured by his simplest criteria, then, Britain presented a worrisome picture to Ferguson. It was quite obviously not a democratic republic. Although not absolutist, like many of its European neighbors, the government was headed by an hereditary monarch and gave many positions of power to men because of ancestry or wealth rather than worth. The Roman Republic had declined and perished; but, according to Ferguson, the energies kindled by Republican times served to sustain a certain measure of greatness,[33] and at least the name of republic had—far into the imperial period—been honored through the lip service of rulers and the tributes of philosophers. In Britain, however, republicanism had never been experienced at all, and any advocacy of such a form was treasonable. Although Ferguson never frankly expressed the concern this must have aroused in him, the present speculation is supported by much that is implicit in his discussion of governmental forms.

But it is not necessary to rely on such uncertain evidence of Ferguson's fears. His defense of republicanism, after all, rested on the contention that this form of government is the keystone of a society which expresses and promotes virtue, and if Ferguson never openly decried the absence of a democratic republic, he was fully explicit in describing other symptoms of Britain's inadequate performance of those functions of society he valued most highly. Ferguson judged society "as a state to be valued from its effects in preserving the species, in ripening their talents, and exciting their virtues."[34] Ferguson found what appeared to him to be serious shortcomings in all three aspects. His own society seemed to be marked by dangerous weakness and disunity, stifling specialization, and corrupt and corrupting indifference about public affairs. Ferguson's study of society constituted an attempt to explain and to cope with these appearances.

The weakness of modern society, its doubtful capacity to protect men, Ferguson saw manifested in two ways. First, the society was, he believed, militarily weak. Relying on professional soldiers to carry the burdens of war, Britain, like other European nations, was faced with a perpetual danger which Ferguson described in the following words:

> In Europe, where mercenary and disciplined armies are everywhere formed, and ready to traverse the earth, where, like a flood pent up by slender banks, they are only restrained by political forms, or a temporary balance of power; if the sluices should break, what inundations may we not expect to behold? Effeminate kingdoms and empires are spread from the sea of Corea to the Atlantic Ocean. Every state, by the defeat of its troops, may be turned into a province; every army opposed in the field today may be hired tomorrow; and every victory gained, may give the accession of a new military force to the victor! [35]

Secondly, according to Ferguson, powerful forces were disrupting the unity which even the Hobbists considered essential to preservation. In opposition to what he believed to be the position of Hobbes, however, Ferguson contended that interest alone can never hold a society together. Moreover, in his view, serious difficulties arise precisely "in a commercial state, where men may be supposed to have experienced, in its fullest extent, the interest which individuals have in the preservation of their country." He continued:

> It is here indeed, if ever, that man is sometimes found a detached and solitary being: he has found an object which

sets him in competition with his fellow creatures, and he
deals with them as he does with his cattle and his soil, for
the sake of the profits they bring. The mighty engine
which we have supposed to have formed society, only tends
to set its members at variance, or to continue their intercourse after the bands of affection are broken.[36]

As a "commercial state," then, indifferent to military skills
and preoccupied with private interest, Britain displayed to
Ferguson a dangerous incapacity to protect its members
against external threats. The very bourgeois values of
pacifism and self-interest which had been extolled by
Hobbes appeared to Ferguson as marks of a society in danger
of destruction.

Commerce, with its attendant specialization of functions,
aroused Ferguson's concern in another respect. Far from
providing opportunities for the exercise and improvement of
man's varied faculties, modern society, he believed, tended
to limit and even to suppress many of man's capacities. This
tendency he remarked particularly in the case of the lower
orders of society, writing:

It may even be doubted, whether the measure of national
capacity increases with the advancement of the arts. Many
mechanical arts, indeed, require no capacity; they succeed
best under a total suppression of sentiments and reason;
and ignorance is the mother of industry as well as of
superstition. Reflection and fancy are subject to err; but a
habit of moving the hand or the foot, is independent of
either. Manufactures, accordingly, prosper most, where the
mind is least consulted, and where the workshop may,
without any great effort of imagination, be considered as
an engine, the parts of which are men.

.   .   .   .

In every commercial state, notwithstanding any pretensions to equal rights, the exaltation of a few must depress
the many. In this arrangement, we think that the extreme

meanness of some classes must arise chiefly from the defect of knowledge, and of liberal education; and we refer to such classes, as to an image of what our species must have been in its rude and uncultivated state. But we forget how many circumstances, especially in populous cities, tend to corrupt the lowest orders of men. Ignorance is the least of their failings. An admiration of wealth unpossessed, becoming a principle of envy or of servility; a habit of acting perpetually with a view to profit, and under a sense of subjection; the crimes to which they are allured, in order to feed their debauch, or to gratify their avarice, are examples, not of ignorance, but of corruption and baseness.[37]

But not even the higher orders of society are immune to the stifling of talents. The following passages express the judgment Ferguson passed on the division between military and civil functions in government:

The subdivision of arts and professions, in certain examples, tends to improve the practice of them and to promote their ends. By having separated the arts of the clothier and the tanner, we are the better supplied with shoes and with cloth. But to separate the arts which form the citizen and the statesman, the arts of policy and war, is an attempt to dismember the human character, and to destroy those very arts we mean to improve. By this separation, we in effect deprive a free people of what is necessary for their safety; or we prepare a defense against invasion from abroad, which gives a prospect of usurpation and threatens the establishment of military government at home.[38]

We may, with good reason, congratulate our species on their having escaped from a state of barbarous disorder and violence, into a state of domestic peace and regular policy; when they have sheathed the dagger, and disarmed the animosities of civil contention: when the weapons with which they contend are the reasonings of the wise, and the tongues of the eloquent. But we cannot, meantime, help to regret, that they should proceed, in search of perfection, to place every branch of administration behind the counter, and come to employ, instead of the statesman and warrior, the mere clerk and accountant.[39]

In these statements, Ferguson indicated some of the considerations which counterbalanced his harsh evaluation of British society; these will be examined later. For the present, it is pertinent to note Ferguson's conviction that, in contrast to "society" in the abstract and to the Roman Republic, the society of his own time apparently failed to provide the stimuli necessary for the full flowering of human talents.

Because the development of human faculties was for Ferguson intimately bound to the emergence of virtue, it is difficult to isolate those of his concerns which relate exclusively to society's failure to promote virtue. Nevertheless, certain phases of his description emphasize that side of the problem, and—as could be expected—these occur in his treatment of political institutions. Leaving aside the question of governmental forms, he repeatedly expressed the fear that a governmental policy directed primarily to the efficient maintenance of prosperity and order would fail, not only to enlist governmental power and influence on the side of virtue, but also to provide men in government with a proper outlet for virtuous activity. His belief that modern states increasingly tended towards such a policy, and his apprehensions about the probable outcome, Ferguson stated in the following terms:

> To the ancient Greek or the Roman, the individual was nothing, and the public every thing. To the modern, in too many nations of Europe, the individual is every thing and the public nothing. The state is merely a combination of departments, in which consideration, wealth, eminence, or power, are offered as the reward of service. It was the nature of modern government, even in its first institution,

to bestow on every individual a fixed station and dignity, which he was to maintain for himself. Our ancestors, in rude ages, during the recess of wars from abroad, fought for their personal claims at home, and by their competitions, and the balance of their powers, maintained a kind of political freedom in the state, while private parties were subject to constant wrongs and oppressions. Their posterity, in times more polished, have repressed the civil disorders in which the activity of earlier ages chiefly consisted, but they employ the calm they have gained, not in fostering a zeal for those laws, and that constitution of government to which they owe their protection, but in practicing apart, and each for himself, the several arts of personal advancement, or profit, which their political establishments may enable them to pursue with success. Commerce, which may be supposed to comprehend every lucrative art, is accordingly considered as the great object of nations, and the principal study of mankind.[40]

When we suppose government to have bestowed a degree of tranquillity which we sometimes hope to reap from it, as the best of its fruits, and public affairs to proceed, in the several departments of legislation and execution, with the least possible interruption to commerce and lucrative arts; such a state, like that of China, by throwing affairs into separate offices, where conduct consists in detail, and in the observance of forms, by superseding all the exertions of a great or a liberal mind, is more akin to despotism than we are apt to imagine.[41]

Not even the wars of modern states, according to Ferguson, represent a genuine public-spirited endeavor. Reporting the amazement of a savage upon hearing of attacks on unarmed "enemy" merchants, Ferguson commented:

It should seem that this simple warrior considered merchants as a kind of neutral person, who took no part in the quarrels of their country; and that he did not know how much war itself may be made the subject of traffic; what mighty armies may be put in motion from behind the

counter; how often human blood is, without any national
animosity, bought and sold for bills of exchange; and how
often the princes, the nobles, and the statesmen, in many a
polished nation, might, in his account, be considered as
merchants.[42]

Although these statements do not explicitly connect these
failures to the absence of republicanism, they do clearly
charge modern political institutions with failure to make
those contributions to virtue which Ferguson elsewhere pro-
claimed as the hallmark of republics.

For Ferguson, it is clear, major shortcomings characterized
the societies of his time, and—although he was occasionally
vague on this point—there can be no question that he
believed that Britain, as a "polished" and "commercial" nation, partook of these imperfections. But it is not enough to
denominate the tendencies antithetical to preservation, human talents, and public spirit as mere "shortcomings" or
"imperfections." They correspond precisely to the factors
Ferguson considered indicative of despotism, the state of
complete corruption which Ferguson described thus:

> If men be anywhere arrived at this measure of depravity,
> there appears no immediate hope of redress. Neither the
> ascendancy of the multitude, nor that of any tyrant, will
> secure the administration of justice: neither the license of
> mere tumult, nor the calm of dejection and servitude, will
> teach the citizen that he was born for candour and affec-
> tion to his fellow creatures. And if the speculative would
> find that habitual state of war which they are sometimes
> pleased to honour with the name of *state of nature*, they
> will find it in the contest that subsists between the despoti-
> cal prince and his subjects, not in the first approaches of a
> rude and simple tribe to the condition and domestic ar-
> rangements of nations.[43]

Highly significant is the parallel between the reference to
the Hobbesian "state of nature" in this passage and the

similar citation in a passage quoted earlier, wherein Ferguson described man's "detached and solitary" condition in a society torn by the competitive striving for interest. Despotism displays to the highest degree a trait already apparent in commercial society—the disruption of genuine fellow-feeling among men. The emergence of mercenary armies, too, Ferguson considered a harbinger of despotism. He wrote:

> The boasted refinements, then, of the polished age, are not divested of danger. They open a door, perhaps, to disaster, as wide and accessible as any of those they have shut. If they build walls and ramparts, they enervate the minds of those who are placed to defend them; if they form disciplined armies, they reduce the military spirit of entire nations; and by placing the sword where they have given a distaste to civil establishments, they prepare for mankind the government of force.[44]

Similarly, in his view, "the separation of professions . . . in its termination and ultimate effects, serves, in some measure, to break the bonds of society" [45] and thus to promote and preserve despotic corruption. Finally, and most importantly, Ferguson maintained that a political system content with the preservation of order leads to despotism and may, in fact, imperceptibly become a despotic one. He argued:

> Corruption, however, does not arise from the abuse of commercial arts alone; it requires the aid of political situations; and is not produced by the objects that occupy a sordid and mercenary spirit without the aid of circumstances that enable men to indulge in safety any mean dispositions they have acquired.
>
> Providence has fitted mankind for the higher engagements which they are sometimes obliged to fulfill; and it is in the midst of such engagements that they are most likely

to acquire or preserve their virtues. The habits of a vigorous mind are formed in contending with difficulties, not in
enjoying the repose of a pacific station; penetration and
wisdom are the fruits of experience, not the lessons of
retirement and leisure; ardour and generosity are the qualities of a mind aroused and animated in the conduct of
scenes that engage the heart, not the gifts of reflection and
knowledge. The mere intermission of national and political efforts is notwithstanding sometimes mistaken for public good; and there is no mistake more likely to foster the
vices, or to flatter the weakness, of feeble and interested
men.

If the ordinary arts of policy, or rather, if a growing
indifference to objects of a public nature, should prevail,
and, under any free constitution, put an end to those
disputes of party, and silence that noise of dissension,
which generally accompany the exercise of freedom, we
may venture to prognosticate corruption to the national
manners, as well as remissness to the national spirit.

The intimate tie between corruption and despotism Ferguson explained in the following passage which, like much
of Ferguson's writing, paraphrases Montesquieu:

Oppression and cruelty are not always necessary to despotic
government; and even when present, are but a part of its
evils. It is founded on corruption, and on the suppression
of all the civil and political virtues; it requires its subjects
to act from motives of fear; it would assuage the passions
of a few men at the expense of mankind; and would erect
the peace of society itself on the ruins of that freedom and
confidence from which alone the enjoyment, the force, and
the elevation of the human mind are found to arise.[46]

Certainly Ferguson's apprehensions were aroused by the gap
between the promise he saw in "society" and the reality he
observed and experienced in his own society. But his fears
were heightened immeasurably by the conviction that the

decisive social and political characteristics he noted in his own time were shared—although in more intense form—by despotic states destructive of all humanity.

Confronted with such a frightening situation, Ferguson could react—one would think—in any one of three obvious ways: he could mentally withdraw from the situation; he could try to change it; or he could deny his impressions. But Ferguson did not choose any one of these alternatives. Elements of each can be found in his writings alongside of arguments which explicitly or implicitly reject each alternative. And a recollection of all that has been said about Ferguson's role and situation can offer a very general explanation of why this should be so. Insofar as his was a life of contemplation, he could well find solace in rational comprehension of ineluctable necessities and in the purity of his own intentions; but he was also a man who longed for effective action. As a man of high humanistic principles, he could well challenge existing evils and search for ways of reforming them; but he was also deeply committed to much in the existing order, and, in any case, he was well aware that he lacked the power to effectuate change. Finally, in his capacity as ally and supporter of the status quo, he could rest content with applying a rationalizing gloss over the problems of his time; but he was also a self-respecting intellectual whose sense of his own integrity had, after all, led him to become aware of these problems in the first place.

Ferguson's complex and conflicting reactions to the dangers he saw in his own society, like the conception of virtue which awakened him to the dangers, rested on the complexity and ambiguity inherent in his social role—internally divided into moralistic, ideological, and intellectual components but ultimately integrated by his position as an intellectual. A further explication of these complex reactions and of their consequences will not only reveal much about the

internal conflicts: it will also bring out the underlying unity
which held together all phases of Ferguson's literary activity.
That unity has already been discussed at several stages of the
present study. Its elements have been seen: first, in historical
and biographical perspective; second, in the light of Ferguson's approaches to technical philosophical problems; and,
third, from the standpoint of his conception of virtue. The
present discussion presupposes all three earlier ones—particularly the last—and can be expected to give the most
comprehensive overview, just as Ferguson most fully expressed his character as intellectual in relating himself to his
society.

The three types of reaction—withdrawal, reform, and
denial—are in a sense simply three new ways of classifying
the elements in Ferguson's conception of virtue. Withdrawal corresponds to passivist virtue in its most purely Stoic
version. From this point of view, societal problems all fade
into insignificance—they concern only those externals
which are irrelevant to true virtue—and man's attention is
directed to the discipline of his own mind. As a reaction to
his situation, Ferguson's reformism refers to the activist
component of virtue in its most discontented and critical
phase. There the call is for action which will enhance the
happiness of beneficiaries as well as actors. Denial reflects
that blend of passivist and activist elements which have
been associated most markedly with Ferguson's homiletic
and ideological roles but which have also been seen to have
had deep roots in his role as intellectual. Since the presence
of all three elements in Ferguson's thought has already been
demonstrated, it is now possible to focus attention on those
manifestations which peculiarly relate to the problems posed
by British society.

In its purest form, as in its Stoic origins, Ferguson's
withdrawal response has definite pessimistic overtones. Al-

though it does, indeed, usually involve some claim of ultimate universal harmony, it also stresses the individual man's helplessness in the face of cosmic forces. Seeing the problems of society from this perspective might well produce fatalistic resignation to an inevitable decline. But such a conclusion Ferguson rejected with great fervor. He denied that societies have a necessary cycle of life from youth to age and death, that social vigor is subject to natural exhaustion, and that "weakness and effeminacy" are natural consequences of "prosperity and plenty." [47] Instead, he insisted on the efficacy of wise institutions, writing:

> Ordinary establishments terminate in a relaxation of vigour, and are ineffectual to the preservation of states; because they lead mankind to rely on their arts, instead of their virtues, and to mistake for an improvement of human nature, a mere accession of accommodation or of riches. Institutions that fortify the mind, inspire courage, and promote national felicity, can never tend to national ruin. [48]

To the extent, then, that withdrawal implied a hopeless abstention from corrective action, Ferguson characteristically found it completely unsatisfactory.

An unequivocal campaign aimed at the creation of wise institutions was, however, almost as uncongenial to Ferguson. Since, in his view, the institutions with greatest influence on virtue are the political ones, [49] the solution of serious social problems necessarily involves political action and—in the gravest cases—a radical transformation of existing political institutions. Within the limits of permissible action established by any prevailing form of government, Ferguson was usually prepared to sanction endeavors for improvement. He hesitated, however, at the thought of any course which might involve a revolutionary change of insti

tutions. At times, indeed, he rested his unwillingness to
counsel such a step on considerations which appear similar
to those he rejected in the passage quoted above. So, for
example, he wrote:

> Like the winds, that come we know not whence, and blow
> whithersoever they list, the forms of society are derived
> from an obscure and distant origin; they arise, long before
> the date of philosophy, from the instincts, not from the
> speculations of men. The croud of mankind, are directed
> in their establishments and measures, by the circumstances
> in which they are placed; and seldom are turned from their
> way, to follow the plan of any single projector.
>   Every step and every movement of the multitude, even
> in what are termed enlightened ages, are made with equal
> blindness to the future; and nations stumble upon estab-
> lishments, which are indeed the result of human action,
> but not the execution of any human design. . . . No
> constitution is formed by concert, no government is copied
> from a plan. . . . The seeds of every form are lodged in
> human nature; they spring up and ripen with the sea-
> son.[50]

But his objections to deliberate revolution were not usually
premised on a flat claim that men's circumstances are
beyond purposive control and that the consequences of human actions completely defy anticipation. Nor was his rejection of a revolutionary course always as sweeping as that
implied in such a claim. More commonly, Ferguson emphasized the basic difficulties inherent in any theoretical approval of revolutions and the risks attendant on any revolutionary course without categorically precluding a recourse to
revolution under some unspecifiable circumstances.

The discussion of revolution in his *Principles of Moral
and Political Science* provides so significant an illustration of his fears as well as of the strength of his commitment
to activism that it is useful to quote some sizeable excerpts.

Having argued that governments require force to perform their functions, he asked, "When the prerogatives which are given for protection are employed to oppress, what new power can be found to redress the grievance?" In place of an answer, he wrote:

> This is accordingly the great problem of political wisdom, and a principal test of national felicity: But after all that can be contrived, or deliberately thought of for this purpose something must be left to the powerful instincts of nature. When the multitude, whose interests so much it is to have settled government, tear down the power by which they themselves are protected, we must suppose that they are either seized with madness, or that by wrongs they are driven to despair. In either case, maxims of science and reason, or principles of justice are inculcated in vain. The reasoner is everywhere surrounded with precipices. If he maintain that the people, in every case, should obey, he delivers over the subject to be oppressed and injured at discretion.
>
> If he admit that the people, in any case, may resist; as there is none but the party himself to judge the case, all government seems to be held at the discretion of those who ought to obey it.
>
> So far are we from being able to state any speculative or abstract position that we may not be abused. And so far are we left to the powerful instincts of nature, for our direction in matters of the greatest moment. . . . The power of necessity is superior to law; and the instinct of nature drives to its end, with a force which speculative maxims can neither withstand nor direct.[51]

This statement, in its emphasis on "the powerful instincts of nature" and the "power of necessity," echoes those of Ferguson's pronouncements which place social and political developments largely out of the reach of human control. But, near the conclusion of the same work, he again raised the question of revolution. This time he answered it in the following way:

To the question, that may be asked in any particular
case, To what government we should have recourse, or
under what roof we should lodge? The first answer, no
doubt, is *The Present!* Nay, but the present government
may have its defects, as the walls or roof of the building in
which we lodge may be insufficient or threaten to fall on
our heads. Then set about the necessary repairs. In respect
to your dwelling, the walls may be renewed or rebuilt in
parts successively; and, in respect to the administration of
government, grievances may be redressed. But in respect to
the one, it is a wise maxim: Beware you take not away so
much of your support at once as that the roof may fall in:
Or in respect to the other, Beware you do not overthrow so
much of your government at once as that the innocent
have no protection against those who may be disposed to
the commission of crimes.

This caution indeed it may be difficult to apply in every
case. In some instances, it may be said of our dwelling, that
the roof is actually falling, and that the whole must be
taken down; in respect to our political situation, that the
oppression of a despotic power, whether in the person of
one or many, is incorrigible, and must be cut short at once;
for, while any measure of such power remains, no reform
can be maintained.

It is indeed the nature of extreme evil to be surrounded
with calamities on every side; insomuch that, in guarding
against mischief on one side, some other must be incurred.
And, although it may happen that the last remedy of
political evil, like a chirurgical operation, may be attended
with more pain than was inflicted by the disease in any
equal portion of time, still the operation nevertheless is to
be preferred to a perpetuity of the complaint.

.   .   .   .

[Nevertheless] it may be safely assumed as a maxim
under every establishment whatever, That the present
order, if tolerable, is to be preferred to innovation, of
which, even in small matters, it may be difficult, and is
often above the reach of human wisdom, to forsee all the
consequences or effects.

Here, however, it must be admitted that, where men are

least disposed to innovation, changes imperceptibly arise, whether in the ordinary course of things, as in the progress of arts, or in the succession of events. And, as men are the actors in this political scene, whether seemingly stationary or transient, it behoves them to know the good of which they are susceptible and the evils to which they are exposed. The sceptic may contest any serious distinction in this matter; and, as men are so variously accommodated, insist that every age or nation should be left to please itself. The slave, we are told, is often more chearful and undisturbed than the citizen of a fair republic: And if we reason from the tastes of men, we must leave every one to chuse for himself. This is pleaded in matters of private as well as public felicity; but so long as human nature has its visible destination, in the perfection or excellence of which it is susceptible, we must be allowed to scrutinize the tastes, as well as the attainments of men.

When, under one species of establishment, we observe the persons and possessions of men to be secure, and their genius to prosper; under another, prevalent disorder, insult, and wrong, with a continual degradation or suppression of all the talents of men, we cannot be at a loss on which to bestow the preference.[52]

If it is permissible to consider Ferguson's assessment of revolution as a magnified reflection of the extent to which his reaction to his own times partook of activism or reformism, then several conclusions can be drawn. First, Ferguson was prepared, in general, to advocate change and even revolution if—but only if—an analysis of all factors relevant to the situation showed conclusively that the change would further public virtue. Second, Ferguson was intensely aware of the restrictions which unregulable conditions placed on deliberate actions. Third, Ferguson was extremely sensitive to the danger that action intended to reform evil conditions might, in fact, unintentionally deprive men of vital advantages. The last two characteristics of Ferguson's thought served, of course, to place severe restrictions around any radical tendency implicit in his writings—and many times to submerge it completely.

It is not necessary to cite again all of the many passages already discussed in the earlier exposition of the ideological component of Ferguson's conception of virtue. Those examples should suffice to show that Ferguson did, on many occasions, resort to a simple denial of any shortcomings—not to speak of critical failures—in British society. Particularly in his later books, he frequently seemed merely to ignore matters which had elsewhere caused him grave concern or to dispose of them with sentences like the following: "as the lot of man is never free of inconvenience, so the inconvenience he suffers is never deprived of all compensation." [53] Not only did he fail to offer harsh criticisms of British political institutions, but he also lavished upon them such unrestrained praise that he was moved to comment:

> After all, it is possible that, in thus attempting to fix canons of estimation in matters of political institutions, we may be partial to those of our own country, and mistake the forms to which we ourselves are accustomed for the models of reason and wisdom. It is however fortunate for a country to have institutions which can be so mistaken by those who experience their effects. [54]

Even commerce, the predominance of which Ferguson so often decried, became, at other times, the object of unqualified praise. So, for example, Ferguson wrote:

> In the progress, as well as in the results of commercial arts, mankind are enabled to subsist in growing numbers; learn to ply their resources, and to wield their strength, with superior ease and success. The resources of wealth are increasing, and, joined to the advantage of a growing energy and skill in the use of them, constitute to nations, who unite the public virtue with commerce, an accession of security and power.

The object of commerce is wealth: But, in this part of the history of man, nevertheless, is evident, what in reality will be found applicable to many other of its parts, namely that the end, he proposed to himself, is not to him so much of value as the pursuit in which it engages him, or the means he is led to employ, in the conduct of that pursuit.

The end of commercial art is, such a supply of accommodation and pleasure, as wealth may procure: But, suppose this end to be attained at once, and without any effort; suppose the savage to become suddenly rich, to be lodged in a palace, and furnished with all the accommodations or means of enjoyment, which an ample estate or revenue can bestow; he would either have no permanent relish for these possessions, or not knowing how to use or enjoy them, would exhibit effects of gross and ungovernable passion, and a brutality of nature, from which amidst the wants and hardships of his own situation, he is in a great measure restrained.

Such we may pronounce to be the effects of mere wealth, unattended with education, or apart from the virtues of industry, sobriety, and frugality, which nature has prescribed as the means of its attainment. But in the use of these means, the industrious are furnished with exercises improving to the genius of man; have occasion to experience, and to return the offices of beneficence and friendship; are led to the study of justice, sobriety, and good order, in the conduct of life. And, thus, in the very progress with which they arrive at the possession of wealth, form to themselves a taste of enjoyment, and decency of manners, equivalent to a conviction that happiness does not consist in the measure of fortune, but in its proper use; a condition, indeed, upon which happiness depends, no less in the highest, than in the lowest, or any intermediate state into which nations are led in the pursuit of these, or any other arts.[55]

This passage merits quotation in full because it illustrates the most common device which Ferguson employed when he sought to gloss over difficulties: he postulated an inevita-

ble, suprahuman logic of continual spiritual as well as material progress.[56] Although the first paragraph of the section
just reproduced qualifies the optimistic prognosis for commercial states, the succeeding paragraphs make it clear that,
in this place at least, Ferguson maintained that the uniting
of "public virtue with commerce" will be brought about by
the inner laws of commercial progress. The effect of this
aspect of Ferguson's work seems to be a bland optimism.

Yet to complete the circle being drawn in this discussion
of Ferguson's responses to the problems he saw in his society,
it is necessary to recall that Ferguson did not and could not
rest at this point: he never lost complete sight of the more
problematical and somber facets of his situation. No matter
how strongly he affirmed the inevitability of progress, Ferguson always returned to the need for wise and good human
judgment—if only (and this was no minor consideration) to
safeguard the realm of human freedom which, as has been
shown in the earlier discussion of his methodology, was
indispensable to the most basic conception he had of himself
and of his task. Accordingly, it was in the same book from
which the preceding passage is drawn that Ferguson
wrote:

> The life and activity of intelligent being consists in the
> consciousness or perception of an improveable state, and in
> the effort to operate upon it for the better. This constitutes
> an unremitting principle of ambition in human nature.
> Men have different objects, and succeed unequally in the
> pursuit of them: But every person, in one sense or another,
> is earnest to better himself.
>
> Man is by nature an artist, endowed with ingenuity,
> discernment, and will. These faculties he is qualified to
> employ on different materials but he is chiefly concerned to
> employ them on himself: Over this subject his power is
> most immediate and most complete; as he may know the
> law, according to which his progress is effected, by con-

forming himself to it, he may hasten or secure the result.

The bulk of mankind are, like other parts of the system, subjected to the law of their nature, and, without knowing it, are led to accomplish its purpose: While they intend no more than subsistence and accommodation, or the peace of society, and the safety of their persons and their property, their faculties are brought into use, and they profit by exercise. In mutually conducting their relative interests and concerns, they acquire the habits of political life, are made to taste of their highest enjoyments, in the affections of benevolence, integrity, and elevation of mind: and before they have deliberately considered in what the merit or felicity of their own nature consists, have already learned to perform many of its noblest functions.

Nature in this as in many other instances does not entrust the conduct of her works to the precarious views and designs of any subordinate agents. But if the progress of man in every instance were matters of necessity or even of contingency, and no way dependent on his will, nor subjected to his command, we should conclude that this sovereign rank and responsibility of a moral agent with which he is vested, were given in vain; and the capacity of erecting a fabric of art, on the foundation of the laws of nature, were denied to him in that department precisely in which they are of the highest account.[57]

Only a few pages before this rejection of completely automatic progress, Ferguson set forth in far stronger terms a denial that change can be invariably equated with genuine progress. In words which recall the extended discussion of despotism in his earlier book and his preoccupation with the decline of Rome, he wrote:

. . . This active nature, in respect to the advantages, whether of knowledge or art, derived from others, if there be not a certain effort to advance, is exposed to reverse and decline. The generation in which there is no desire to know more or practice better than its predecessors, will probably neither know so much nor practice so well. And the decline of successive generations, under this wain of

intellectual abilities, is not less certain than the progress
made under the operation of a more active and forward
disposition.[58]

When the fearful warning expressed in this statement is
combined with the convictions which Ferguson put forth
elsewhere, that social decline can be moral as well as intellectual and that decline can set in as the uncontrollable and
unpredictable consequence of deliberate human action,
then the way is clear to a withdrawal from the corrupt social
scene and a search for refuge in disinterested intellection
and pure intention.

This survey of Ferguson's responses to his situation, then,
reveals that they ran the gamut from withdrawal to reform
to denial and that none was expounded without, at the same
time, suggesting some other one, incompatible with itself.
But this is an untenable and incomprehensible situation. It
is true that the basic thesis of this study—viz., that Ferguson's thought can best be understood as the orientation of an
intellectual, rather than as a mutilated philosophic system or
imperfectly objective sociology—does not require or expect
Ferguson's writings to be free of inconsistencies; nevertheless, the contention has been advanced that Ferguson
worked out a position which could guide his relationship to
most situations and that the ambivalences which do manifest themselves are sufficiently few in number and clearly
enough patterned so that they can be encompassed and
explained by the central concept of the intellectual's role.
Bluntly juxtaposed as they have just been, Ferguson's various responses are comprehensible only in the vaguest way,
and they could in no way be seen to form part of a coherent
pattern of ideas. These difficulties arise, however, only because the analysis has not been completed. Ferguson did not
respond to every problem in each of the ways outlined
above. The variety of his responses reflects, not only the

variety of elements constituting his social role, but also the differing assessments of differing problems which he made in the course of a social analysis more circumstantial and more pointed than the general pronouncements about the nature of society which have already been examined.

Ferguson's responses to those problems of his own society which his conception of virtue had enabled him to define can, in short, be explained only in conjunction with his attempt to understand specific characteristics of particular societies. It is to this attempt that attention must now turn. The truly significant ambivalences in his thought will be perceptible only after many apparent incompatibilities among the responses of withdrawal, reform, and denial have been shown to be far less incoherent than they appear to a surface inspection. But this is not to say that the catalogue of responses was introduced prematurely into the present analysis. Even—and especially—in its overly universalized form, it can help to clarify the concerns which animated Ferguson's social and political analysis.

The basic concerns, as has been noted above, were defined by the relationship between virtue in general and society in general. In line with his conception of that relationship, it has been pointed out, Ferguson considered society as a medium for man's perfection—as an aid for his self-preservation, a school for his faculties, and a source of stimulation for his virtues. His general approach also called attention to the importance of social habit and to the primacy of political institutions and political activity. The responses now surveyed—corresponding roughly, it will be recalled, to divergent components of his general conception of virtue—suggest a more refined, and therefore more complex, formulation of the questions which can be seen to have directed Ferguson's inquiries. Withdrawal could be considered a tenable response by a socially concerned intellectual [59] only to the extent that he believed social phenomena to be governed by ineluctable necessity; Ferguson's response of reform presupposed a range of free human action, a possibility for the efficacious exercise of ingenious power; and the denial of shortcomings—if it was not to be simply an abdication of integrity—could only rest on the discovery of persuasive compensations. When Ferguson turned to the study of societies in particular— goaded by the nagging uneasiness aroused by the patent incapacity of his own society to fulfill the promise inherent in society in general and by the specter of despotism— he was prepared to see the promise qualified by necessity, unfulfilled because of improper use of power, and translated into terms which, although they differed from the general ones, might well be fully as valuable.

Ferguson, then, was led to view society, not simply as the fulfillment of a promise, but rather as a structure of necessity, controllable human power, and changing (though equivalent) values. Societies, in this view, were seen as varying and changing patterns of limitations and opportunities, and the science of society, consequently, was developed as a tool flexible enough to cope with variety and change. But his ultimate concern with the problems of virtue Ferguson never abandoned, and his core demands Ferguson could not alter without totally betraying his self- and socially-imposed tasks. Societies were not merely examined: they were put to the question. Every society had to justify its existence and form before the bar of human virtue; and, as a corollary, no despotic order was ever considered as an admissible mode of human organization. Sociology and political science, considered as empirical and descriptive disciplines, became relevant for Ferguson only as aids to a task which was primarily evaluative in character. Ferguson's contributions to the empirical analysis of social and political phenomena can be placed in correct perspective and properly assessed only in the light of all the foregoing considerations.[60]

The Analysis of Social Development

Bearing in mind the actuating problems and the structural guides they provide, it is now possible to consider Ferguson's explanations for the two related phenomena which, because they encompass all of his concerns, demanded Ferguson's concentrated attention—viz., social variety and social change. Since, in his view, societies express as well as mold human nature, the explanation for variety among societies involves, at the same time, the explanation of different forms of human nature. To approach these phenomena, Ferguson set forth several fundamental maxims. The most basic of these he set forth when he wrote, "Human nature nowhere exists in the abstract." [61] Secondly, Ferguson maintained, "If in human nature there are qualities by which it is distinguished from every other part of the animal creation, this nature itself is in different climates and in different ages greatly diversified." [62] The third maxim is less a distinct principle than an amplification of the preceding one; it holds that:

> Persons who are occupied with different subjects, who act in different scenes, generally appear to have different talents, or at least to have the same faculties variously formed, and suited to different purposes. The peculiar genius of nations, as well as individuals, may in this manner arise from the state of their fortunes.[63]

The differences among societies, then, as well as the differences among various expressions of human nature, Ferguson ascribed to differing "states" of men's "fortunes."

Like Montesquieu, and like many other writers of his time, Ferguson believed that certain physical features play an important part in determining a society's situation. Paramount among these, in his view, is climate; "the intermediate climates. . . ," he wrote, "appear most to favour [human] nature." [64] Other influential physical factors were often closely connected with climate in Ferguson's mind. Thus, he assimilated racial differences to differences of climatic conditions and extolled the stimulating powers of physical conditions which confront men with "certain difficulties to surmount." [65] Finally, convinced that "human nature, in states of moderate extent has prospered and excelled; but in a state overgrown, has generally declined and degenerated," [66] Ferguson placed high value on "every circumstance which enable [nations] to divide and maintain themselves in distinct and independent communities." [67] Although Ferguson never doubted whether such physical factors as climate, race, natural resources, and geographic situation help to distinguish societies from one another, he did not find this type of explanation as useful as that suggested in the following passage:

> As nature seems to try the ingenuity of man, in a variety of problems, and to provide that the species, in different countries, shall not find any two situations precisely alike; so the generations that succeed one another, in the same country, are in the result of their own operations, or the operations of those that went before them, ever made to enter upon scenes continually varied. The inventions of one age prepare a new situation for the age that succeeds; and, as the scene is ever changing, the actors proceed to change their pursuits and their manners, and to adopt their inventions to the circumstances in which they are placed.[68]

Ferguson preferred explanations based on non-physical factors because, in his view, the operations of a "supposed physical source of [men's] dispositions" are far less clearly understood than the effects of other "circumstances [in the situation of a people] which by determining their pursuits, regulate their habits." [69] Such modesty based on the demands of scientific rigor did not impede Ferguson's speculative verve in other places, however, and would probably not have done so here if there had not been a second, more basic, reason for discovering further explanations of social variety. Physical factors are, after all, relatively stable and cannot help to explain precisely those variations and fluctuations which it was Ferguson's main purpose to explain. As if to underline this point, Ferguson concluded his discussion of climatic influence with the following observation:

> They have raised the fabric of despotic empire to its greatest height, where they had best understood the foundations of freedom. They perished in the flames which they themselves had kindled; and they only, perhaps, were capable of displaying, by turns, the greatest improvements, or the lowest corruptions, to which the human mind can be brought.[70]

Ferguson relied on physical factors to distinguish those societies which display relatively little energy from those which, stimulated by their situation, strike out in ever-new directions and constantly change the patterns of habit and activity. Physical factors, in short, explain the difference between those societies Ferguson considered stagnant and those he denominated "progressive." The mode and character of progress itself, however, required a different order of explanation.

The variables which Ferguson took to be decisive for distinguishing one form of progressive society from another are characteristics of social life itself. By recalling the earlier examination of Ferguson's approach to society in general, it is possible to anticipate, in some measure, the kinds of characteristics which Ferguson would single out for particular attention. First, since Ferguson believed that all societies must contribute to the preservation of the individual, it is clear that he would emphasize those aspects of social life which comprise man's "interested" activities—most basically, those which satisfy his physical needs. Secondly, conceiving society not as a mechanically interrelated mixture of individual activities but as an organically integrated compound, Ferguson would, as a matter of course, seek out the integrating factors in each society. Thirdly, inasmuch as every society, according to Ferguson, stimulates men to the pursuit of some conception of perfection, he can be expected to have distinguished societies according to their differing opinions about the proper goals of human endeavors. These expectations are, as will be seen, clearly fulfilled in Ferguson's attempt to account for variety and change in progressive societies.

Ferguson grouped societies in three fundamental categories—savage, barbarous, and polished; he defined each category in terms of characteristic economic activities, patterns of social subordination, and constellations of opinions. The correspondence between these variables and those anticipated above is, on the whole, quite obvious, although the second one may require some clarification. Ferguson maintained that the interplay of sociable and antagonistic impulses which constitutes every society tends to take a more or less clearly articulated form. Different groups in society attain differing positions in a complex structure of superordination and subordination. In consequence, for Ferguson, the integration of society is always to be expressed as a function of some characteristic class structure, as well as of a typical form of economic activity and of a peculiar body of habitual opinion.

As indicated by his use of the term "progress" and as

suggested by the names of the major types, Ferguson tended to picture the main varieties of social forms as successive stages in a historical development. This statement must be qualified immediately in two ways. First, it must be recalled that Ferguson conceded the existence of non-progressive societies, societies which, because of their special physical circumstances, never enter on a career of development or which interrupt this career at some early stage. Second, and the importance of this qualification will become increasingly clear, it must be noted that, insofar as despotism constitutes a fourth category, the chain of progress can be broken at any point. Further qualifications and ambiguities will be touched on later; but, speaking generally of progressive and normal societies, Ferguson believed that they all began in a savage condition and progressed through barbarism to a polished and civilized stage of development. This conviction, rich in many consequences, first of all determined Ferguson's method. Rejecting all attempts to reconstruct the earliest periods by logical deduction,[71] he insisted that empirical information about the savage state in the development of every society can be gathered from historical inferences and evidence and from the reports of travelers who have observed extant, non-progressive societies. "The suggestions of nature, which directed the policy of nations in the wilds of America," he wrote, "were followed before on the banks of the Eurotas and the Tyber." [72] While, in his speculations about the prehistory of Rome, Ferguson relied primarily on inferences drawn from available historical evidence,[73] his depiction of savage society in general rested heavily on travelers' books and bears clear marks of those sources.

Although Ferguson vehemently denied both the possibility and the desirability of any return to some pristine and primeval state of society, it is clear that he, like many of the

SAVAGES

travelers he cited, did not consider savagery as a completely
abhorrent condition and that he even found much to admire
in it. The basic economic activities of savage society he
described in the following words: "Nations that know least
of the means of subsistence, have recourse to hunting and
fishing; or rely on the spontaneous growth of the field in
herbs or fruit." [74] Intimately connected with this economic
pattern, a pattern in which men "have little attention to
property," [75] is a very loosely defined structure of subordination. Ferguson wrote:

> If mankind, in any instance, continue the article of prop-
> erty on the footing we have now represented, we may
> easily credit what is farther reported by travellers, that they
> admit of no distinction of rank or condition; and that they
> have in fact no degree of subordination different from the
> distribution of functions, which follows the differences of
> age, talents, and dispositions. Personal qualities give an
> ascendant in the midst of occasions which require their
> exertions, but in times of relaxation, leave no vestige of
> power or prerogative.[76]

Corresponding to these typical activities and typical structures, in Ferguson's view, every savage society exhibits characteristic habits of thought. First, he echoed—but
reinterpreted—the common assertion that savages are ignorant and superstitious; he wrote:

> [Being] able masters in the detail of their own affairs, and
> well qualified to acquit themselves on particular occasions,
> they study no science, and go in pursuit of no general
> principles.
>
> . .   .   .
>
> In what depends on the known or the regular course of
> nature, the mind trusts to itself; but in strange and uncom-
> mon situations, it is the dupe of its own perplexity, and,
> instead of relying on its prudence or courage, has recourse

to divination, and a variety of observances, that, for being irrational, are always the more revered. Superstition being founded in doubts and anxieties, is fostered by ignorance and mystery. Its maxims, in the mean time, are not always confounded with those of common life; nor does its weakness and folly always prevent the watchfulness, penetration, and courage, men are accustomed to employ in the management of common affairs.[77]

Secondly, he maintained that men in savage society possess fierce independence coupled with a capacity to bestow unstinting love and hate. In this respect, according to Ferguson, savage societies clearly surpass more advanced societies—so much so that, even in the absence of a structure of subordination, they can be held together by the strength of personal attachments and dedication to the common good.[78] This is true, in large measure, because without property men do not develop opinions which place personal interest above everything else.[79] The absence of property, in turn, Ferguson explained by noting that "the indolence of mankind, or rather their aversion to any application in which they are not engaged by immediate instinct and passion, retards their progress in extending the notion of property." [80]

In summary, then, it can be noted that Ferguson viewed savage society as a form of organization which meets man's physical needs at a very elementary level, which is integrated without the emergence of unequal classes, and which displays social habits of skill and ignorance, independence and passion, selflessness and laziness. Consistently with his general dicta about the harmony between human nature and society he insisted that such a situation is in no sense wholly inimical to virtue; [81] he believed, rather, that some of the most important constituents of virtue it fosters to the highest degree. At the same time, however, he insisted just as strongly that it is a type of society which institutionalizes a failure to foster many important human capabilities and that, in any case, it can only exist among men who have not begun to develop their faculties.

Unless physical conditions are such as to suppress or obviate effort, societies will not, in Ferguson's view, remain at this level. They tend to progress to that barbarian condition whose principal characteristics Ferguson set forth in the following words:

> [Nations] having possessed themselves of herds and depending for their provision on pasture, know what it is to be poor or rich. They know the relations of patron and client, of servant and master, and suffer themselves to be classed according to their measures of wealth. This distinction must create a material difference of character, and may furnish two separate heads under which to consider the history of mankind in their rudest state; that of the savage, who is not yet acquainted with property; and that of the barbarian, to whom it is, although not ascertained by laws, a principal object of care and desire.
>
> It must appear very evident, that property is a matter of progress. It requires, among other particulars which are the effects of time, some method of defining possession. The very desire of it proceeds from experience; and the industry by which it is gained, or improved, requires such a habit of acting with a view to distant objects, as may overcome the present disposition either to sloth or enjoyment. This habit is slowly acquired. . . .[82]

Little needs to be added to Ferguson's own summary statement. He pointed to the transformation of a food-gathering economy into a pastoral economy characterized by private property; he noted the creation of classes defined by economic inequality; and he called attention to the emergence of new capabilities for understanding and new habits of industry. Barbarian society, thus, representing an advance

in human skills and a consequent extension of human desires [83] marks an irreversible step in man's history. But this
progress, and there can be no question that Ferguson considered an unfolding of human talents to be progressive in an
evaluative as well as descriptive sense, is not purchased
without some cost to primitive virtue. In place of the love of
equality, the distribution of function according to merit, and
the general sense of communal fellowship, there emerges a
situation which Ferguson described as follows:

> In passing from the condition we have described, to this we
> have at present in view mankind still retains many parts of
> their earliest character. . . . But we may apprehend, that
> the individual having now found a separate interest, the
> bands of community must become less firm, and domestic
> disorders more frequent. The members of any community,
> being distinguished among themselves by unequal shares
> in the distribution of property, the ground of a permanent
> and palpable subordination is laid.[84]

Ferguson believed, as will be seen, that the shortcomings of
barbarism are far outweighed by the inestimable advantages
resulting from the rise of political institutions, which, in his
view, depends on the existence of these very shortcomings.
But it is not necessary to anticipate those considerations in
order to note that, for Ferguson, the establishment of private
property—whatever its concomitant disadvantages—constitutes a major gain for mankind. His conviction on this
score was, in fact, so strong that in some passages in each
of his books he disregarded that he had elsewhere designated a historical origin for the sense of private property
and he treated it as a universal and instinctive impulse.[85]
In any case, it is perfectly clear that Ferguson viewed
private property as an essential object of a fundamental
human right and that he, therefore, hailed the type of
society which brought it to the fore.

Once established, according to Ferguson, the pattern of exercising economic tasks through the medium of privately appropriated objects expands to land as well as herds. Men abandon their migrations and societies become settled and agricultural.[86] Thus is prepared the way for the third major transformation of society. "As the property of land excites to invention in agriculture," Ferguson noted, "it likewise excites to invention in other arts. They who have no land betake themselves to manufacture, that they may have wherewith to buy the produce of land."[87] Although, in his view, a certain amount of manufacturing takes place in all societies, the type of society which takes its main character from a manufacturing economy can be readily identified by two related hallmarks. "Polished" societies, according to Ferguson, are those in which, first of all, the people "have separated, and committed to different persons, the several tasks, which require a peculiar skill and attention."[88] "By the separation of arts and professions," Ferguson continued, "the sources of wealth are laid open; every species of material is wrought up to the greatest perfection, and every commodity is produced in the greatest abundance."[89] The second decisive aspect of the most advanced economies is their reliance on commerce, a feature which Ferguson described in the following words:

> Among the circumstances, therefore, which were formerly mentioned, as attending the progress of commercial arts, none is of more consequence to their advancement, than the separation of callings, and the subdivision of each into a convenient number of different branches. . . . But to this separation of tasks, as well as to circumstances in the original lot of man, it was observed, that *commerce*, or the exchange of commodities, was necessary. . . .
> With the benefit of commerce, or a ready exchange of commodities, every individual is enabled to avail himself, to the utmost, of the peculiar advantage of his place; to

work on the peculiar materials with which nature has furnished him; to humour his genius or disposition, and betake himself to the task in which he is peculiarly qualified to proceed.[90]

Societies of the third type, then, characteristically exhibit a wealthy manufacturing economy resting upon commerce and a complex division of labor.

Ferguson asserted that, just as the structure of subordination in savage and barbarian societies is conditioned by the characteristic economic activities, so in advanced societies the most common "ground of subordination" is "in the habits which are acquired by the practice of different arts." [91] To explain and at the same time justify this state of affairs, Ferguson urged the following:

> Some employments are liberal, others mechanic. They require different talents, and inspire different sentiments; and whether or not this be the cause of the preference we actually give, it is certainly reasonable to form our opinion of the rank that is due to men of certain professions and stations, from the influence of their manner of life in cultivating the powers of the mind or in preserving the sentiments of the heart.[92]

Although, according to Ferguson, innate capacity and property continue to play some part in determining men's places in a social hierarchy, the most usual determinant in a polished society is the task performed in the division of labor; men's social power is a function of their social role. At times, Ferguson suggested that each man's social role will, in turn, reflect his true capabilities, but in general he seemed to assume that the division of labor will arise "casually" and that men will be bred to the habits appropriate to the position they happen to occupy by the experiences and exigencies of that position.[93]

The most important attribute, then, which Ferguson ascribed to habits of thought in the most advanced societies is
the dissimilarity of opinion and range of knowledge to be
encountered among differing levels of society. But certain
qualities are, in his view, universally shared by the habits of
all men in such societies. Thus, he believed, all or most men
in commercial societies come to acquire habits of industry
and a sense of interest.[94] Moreover—and this characteristic
of polished opinion Ferguson attributed in some measure to
the peculiar Christian and feudal antecedents of modern
commercial societies [95]—"what are commonly termed the
polite ages of mankind [are] characterized by mildness of
manners." [96] Men tend to be less buffeted by extreme passions than they are in "rude" stages of social development;
advanced society is, in short, marked by "civilization." [97]

Earlier discussions have shown that, on one level at least,
Ferguson expressed grave doubts about the worth of the
civilization purchased through commerce, and these doubts
will have to be examined again after the political dimension
of Ferguson's analysis has been set forth. But it is not
necessary to wait until then to note that, in the final analysis
and on the basis of the most central feature of the activist
conception of virtue, Ferguson's position eventuated in a
vindication of commercial society. The argument presented
to sustain this point is so vital to an understanding of Ferguson's total orientation, and his presentation is so unusually
clear and frank, that the passage merits extensive quotation.
Ferguson wrote:

> [We] may fancy it to be the object of commerce, or the
> effect it might serve to produce, were its efforts completely
> successful, to level the conditions of men in all the variety
> of their situations; to compensate original defects by adven-
> titious supplies; and to give every commodity a current,

from the place at which it is superfluous or abounds, to any other at which it is wanted.

Here, indeed, is a lofty pretension of human art; and the effect is actually such as to raise mankind, in the ages of commerce far above the level of that condition, which they held in a more early state of their progress: But, when we observe them in either extreme of simplicity and rudeness, or of accommodation and art, or under any of the gradations which lead from the one to the other, they seem to be equally satisfied, or rather equally dissatisfied, in all the varities through which they are known to pass. They have their different habits that reconcile them equally to the state in which they are accustomed to live; and whatever that state may be, they have their feeling of wants, or their desire of something better than the present, which ever prompts them to urge on their way; insomuch that, possibly, the sum of gratification or disappointment may be equal in all the different situations of men.

On this supposition it may be asked, what does the species gain in the result of commercial arts, and at the expense of so much invention and labour.

This problem is likely to occur only among speculative men in some advanced state of the very arts, of which the value is brought into question, and the merits, when tried before such judges, may be pronounced very different from what they would be found before a different tribunal.

On this subject, however, there are fixed principles to which we may recur, and on which, without being under a necessity to prove, that the measure of human enjoyment is increased in any particular age of commerce, we may nevertheless justify the efforts of mankind to multiply their accommodations, and to increase their stores.

First of all, we may observe, that progress itself is congenial to the nature of man; that whatever checks it, is distress and oppression; whatever promotes it, is prosperity and freedom. . . .

Even, if we should thus be disposed to give up any superiority of enjoyment, derivable from one set of personal accommodations, in preference to another, the invention and practice of arts relating to such accommodations, have unquestionable value, in the exercise they furnish to the active nature and intelligent power of man.

Such is the nature of man, the party concerned in this question, that, although by erecting the fabric of commercial arts, and by accumulating the wealth which they bestow, he should not, in the mere circumstance of fortune, find the sum of his enjoyment increased; yet, it would not follow, that he has laboured in vain, whether in cultivating the ground, or in working the materials which the Author of nature has supplied for his use. It is, indeed, mostly in some active exertions that his happiness consists. . . .[98]

In the case of polished society, then, as in the cases of savage and barbarian societies, Ferguson was persuaded that the pattern of economic activity, social subordination, and habitual opinion constitutes an integral whole which demands understanding in view of its important consequences and which merits respect in view of its contributions to man's striving for perfection.

Political Institutions

On the basis of his study of variety and change in society, Ferguson could reappraise the functions, forms, and obligations of political institutions and arrive at conclusions far less disheartening than those derived from his examination of political institutions as the apex and culmination of society in general. There, it will be recalled, he was compelled to argue that only democratic republican institutions resting on disinterested beneficence truly serve the cause of society and virtue—an argument which placed him in the untenable position of implacable hostility to the institutions of his own time without providing him either the knowledge necessary to cope with the problem of despotism or the guidance appropriate to practical activity in support of the designated goal. The political theory based on a general view of virtue and necessity, in short, failed to perform precisely that function which Ferguson required of all his speculations: it could in no sense contribute to a tenable orientation to practice. Although, as will be seen, Ferguson's new approach to politics did not (and could not) solve all of the problems inherent in his situation, it did enable him in some measure to make sense of his situation and to make his peace with his activities. When he had come to the end of his last discussion of the "political science"—the concluding portion of each of his published works—he had gone as far as he could go in his role as intellectual. That only two of his unpublished manuscripts deal with political topics reveals the limitations placed on the fulfillment of the role by factors both internal and external to it which precluded its becoming a medium for complete and stable satisfaction. It was, and perhaps always is, a role which tends to liquidate itself. But these asseverations anticipate the conclusions of the present analysis: they cannot be substantiated at this time; they are raised here only to call attention to the significance of the succeeding examination of Ferguson's thoughts about political institutions and to reassert that, despite all retreats into extramundane realms of pure contemplation and private worlds of pure intention, Ferguson the intellectual was by commitment a political man and that his orientation was most characteristically a political orientation to a political world.

As was made clear even in Ferguson's most general discussion of politics, however, he denied that the political realm could be discussed apart from other aspects of social life. "Society is the natural state of man," he wrote, "and political society is the natural result of his experience in that state of society to which he is born." [99] This assertion constitutes the foundation upon which he constructed his attempt to comprehend and evaluate political institutions in the light of varied and changing social situations. Continuing the argument to show that he is not dealing with abstract and universal concepts, he maintained, "Political establishments . . . which began to be formed in the first and simplest ages, continue in a state of gradual formation, as the experience of every age directs. . . ." [100] The original experience impelling men to establish authoritative centers of power, according to Ferguson, was as compelling as that which initiated the refinement of economic skills. The experience and the analogy Ferguson described in the following words:

> Man is born naked, defenceless, and exposed to greater hardships than any other species of animal; and though he is qualified to drag a precarious existence under these disadvantages yet as we find him, in the situation of his greatest defect, urged by motives to supply it, no way short of necessity, so we find him, by a continued application of this motive, which we term ambition, still urged to proceed in every subsequent state of his progress. His society, also, prior to any manner of political establishment, we may imagine exposed to extreme disorder; and there, also, we may fancy the spur of necessity no less applied than in the urgency of his mere animal wants. From these motives, accordingly, we admit the arts of human life, whether commercial or political, to have originated, and suppose that the consideration of necessity must have operated prior to that of convenience. . . . [101]

Two observations must be offered about this passage. First, it seems to display Ferguson's characteristic carelessness about important points when those points are not immediately relevant to the argument at hand and when the rhetorical effect would be damaged by more precise formula-

tions. This is said because Ferguson here disregarded all of
his assertions about the spontaneous community which allegedly makes government superfluous in savage societies.
But even if the omission of that qualification was the product of design rather than carelessness—and it is certainly
true that Ferguson's later books (perhaps because they
were directed less against the derogation of instinctive human nature which Ferguson ascribed to Hobbes than
against the disdain of progress and civilization which, in
his view, characterizes the writings of Rousseau) pay little
attention to that vindication of savage society which played
an important part in the *Essay on Civil Society*—it will not
be considered as indication of a significant shift in Ferguson's position. The decision to refrain from such an interpretation is dictated, not only by contemplation of the
infinite amount of useless labor which would be required to
explicate Ferguson's text each time it departs from the
main lines of his argument, but also because the analogy
presented in this very passage recalls the crucial point
which a rigorous statement would have made explicit. This
consideration, the second elicited by the quoted passage,
leads to Ferguson's more circumstantial account of the
origin of political institutions.

Both the necessity for government and the possibility of
establishing one arose, according to Ferguson, in the second
stage of social development, after the emergence of private
property and together with the subordination and habits
appropriate to it. In a passage which, but for the historical
account which it presupposes, has a genuine Hobbesian
ring, Ferguson explained the "disorder," demanding remedy
through authoritative and powerful rules. He wrote:

> [Man] apprehends a relation between his person and his
> property, which renders what he calls his own in a manner

a part of himself, a constituent of his rank, his condition, and his character, in which, independent of any real enjoyment, he may be fortunate or unhappy; and, independent of any personal merit, he may be an object of consideration or neglect; and in which he may be wounded and injured, while his person is safe, and every want of his nature is completely supplied.

In these apprehensions, while other passions only operate occasionally, the interested find the object of their ordinary cares; their motive to the practice of mechanic and commercial arts; their temptation to trespass on the laws of justice; and, when extremely corrupted, the price of their prostitutions, and the standard of their opinions on the subject of good and evil. Under this influence, they would enter, if not restrained by the laws of civil society, on a scene of violence or meanness, which would exhibit our species, by turns, under an aspect more terrible and odious, or more vile and contemptible than that of any animal which inherits the earth.[102]

The source of the illness, however, also provides, in Ferguson's view, a means for a cure. The creation and accumulation of wealth in private hands tend to transform the leaders, whom savages choose only for limited purposes and terms, into regular political rulers. Ferguson remarked:

Before this important change is admitted, men must be accustomed to the distinction of ranks; and before they are sensible that subordination is requisite, they must have arrived at unequal conditions by chance. In desiring property, they only mean to secure their subsistence: but the brave who lead in war, have likewise the largest share in its spoils. The eminent are fond of devising hereditary honours; and the multitude, who admire the parent, are ready to extend their esteem to his offspring.[103]

This is not to say that Ferguson simply equated the spontaneously emerging pattern of subordination with the organized hierarchical structure of government. It means, rather, that the power which political institutions wield must be generated and accumulated through casual social processes before it can be controlled by governors and used to adjust relations and that social subordination provides the basic definition of power in every society.

Social circumstances, then, underlie the formation of political institutions, as they prescribe the primary tasks of government. It has been noted above that Ferguson believed that the disorder bred by "interested" conflict gave the first impetus to political organization, an impetus strong enough to be denominated "necessity." In the following passage, Ferguson expanded his conception of the necessary functions which every government must perform:

> While the mode of subordination is casual, and forms of government take their rise, chiefly from the manner in which the members of a state have been originally classed, and from a variety of circumstances that procure to particular orders of men a sway in their country, there are certain objects that claim the attention of every government, that lead the apprehensions and the reasonings of mankind in every society, and that not only furnish an employment to statesmen, but in some measure direct the community to those institutions, under the authority of which the magistrate holds his power. Such are the national defence, the distribution of justice, the preservation and internal prosperity of the state. If these objects be neglected, we must apprehend that the very scene in which parties contend for power, for privilege, or equality, must disappear, and society itself no longer exist.[104]

Although all of these functions are, in Ferguson's view, indispensable, the one which is most consequential for Ferguson's argument is the second one, the distribution of justice. The necessity of performing the others had important implications for his conception of political institutions (and some of these will be examined below), but this one

provided him with the most important key to the explanation and justification of governmental activity.

In Ferguson's terminology, justice is essentially equivalent to liberty or freedom and "security is the essence of
freedom. . . ." [105] All governments, therefore, which are
compatible with the continued existence of society will,
according to Ferguson, take action to preserve the "rights of
property and of station" which men have casually acquired.
Only through the promulgation of laws to regularize the
acquisition and exchange of property, the mobilization of
coercive machinery to prevent and punish the violation of
these laws, and the institution of normal procedures for
defining the paths to and privileges of social superiority—
only through these characteristically governmental steps
can society be preserved from the divisive forces loosed
by the emergence of private property. Ferguson, then,
tended to equate the establishment of government with
the establishment of coercive laws defining and protecting
rights and privileges.

This paraphrase of Ferguson's position requires considerable qualification and amplification. In the first place, it
must be noted that, in his view, the establishment of full
liberty under law cannot be expected to take place at the first
institution of government. As the following passage makes
clear, he asserted that the "political arts" must first reach a
certain level of development, progressing usually so as to
keep pace with the general development of society. He
wrote:

> Liberty, in one sense, appears to be the portion of polished
> nations alone. The savage is personally free, because he
> lives unrestrained, and acts with the members of his tribe
> on terms of equality. The barbarian is frequently inde-
> pendent from a continuance of the same circumstance, or
> because he has courage and a sword. But good policy alone

can provide for the regular administration of justice, or
constitute a force in the state, which is ready on every
occasion to defend the rights of its members.

It has been found that, except in a few singular cases,
the commercial and political arts have advanced together.
These arts have been in modern Europe so interwoven,
that we cannot determine which were prior in the order of
time, or derived most advantage from the mutual
influences with which they act and re-act on each other. It
has been observed, that in some nations the spirit of commerce, intent on securing its profits, has led the way to
political wisdom. A people possessed of wealth, and become jealous of their properties, have formed the project of
emancipation, and have proceeded, under favour of an
importance recently gained, still further to enlarge their
pretensions, and to dispute the prerogatives which their
sovereign had been in use to employ.[106]

Secondly, the intimate connection between the prepolitical
distribution of power in society and the order established by
government, as well as the accession of new power accruing
to those who gain the leading positions, entail the probabil-
ity that the governors themselves will disrupt, through an
abuse of power, the established order by disturbing the
established rights of subordinates. This danger, in Ferguson's view, can never be wholly eliminated; but the abuse
of power can be checked, he believed, through the asser-
tiveness of the victims, and, in time, constitutions can
emerge which reflect a new distribution of social power and
which provide for a reasonably secure maintenance of
rights. Ferguson explained this point in the following
words:

There are, in most communities that have made any progress in political arts, certain primary articles, which may
be termed fundamental laws of the constitution.

Such fundamental laws, or conventions are neither the

foundations upon which society was originally formed, nor
do they always follow soon after its first institution. They
come in the sequence of circumstances into which men
have passed, without any view to political establishments,
as in the sequel of casual subordination of ranks, arising
from personal qualities, birth, education, or fortune. They
are sometimes the result of amicable deliberations, and
sometimes such as prevailing parties may have obtained by
force. Mankind are known to live for many ages in society
together, before they are sensible of the inconveniences,
whether arising from the abuse of prerogative or the abuse
of privilege, for which political law is intended as a remedy. The evils have sometimes taken deep root, before
the attempt is made to remove them, and civil war is
frequently the prelude to the establishment of order upon
any permanent footing. Thus the great charter of England; many of the political capitulations in Germany,
the pacification of parties at Rome, and what may be
termed the fundamental political law in the instance of
many other states, was the result of war or contention that
arose after many ages of society had elapsed.[107]

Although it is true that, for Ferguson, every government
must secure some kind of order, and therefore guarantee
some measure of justice and liberty, it is equally true that
the degree of security achieved and the extent of satisfaction
granted to men's claims vary widely in different situations.

The most significant index of the adequacy of a particular
political institution is, according to Ferguson, its form. He
was convinced that certain forms are far more conducive to
the fullest possible enjoyment of liberty than others. But
before these forms can be discussed, it must be made clear
that, in Ferguson's view, forms of government cannot be
assessed simply by the extent to which they perform all of
the political functions in an ideal way. Rather, the forms
must be taken in relation to the social circumstances from

which they arise and which they are expected to maintain. The desirable forms can never be more than an index of desirable circumstances; the less desirable forms may well represent, he maintained, the only possible manner in which any political functions can be performed at all.

To some extent, this has already been shown above where Ferguson was quoted as saying that normally a genuine rule of law can arise only in conjunction with the development of a polished and commercial society. Ferguson, however, had a great deal more to say on this subject (much of it admittedly no more than a restatement of the most familiar contentions in Montesquieu's *Spirit of the Laws*); [108] and his discussion of the relationship between varying social situations and their appropriate political forms constitutes the crucial step in his attempt to dismiss the bogy of democracy without abandoning completely the commitment which had raised it in the first place. Ferguson opened his discussion of governmental forms by writing:

> Forms of government are supposed to decide of the happiness or misery of mankind. But forms of government must be varied, in order to suit the extent, the way of subsistence, the character, and the manners of different nations. In some cases, the multitude may be suffered to govern themselves; in others, they must be severely restrained. The inhabitants of a village in some primitive age, may have been safely entrusted to the conduct of reason, and to the suggestion of their innocent views; but the tenants of Newgate can scarcely be trusted, with chains locked to their bodies, and bars of iron fixed to their legs. How is it possible, therefore, to find any single form of government that would suit mankind in every condition? [109]

In view of Ferguson's concerns and in view of the general familiarity of the material he borrowed from Montesquieu, it is not necessary here to describe at length Ferguson's restatement of the tie between aristocracy and small states, marked by substantial inequalities but tempered by a spirit of moderation, or of that between monarchy and large states, characterized by an elaborate status hierarchy, in which men are motivated by a craving for honor.[110] Each of these forms is, in his view, appropriate to a different stage and condition of social development; and, under the specified circumstances, provides the only attainable assurance that political functions will be performed. Ferguson's main interest, however, lay in the analysis of democracy, "mixed monarchy," and despotism. It is on these analyses that the present discussion will focus.

Democracies, according to Ferguson, are systems of government in with every individual is equally eligible to participate in the conduct of public affairs and in which major decisions are made by popular assemblies. They arise in small communities where all citizens can know one another and correspond to a situation in which economic inequality is very slight; i.e., they presuppose a low level of social progress.[111] Under such circumstances, he believed, there may be found habits of self-sacrifice and public spiritedness sufficiently widespread among the members of society so that it can actually be said that the structure is integrated by the principle of virtue. Whatever subordination exists, and some measure of it is necessary if there is to be government at all, is determined by natural inequalities of ability and merit.[112] Ferguson's description of democracy, in short, encompasses all the qualities which he ascribed to political institutions as such in the passages which extoll them as the apex of society, as a school for virtue.

But remarkably enough, when the social characteristics of democratic states are scrutinized, they reveal precisely those qualities which Ferguson ascribed elsewhere to societies at the level of savagery. Ferguson himself noted the similarity, commenting, "From the description contained in the last section, we may incline to believe, that mankind, in their simplest state, are on the eve of erecting republics"; but he rejected that suggestion on the grounds that "the resolution of chusing, from among their equals, the magistrate to whom they give from thence-forward a right to controul their own actions, is far from the thoughts of simple men." [113] Presumably, then, societies which display democratic forms must first have undergone the experience of submission to rulers elevated to positions of authority casually; they must, in other words, first make some advance in the direction of property and subordination. Nevertheless, if it was to have been possible for a people rebelling against abuses of power to return to a state of near equality, they cannot have been very far removed from the most primitive conditions.

This explanation leaves unanswered two related questions: how can a people advance far enough to develop habits of obedience to government without, at the same time, developing economic skills and needs—with their attendant subordination—to a point where equality becomes inconceivable; and what activities constitute the functions of a government which is not needed to regulate conflicts among interested men? Although Ferguson never expressly addressed himself to these questions, it is possible to infer his answers from his treatment of Roman history. The characteristic of Roman society which Ferguson considered most significant is its policy of militarist expansionism. It was this element in Roman life which Ferguson cited when he sought to explain the logic of the revolution ousting the Tarquin kings. Ferguson wrote:

So far it appears that while every successive prince gratified his own ambition by subduing some neighboring

district or village, and brought an accession of riches or
territory to his country, the genius of monarchy was favorable to the growth of this rising empire. But when princes
became satiated with conquests abroad, or began to medi-
tate schemes to increase their own importance at home,
their ambition took a different direction, and led them to
aim at making the kingdom hereditary, and the people
more subservient to their own pleasure. Under this direction of the monarch's ambitions, the state, as Montesquieu
observes, was likely to become stationary or even to decline. A revolution, therefore, became necessary, in order
to prolong its progress.[114]

This suggests that, in Ferguson's view, Rome was a society
whose progress took the form of warlike aggrandizement
and whose democratic institutions were intimately tied to
its militarism.

If this is taken as an indication of Ferguson's general
position with regard to democratic republics, then the questions raised above admit of an answer generally consistent
with the main lines of Ferguson's analysis. It can be said that
a progress based on military exploits can accustom men to
obedience without at the same time creating wide economic
inequalities and that a military society will naturally retain
greater respect for talents than for wealth. Furthermore, it
can also be concluded that the principal objects of democratic governments are the conduct of foreign affairs and the
equitable distribution of spoils.[115] From this point of view, it
is clear that the existence and maintenance of a democratic
constitution depend on the existence and continuation of
very special circumstances; and—paradoxically—that the
very existence of the requisite circumstances will, by virtue
of a necessary inner dynamic, militate against their continuation. That is to say that the successful pursuit of a national policy of military expansionism will in time expand

the area of a society beyond that appropriate to democracy and will enrich the society to a point where commerce and inequality inevitably arise.[116] As a form of government for actual states, then, Ferguson considered democracy a very rare and tenuous possibility.

But it is not necessary to rely on inferences to show that Ferguson did not consider democracy a viable form of government for progressive societies. Somewhat wistfully he wrote:

> Candour, force, and elevation of mind, in short, are the props of democracy; and virtue is the principle of conduct required to its preservation.
>
> How beautiful a pre-eminence on the side of popular government! and how ardently should mankind wish for the form, if it tended to establish the principle, or were, in every instance, a sure indication of its presence!
>
> But perhaps we must have possessed the principle, in order, with any hopes of advantage to receive the form; and where the first is entirely extinguished, the other may be fraught with evil, if any additional evil deserves to be shunned where men are already unhappy.[117]

In a more assertive tone, he stated flatly:

> The principal objections to democratical or popular government, are taken from the inequalities which arise among men in the result of commercial arts. And it must be confessed that popular assemblies, when composed of men whose dispositions are sordid, and whose ordinary applications are illiberal, however they may be intrusted with the choice of their masters and leaders, are certainly in their person, unfit to command. How can he who has confined his views to his own subsistence or preservation be intrusted with the conduct of nations? Such men, when admitted to deliberate on matters of state, bring to its councils confusion and tumult, or servility and corruption;

and seldom suffer it to repose from ruinous factions, or the
effect of resolutions ill formed or ill conducted.

. . . .

   Whether in great or in small states, democracy is preserved with difficulty, under the disparities of condition,
and the unequal cultivation of the mind, which attend the
variety of pursuits and applications, that separate mankind
in the advanced state of commercial arts. In this, however,
we do but plead against the form of democracy, after the
principle is removed; and see the absurdity of pretensions
to equal influence and consideration, after the characters
of men have ceased to be similar.[118]

In general, his conclusion was that the attempt to establish or to maintain a democratic republic under advanced
social conditions is bound to be, at worst, a plunge into chaos
and eventual despotism, or, at best, no more than a sham.
The first of these alternatives is clearly implied in the fears
Ferguson expressed about any move to destroy the mode of
subordination he alleged to be inherent in a polished society,
and such a move is prerequisite to any grant or assumption
of genuine power to or by the lower classes. The second
alternative—and this is the one which Ferguson considered
the more likely—rests on his conviction that an established
advanced social order, supported by all of the motives, institutions, habits, and power which progress entails, can be
uprooted, if at all, only under extremely unusual circumstances.[119] On this basis, Ferguson wrote:

In every society there is a casual subordination, independent of its formal establishment, and frequently adverse to
its constitution. While the administration and the people
speak the language of a particular form, and seem to admit
no pretensions to power, without a legal nomination in one
instance, or without the advantage of heriditary honours in
another, this casual subordination, possibly arising from
the distribution of property, or from some other circum-

stance that bestows unequal degrees of influence, gives the
state its tone, and fixes its character.[120]

The appropriate form must build on the realities of the
situation. It must accord, first of all, with the possibilities of
the social power structure inherent in every advanced society. Secondly, because "the authority of government itself,
under every political establishment, rests on the habits of
thinking, which prevail among the people," it must base
itself on the opinions which men actually hold in commercial states. In the third place, in keeping with the almost
universal characteristic of modern polished nations, the
form must have a focal point of power distinct and strong
enough to hold together the numerous inhabitants of a large
country. As has been shown, Ferguson held that democratic
institutions must fail in all of these respects; that monarchy
is only very doubtfully consistent with "the maxims of commerce"; and that aristocracy—in either its traditionalist or
oligarchical variant—is probably not suited to the inequalities derived from the division of labor (rather than birth or
wealth) and is certainly not adequate to the rule of a large
area. None of the simple forms of government which are
capable of performing the essential functions of all governments, then, can solve the problems Ferguson believed to be
set by social progress; and, as the example of Rome illustrates, failure to solve these problems can only lead to despotism, a form which is not only injurious to all virtue but also
ultimately unable to maintain society.

But Ferguson denied that the situation is at all hopeless.
Following Montesquieu and a tradition which extends
(although with significant variations) from Plato, Aristotle,
Polybius, and Cicero, he urged the appropriateness of a
"mixed" constitution, specifically that of "mixed monarchy."[121] Such a form, according to Ferguson, comprises

a hereditary king who commands the force of society, and representative assemblies, drawn from each of the major classes in society, whose assent is requisite to the enactment of every law. Ferguson maintained that "mixed monarchy" meets all of the requirements set by the commercial stage of social development, and, most importantly, he argued that it is the form better suited than any other to the performance of all the necessary functions of government. The second of these conclusions, already implicit in much that has been said, will be examined below; first, it is necessary to show that, in Ferguson's view, this constitution is a very likely concomitant of the power relations, opinions, and size of advanced societies.

When Ferguson undertook to describe the polished structure of subordination in a political context, his categories, although related to the sociological generalization which derives subordination from the "separation of professions," were expressed in historical terms. Focusing his attention on England, he pointed out that its barbarian stage had been marked at first by the emergence of aristocratic governments based originally on inequality of wealth. Subsequently, the king—the leader of the most powerful and ambitious noble family—increased his power by forging an extended governmental unity by force, utilizing wealth to transform nobles into dependent agents, and gaining the support of the people, who were eager to have royal assistance against the nobles' infringements on rights.[122]

In the period of monarchy, however, according to Ferguson, forces destined to limit royal power were at work. The nobility was never completely broken; the importance of the people was enhanced by the encouragement which the national pacification achieved by the king gave to the "practice of commercial and lucrative arts." The pattern of subordination, then, gradually changed from one defined by inequality of wealth and force to one defined by a difference of function. The king and his closest followers were engaged in the actual performance of governing functions; the nobles maintained their roles as heads of estates and participated to some extent in government; and "the people" were engaged in the production of new and increasing wealth. Although this distribution of tasks, according to Ferguson, clearly ranged men in groups of varying power, the new structure was composed of elements more nearly equal than those in any earlier situation. The scene was thus set, Ferguson believed, for a conflict which eventuated in a new form of government.

The general relationship between a social power structure and a governmental form, Ferguson described in the following words:

> Mankind must be contented to act in the situations in which they find themselves placed; and, except when urged by great occasions, seldom project, and rarely at once obtain, any great innovation. The party which has an advantage in the actual state of society endeavour to avail themselves of it; and the party that is aggrieved, strives to obtain relief. The effect is, to preserve the establishment where parties are equally balanced, or to procure some change, where either prevail. . . .[123]

Within the limits thus set on the extent to which political institutions can depart from the casual pattern of subordination, Ferguson felt that he could explain the emergence and persistence of "mixed monarchy." It is a form, in his view, which takes institutional cognizance of the actual conflicts among men in commercial societies—and in those conflicts men group themselves into parties [124]—without ignoring the actual inequalities among the contending forces. Mixed monarchy, in short, represents the establishment of orderly, non-violent channels for the carrying on of party conflict.[125] The monarch continues to enjoy the prerogatives inherent in his function; the nobles can protect their privileges; and the people—through the instrumentality of representation—can safeguard their interests.

In view of all that has been said, it is not necessary to labor that Ferguson obviously believed that mixed monarchy corresponds to both the state of actual opinion and the exigencies of a large territory. Men respect the position of the king because they have been habituated to do so by long experience of monarchical rule, because the position is endowed with pomp and splendor calculated to awe the common people, and because they are persuaded of the importance of the tasks he performs. Similar considerations operate to shore up the influence of the aristocracy; and the representatives of the people—although largely denied the support of tradition and pomp—are able to assert themselves on the basis of the respect which the ruling groups are bound to accord the wealth and crucial activities they represent. Likewise, according to Ferguson, each party is actuated to assert its claims to political consideration by habits inextricably entwined in its social role. In the case of the king and the nobles, this is true almost by definition of the role; in the case of the people, it is consequent upon the constant increase in their sense of interest accompanying the rise of commerce. When to these considerations is added the monarchical element in this mixed constitution, which fits it to the governance of an extended territory, then Ferguson's reasons for considering the mixed monarchy appropriate to the conditions of advanced societies become completely clear.

This form, moreover, corresponds most fully to that rule of law which, in Ferguson's view, manifests the most effective performance of the crucial function of all government, the preservation of order through the protection of established rights. Ferguson wrote:

> Nations . . . have been fortunate in the tenor, and in the execution of their laws, in proportion as they have admitted every order of the people, by representation or otherwise, to an actual share of the legislature. Under establishments of this sort, law is literally a treaty, to which the parties concerned have agreed, and have given their opinion in settling its terms. The interests to be affected by a law, are likewise consulted in making it. Every class propounds an objection, suggests an addition or an amendment of its own. They proceed to adjust by statute, every subject of controversy; and while they continue to enjoy their freedom, they continue to multiply laws, and to accumulate volumes, as if they could remove every possible ground for dispute, and were secure of their rights, merely by having put them in writings.[126]

Stating the matter even more positively, he asserted that the political processes of a mixed monarchy—despite and even because of the selfish interests which animate them—assure the greatest possible achievement of the "public interest," guarantee the maximum of "liberty" which can ever be attained.[127]

Not only did Ferguson deny, therefore, that commercial society presents insoluble political problems, he argued that precisely such a situation provides the conditions under which the best solutions to all the most basic political problems can—and probably will—be put into effect. It must be recalled, however, that Ferguson did not deny the adequacy of other forms for other situations. Aristocracies and monarchies, too, may establish some sort of law and order.[128] His points are, rather, that the law which is a treaty will be more stable and more satisfying to all parties than any other kind and that a legislative process which is analogous to a treaty-making process will provide greater assurance that rulers will not abuse their powers than will any exclusive repository of legislative authority.[129] Ferguson, thus, saw commercial society as the type of society conducive to mixed monarchy and saw such a constitution as the ideal manner of performing the most decisive function of actual political institutions.

Reassessment of Promise and Threat

On this basis, Ferguson could reassure himself about the consequences of progress and, more specifically, reassess the conditions he found in British society. Even at the cost of some repetition, it is useful to survey and clarify the contributions made to Ferguson's orientation by his analysis of society as a structure of necessity, human power, and translated values. As necessary truths of actual social life, Ferguson listed the dependence of government on social subordination and social opinion, the general link between subordination and advancing economic institutions (particularly property), the correspondence between economic progress and a rising sense of interest among men, and the violent conflicts which mark the unregulated relations among interested men. These factors, in Ferguson's view, define all social situations and place restrictions not subject to human control on men's capacity to achieve perfection. Furthermore, he maintained, societies advance from one type to another in a course of irreversible cumulative development, which entails change in their structures of subordination, their patterns of opinion, and their economic activities. Unless the society is one which, because of peculiar physical circumstances, fails to be susceptible to progress, the only alternative to continuing progress is despotism and the eventual ruin of society.[130]

It is important to note that, in Ferguson's view, despotism is not only corrupt in a moral sense but also incapable (in the long run) of sustaining social life. In a passage which speculates on the termination of despotism, he presented a fairly clear exposition of this view, although, like so many others, the first statement is marred by a qualification which can have little meaning in the context of the general argument there presented. He wrote:

> Were despotic empire, meantime, to continue for ever unmolested from above, while it retains that corruption on which it was founded, it appears to have in itself no principle of new life, and presents no hope of restoration to freedom and political vigour. That which the despotical master has sown, cannot quicken unless it die; it must languish and expire by the effect of its own abuse, before the human spirit can spring up anew, or bear those fruits which constitute the honour and felicity of human nature.
>
> .   .   .   .
>
> The commercial arts, which seem to require no foundation in the minds of men, but the regard to interest; no encouragement, but the hopes of gain, and the secure possession of property, must perish under the precarious tenure of slavery, and under the apprehension of danger arising from the reputation of wealth. National poverty, however, and the suppression of commerce, are the means by which despotism comes to accomplish its own destruction. Where there are no longer any profits to corrupt, or fears to deter, the charm of dominion is broken, and the naked slave, as awakened from a dream, is astonished to find he is free.[131]

Putting aside the marginal qualifications, it becomes clear that, for Ferguson, societies which fail to establish and sustain institutions appropriate to progress are doomed to an agonizing collapse.[132] Practically speaking, then, the need to maintain progress and to avert despotism approaches the same degree of necessity, in Ferguson's view, as the other necessary social laws—although some of them are literally necessary in the sense that men are powerless to resist them. Failure to meet the need spells the dissolution of the society.

The real efficacy of deliberate human power is, according to Ferguson, restricted to the area defined by these ineluctable limits. The attempt to overstep them is futile in most cases; where it is not, it is bound to have disastrous consequences, whatever the intention. But this does not mean, according to Ferguson, that the sphere of decisions and purposive action is an insignificant one. Men are not only called upon to abstain from fatally improper uses of power; they are also required to make wise adjustments to changing circumstances and to ensure the proper functioning of their present institutions. It must be recalled, moreover, that he did not reject completely the possibility that revolution and deliberate convention may sometimes be effectual and even necessary to establish political institutions more appropriate to actual conditions than those which exist. This was, in fact, the basis upon which he justified the two Whig causes, the embarrassing Civil War and the Glorious Revolution.

More frequently, however, he considered a revolutionary course unnecessary, as well as excessively risky and costly. He was prepared to concede its appropriateness only when there exist unmistakable signs of a sharp divergence between conditions and institutions and when there exist substantial reasons for believing that the revolutionists actually represent the forces working for proper adjustment. Revolutionists and the "spirit of reformation" in general he distrusted, believing that, as a rule, they represent corruption or well-intentioned but misguided attempts to do the impossible.[138] He was bolstered in his opposition to radical innovations by his conviction that major institutional adjustments are usually the unanticipated consequences of an accumulation of numerous relatively minor adjustments made in the normal course of social development.

The crucial decisions which, according to Ferguson, lie in man's discretionary power under most circumstances are much less concerned with the introduction of proper institutional innovations than with the maintenance of existing institutions and with continued progress within the established order. With respect to both concerns, Ferguson set forth a number of specific principles to govern the conduct of affairs in advanced commercial states possessing a mixed monarchical constitution. First, he believed that—to perform every state's task of preserving prosperity and of encouraging progress—rulers must adopt a correct economic policy. This he described in the following words:

> Men are tempted to labour, and to practice lucrative arts, by motives of interest. Secure to the workman the fruits of his labour, give him the prospects of independence or freedom, the public has found a faithful minister in the acquisition of wealth, and a faithful steward in hoarding what he has gained. The statesman in this, as in the case of population itself, can do little more than avoid doing mischief. It is well, if, in the beginnings of commerce, he knows how to repress the frauds to which it is subject. Commerce, if continued, is the branch in which men committed to the effects of their own experience, are least apt to go wrong.
>
> .   .   .   .
>
> In matters of particular profession, industry, and trade, the experienced practitioner is the master, and every general reasoner is a novice. The object in commerce is to make the individual rich; the more he gains for himself, the more he augments the wealth of his country. If a protection be required, it must be granted; if crimes and frauds be committed, they must be repressed; and government can pretend to no more.[134]

Ferguson proscribed, not only all governmental policies
which tend to interfere directly with the unhampered conduct of commerce and industry, but also any law which
tends to hinder economic activity indirectly by disturbing
the privileges whose attractiveness stimulates men's ambition and industry. Above all, he inveighed against "sumptuary laws" to limit the enjoyments of the wealthy and
against any measures aiming at an "equal division of
wealth." Because both of these topics recur constantly
throughout Ferguson's writings and because the following
passages forcefully state and dolefully dismiss all of the
arguments for such laws which Ferguson considered important, it is thought justified to present several lengthy excerpts from his discussion of both matters. Ferguson
wrote:

Many of the establishments which serve to defend the
weak from oppression, contribute, by securing the possession of property, to favour its unequal division, and to
increase the ascendant of those from whom the abuses of
power may be feared. Those abuses were felt very early
both at Athens and Rome.

It has been proposed to prevent the excessive accumulation of wealth in particular hands, by limiting the increase
of private fortunes, by prohibiting entails, and by with-
holding the right of primogeniture in the succession of
heirs. It has been proposed to prevent the ruin of moderate
estates, and to restrain the use, and consequently the desire
of great ones, by sumptuary laws. These different methods
are more or less consistent with the interest of commerce,
and may be adopted, in different degrees, by a people
whose national object is wealth: and they have their degree
of effect, by inspiring moderation, or a sense of equality,
and by stifling the passions by which mankind are
prompted to mutual wrongs.

. . . .

It appears to be, in a particular manner, the object of
sumptuary laws, and of equal division of wealth, to pre-

vent the gratification of vanity, to check the ostentation of superior fortune, and, by this means, to weaken the desire of riches, and to preserve in the breast of the citizen, that moderation and equity which ought to regulate his conduct.

This end is never perfectly attained in any state where the unequal division of property is admitted, and where fortune is allowed to bestow distinction and rank. It is indeed difficult, by any methods whatever, to shut up this source of corruption.

. . . .

The subjects of property, considered with a view to subsistence, or even to enjoyment, have little effect in corrupting mankind, or in awakening the spirit of competition and of jealousy; but considered with a view to distinction and honour, where fortune constitutes rank, they excite the most vehement passions, and absorb all the sentiments of the human soul; they reconcile avarice and meanness with ambition and vanity; and lead men through the practice of sordid and mercenary arts to the possession of a supposed elevation and dignity.

Where this source of corruption, on the contrary, is effectually stopped, the citizen is dutiful, and the magistrate upright. . . . [On] this supposition, experience and abilities are the only guides and the only titles to public confidence; and if citizens be ranged into separate classes, they become mutual checks by the difference of their opinions, not by the opposition of their interested designs.

. . . .

We must be contented to derive our freedom from a different source; to expect justice from the limits which are set to the powers of the magistrate, and to rely for protection on the laws which are made to secure the estates and the person of the subject. We live in societies where men must be rich, in order to be great; where pleasure itself is often pursued from vanity; where the desire of a supposed happiness serves to inflame the worst of passions, and is itself the foundation of misery; where public justice, like fetters applied to the body, may, without inspiriting the

sentiments of candour and equity, prevent the actual commission of crimes.[135]

Although this discussion (included in Ferguson's first book)
leaves little doubt about where Fersuson's real sympathies
lay and about the bitterness with which he accepted the
limitations of his time, discussions of the same topics in later
works display no regret about the inevitable and inviolable
character of economic inequality in progressive societies. He
went so far, in fact, as to deny completely the value of
ancient precedents, remarking:

> The antient republics, amongst whom it was proposed, in
> some instances to equalize the fortunes of citizens, had
> recourse to the labour of slaves, and the object, without
> this provision would have been altogether chimerical and
> wild.[136]

In general, then, Ferguson stressed the importance of pursuing policies to sustain commerce and the pattern of subordination appropriate to it, and these policies usually turned
out to be best characterized as restraint of interference with
existing social conditions.[137]

But the preservation of commerce alone cannot, according to Ferguson, guarantee the maintenance of a free society. In a passage strongly flavored by his conception of true
virtue, he remarked:

> Wealth, commerce, extent of territory, and the knowledge
> of arts, are, when properly employed, the means of preser-
> vation, and the foundations of power. If they fail in part,
> the nation is weakened, if they were entirely withheld, the
> race would perish: their tendency is to maintain numbers
> of men, but not to constitute happiness. They will accord-
> ingly maintain the wretched as well as the happy. They

answer one purpose, but are not therefore sufficient for all; and are of little significance, when only employed to maintain a timid, dejected, and servile people.[138]

Elsewhere, however, he made it clear that, although in his view all states have the task of encouraging the formation of proper character among their citizens, the definition of propriety cannot be an absolute one. The passage which was quoted at the very beginning of this discussion, "Human nature no where exists in the abstract," concludes, "and human virtue is attached, in every particular instance, to the use of particular materials, or to the application of given materials to particular ends." [139] More specifically and less ambiguously, he suggested that the main object of wise statesmanship is not, in general, the development of men's "moral character" as such; it is, rather, the formation of an appropriate "political character." [140] In consequence, he urged:

> In states where property, distinction and pleasure, are thrown out as baits to the imagination, and incentives to passion, the public seems to rely for the preservation of its political life, on the degree of emulation and jealousy with which parties mutually oppose and restrain each other. The desires of preferment and profit in the breast of the citizen, are the motives from which he is excited to enter on public affairs, and are the considerations which direct his political conduct. The suppression, therefore, of ambition, of party-animosity [sic], and of public envy, is probably, in every such case, not a reformation, but a symptom of weakness, and a prelude to more sordid pursuits, and ruinous amusements.[141]

The educational task, then, assigned to governments is virtually indistinguishable from that of maintaining the order

and progress of existing arrangements. But it is deserving of
separate comment that, for Ferguson, it was not enough that
political forms reflect the general pattern of opinion in a
society: it was necessary that the prevalent habits be constantly reinforced by appropriate deliberate action. Ferguson's reasons for holding this view are clear. He argued:

> Liberty results, we say, from the government of laws; and
> we are apt to consider statutes, not merely as the resolu-
> tions and maxims of a people determined to be free, not
> as the writings by which their rights are kept on record;
> but as a power erected to guard them, and as a barrier
> which the caprice of man cannot transgress.
>
> If forms of proceeding, written statutes, or other consti-
> tuents of law, cease to be enforced by the very spirit from
> which they arose; they serve only to cover, not to restrain,
> the iniquities of power. . . . And the influence of laws,
> where they have any real effect in the preservation of
> liberty, is not any magic power descending from shelves
> that are loaded with books, but is, in reality, the influence
> of men resolved to be free; of men, who, having adjusted in
> writing the terms on which they are to live with their state,
> and with their fellow subjects, are determined, by their
> vigilance and spirit, to make these terms be fulfilled.[142]

Following a parallel line of reasoning, he set another important task before the statesmen of advanced societies. He
reverted to one of his most persistent themes, the desirability
of a militia, and wrote:

> Law without force, is no more than a dead letter; and force,
> if improperly lodged, will frustrate all the precautions of
> the legal establishment. It is no less dangerous in the hands
> of a profligate rabble who would level the conditions of
> men, than it is in the hands of an usurper who would
> render them subject to his will. In order to obviate the
> danger from either of these quarters, the same guard that is

or ought to be set over the sources of the legislative power, namely that every respectable order in the state may have a proper share in it, and that every improper person be excluded from the trust, ought also to be set over the distribution of arms or of force in the community. Where the law originates there also is the proper depository of the national force; and whoever has not the proper interest in the laws of his country is but ill entrusted with its defence.

In ordinary times, military service, like the profession of law, divinity or medicine, may be entrusted to persons who make it an honourable calling. But, it does not by any means follow, that they who have a real stake in the preservation of an order established should forego the use of arms, and profess their inability to defend themselves on their state upon any emergency whatever. Or, if this should be thought necessary, at any period of national progress, we cannot any longer be at a loss to account for the vicissitudes of human affairs, or the fatal reverses in which the established order is sometimes overturned.[143]

This recommendation pretty nearly exhausts the catalogue of the areas in which discretionary human power was considered by Ferguson to be a major determinant of events, and even the actions in these areas—it must be noted—can properly be referred to acquiescence in the dictates of situational necessity.[144] In advanced states engaged in commerce and ruled by law, then, the primary purposes to which discretionary public authority can and ought to be put, in Ferguson's view, are those which preserve the social conditions on which the political structure rests.

Within that structure itself, the primary task is the settlement of disputes between the contending groups which constitute society. The maintenance of order and the adjudication of conflict, not the fostering of true virtue, are the aims of the rule of law. Making this point perfectly explicit, Ferguson wrote:

We are not to expect, that the laws of any country are to be framed as so many lessons of morality, to instruct the citizens how he may act the part of a virtuous man. Laws, whether civil or political, are expedients of policy to adjust the pretensions of parties, and to secure the peace of society. The expedient is accommodated to special circumstances, and calculated to repress the specific disorders peculiarly incident to particular situations.[145]

If this is true and if the rule of law is the very culminating achievement of the society Ferguson has been describing, then what is its moral justification? In what sense did Ferguson believe that this order represents a valid translation of his basic evaluative criteria and no mere fact of existence? At times, Ferguson appears to have been willing to beg these questions altogether, assimilating reality to the assumption of a wholly beneficent natural order. Thus he wrote: "The essential obligations of men in society are founded in what nature has done for them, not in what they themselves have agreed to perform. . . ."[146] More commonly, however, he refused to rely on such a general claim, a claim which provides no way of distinguishing legitimate situations from illegitimate ones. Ferguson expressed his unwillingness to proceed in such a naturalistic fashion in the following words:

> Inequalities of strength, whether of mind or body, constitute a relation of dependence and power, forming a species of government, which we may term instinctive, because it is prior to any concerted design or institution on the part of those concerned.
>
> .   .   .   .
>
> We must not, however, confound the effect of these inequalities in forming a species of actual government, with any supposed right to command in one, or obligation to obey in another.[147]

As a rule, then, Ferguson felt called upon to establish a "right" as authority for government.

He believed—and this has, of course, been implicit in much of the foregoing discussion—that the rights of property and station which men actually come to claim have real moral justification and that the necessary governmental function of preserving rights serves, at the same time, to endow rulers with true moral authority. Ferguson maintained that it is a "self-evident . . . maxim, That every innocent person may defend himself"; "to which we may join," he added, "what is equally evident, that every one having power, may employ it in defense of any other innocent person," [148] From such maxims, he concluded:

> If, therefore, in considering the variety of forms under which societies subsist, the casuist is pleased to enquire, What title one man, or any number of men, have to controul [sic] his actions? he may be answered, None at all, provided that his actions have no effect to the prejudice of his fellow-creatures; but if they have, the rights of defence, and the obligation to repress the commission of wrongs, belong to collective bodies, as well as to individuals.[149]

These considerations underlay Ferguson's equation of justice with liberty and his ability to retain for those words (which he also used as purely descriptive terms) their traditional normative connotations.

This explanation, however, fails to clarify three basic issues—the relationship between the moral stature of rights and the general structure of virtue, the definition and scope of rights, and the justification for the particular way in which any particular system distributes rights and authority—issues which Ferguson had to resolve if he was to demonstrate that the dedication to commerce, inequality, and liberty is a valid manifestation of the morally beneficent attributes he ascribed to society in general. The first of these three remaining tasks Ferguson approached in the following manner:

> [If] force could be effectual to inspire benevolence, even the sword and the mace should be employed to make men love one another. But benevolence is a modification of the will, which no application of force can procure: Even the external effect, if obtained in this manner, would lose the character of virtue. . . . To bestow the felicity of a willing mind, force is not only inadequate, but, by alienating the affections of those against whom it is employed, would have a contrary tendency.
>
> All that the magistrate can do in this matter is, by shutting the door to disorder and vice, to endeavour to stifle the ill disposition of men; and by securing the paths of integrity and marking them with considerations of distinction and honour, to facilitate and encourage the choice of virtue, and to give scope to the best dispositions which nature has furnished, or which the ingenuous mind is able to cultivate for itself.[150]

That is to say, Ferguson considered the primary resources available to rulers in terms of force and coercion, rather than education and leadership in joint activities, and that, consequently, he saw the relevance of politics to virtue as limited to a small range—actually to a mere precondition for the existence of virtuous men.[151]

Ferguson's examination of actual political institutions in actual societies led him to shift his emphasis from a conception of politics as a morally cultivating expression of social solidarity to a conception of politics as a coercive manifestation of power in society. Corresponding to this shift, then, was one which turned attention from the expression and stimulation of virtue—especially beneficence, the apex of activist virtue—to the preservation of innocence and rights.

The transformation was, of course, never complete; it could not be so without a total abandonment of elements crucial to Ferguson's basic commitments. It however does point to Ferguson's reluctant denial of potency to beneficence and the transformation of virtue from a principle of public action into a principle of private intention. The emphasis on rights rather than virtue as a whole, in short, corresponds, peculiarly enough, to the persistence of passivist elements in Ferguson's conception of virtue.[152]

Ferguson's definition of rights themselves makes it clear that the suggestion of such a correspondence is both paradoxical and one-sided, because that definition builds (at least in part) on the most activist claims made in man's behalf. In a passage which provides, at once, a listing of the elements comprising man's "original" rights and a definition of the term "right," Ferguson stated:

> [A] person has a right to use of his faculties and powers; he has a right to enjoy the light of the sun, and the air of the atmosphere; he has a right to the use of his property, and the fruits of his labour. These are self-evident propositions, and the meaning of the term right, which occurs in all of them, may be collected from its uniform signification in each. Agreeably to this rule, right is the relation of a person to a thing, in which no alteration ought to be made, without his consent.[153]

To these, Ferguson added several types of "adventitious" rights, including the rights of "possession, property or command," founded on "occupancy," "labour," or "contract." [154] Except for the treatment of "command," which will be examined below, Ferguson's explanation of these rights needs no exposition here: he followed the familiar outlines of standard eighteenth-century textbook jurisprudence. The important point is that, in Ferguson's view, only the original rights are absolutely inalienable and universal; the others are given validity only because a denial of the "adventitious rights"—which grow up as a result of man's exercise of his original rights—necessarily entails a violation of original ones.

The significant consequences which Ferguson drew from this conception of rights (with its distinction between a primary "original" level and a derivative "adventitious" level) are, first, a rejection of all attempts to construe promise or contract as the ultimate basis of all rights, and secondly, the justification of the varying ways in which property rights are defined by different societies, as well as of the gross inequality of property. The first of these appears to be an attempt to meet Hume's objections to the view that conceptions of justice and the obligation to respect rights have any ontological validity—objections which rested on Hume's demonstration that the authority of promises upon which liberal theory had built its claims presupposes a prior conventional definition of rights, whose obligatory character, according to Hume, rests on nothing more than its utility.[155] In resting his argument on a prior conception of qualities inherent in all human integrity, Ferguson sought to vindicate justice and property by an argument more compelling and more in keeping with his view of man's high place in the universe than the appeals to actual nature and reasonable utility which he found in Hume, without at the same time rejecting Hume's insistence that promise and contract cannot be viewed as the ultimate basis of social ties, an insistence wholly congenial to Ferguson's own emphasis on the social character of man.

The difference between Hume and Ferguson on this point—as is true of almost every one of the differences between them—turns less on the substantive conclusions each drew from his arguments than on the implications which, in Ferguson's view, inhered in their respective approaches. Ferguson's theory of rights, no matter how conventional its conclusions, is always imbued with a sense of man's special dignity and peculiar worth—a sense which, in his view, Hume's arguments lacked. But it is not the present purpose to undertake a comprehensive comparison between the writings of Ferguson and those of his mentor, friend, and adversary, David Hume: the contrast between them has been raised only to indicate the extent to which Ferguson's reliance on a theory of rights does not represent a simple abdication of the grand vision of man's destiny which animated his conception of virtue and, in fact, his entire intellectual effort.

The second major conclusion which Ferguson drew from his conception of rights, on the other hand, indicates the solid barriers which Ferguson sought to erect against any attempt to attack existing social relations by an appeal to rights. Since, according to Ferguson, all property rights are by definition adventitious, no man can lay any claims to property which he does not acquire in the normal course of social development; nor can there be any valid challenge to the rights of those who have acquired property without violating the original rights of others. Ferguson wrote:

> [Liberty] . . . does not consist in the equality of station or fortune. In this sense, liberty were a mere chimera or vision, never realized in the state of mankind. The nations who contended most for the equality of citizens, in admitting the institution of slavery, trespassed most egregiously on the equality of mankind.
>
> .   .   .   .
>
> The only respect in which all men continue forever to be equal, is that of the equal right which every man has to defend himself; but this involves a source of much inequality in respect to the things which any one may have a right to defend.[156] Whilst we admit, therefore, that all men have

an equal right to defend themselves, we must not mistake
this for an assumption that all men have equal things to
defend, or that liberty should consist in stripping the
industrious and skillful, who have acquired much, to enrich the lazy and profligate, who may have acquired nothing, or who may have wasted all they could reach. It is
impossible to restrain the influence of superior ability, of
property, of education, or the habits of station. It is impossible to prevent these from becoming to some degree hereditary; and of consequence, it is impossible, without
violating the principles of human nature, to prevent
some permanent distinction of ranks: And, if this were
possible, it is far from expedient in the circumstances of
human life. In these inequalities we find the first germs of
subordination and government so necessary to the safety
of the individuals and the peace of mankind; in these also
we find the continued incentive to labour and the practice
of lucrative arts.

As liberty consists in the communication of safety to all,
nothing could be more repugnant to it than the violation of
right in any part, in order to level the whole. It is true that
great inequalities of fortune are adverse to some species of
political institution; that great distinctions of rank,
founded on birth alone, to the exclusion of merit, or to the
suppression of all the efforts of distinguished ability in
public service, is a corruption fatal to mankind; that unrestrained possession of arbitrary power of any sort, is for the
sake of liberty and justice to be carefully watched and
stopped short of the extreme to which it may tend; But as
everyone has a right to the condition in which, by the
ordinary course of human nature, he is fairly placed, in
which he is in no way injurious to his fellow creatures, it
must follow that liberty, in every particular instance, must
consist in securing the fairly acquired conditions of men,
however unequal.[157]

Inequality of property and station, thus, is not only compatible with human rights but also inextricably bound up with
them.

But this line of argument is not sufficient, according to Ferguson, to establish the authority of rulers. Insofar as governments function simply to prevent wrongs, they do not require any additional justification, as has been shown.[158] As Ferguson knew, however, governments also exercise command functions—defining rights, monopolizing the defense of rights, collecting taxes, organizing the national defense, and so forth—and, in his words, "The right to command . . . cannot arise . . . [except] by consent so far as one person may, by compact, bind himself to obey the commands of another." [159] The problem of reconciling this demand with Ferguson's evident desire to vindicate the authority of actual governments he attempted to solve by a recourse to the familiar notion of "tacit consent." He wrote:

> There is indeed, by institution of Providence, and by an original distinction of dependence and power, in every society, a government *de facto*. And the same may become a government *de jure*, also, if the parties concerned, upon trial of the situation in which they find themselves placed, agree to the conditions which are required in the exercise of government. . . .
> We may be asked, then, under what government did the people assemble in a body, to give the consent necessary to found such a plea of right to command them? We may answer: No where. And yet this is the only plea upon which the right to command can be supported. We are therefore bound to verify the plea, before we can urge it in behalf of any government whatever.
> The consent, upon which the right to command is founded may not be prior to the establishment of government; but may be obtained under the reasonable exercise of an actual power, to which every person within the community, by accepting of a customary protection, becomes bound to pay the customary allegiance and submission. Here is a compact ratified by the least ambiguous of

all signs, the whole practice, or continued observance of an
ordinary life. The conditions here are ratified, in every age,
and by every individual for himself; not merely stipulated
in remote age, and for a posterity over which the contract-
ing party had not any controul [sic].[160]

Ferguson thus found no incompatibility between the facts
of political development and the requirement that command
be authorized by consent, and he believed that his argument
obviated all need to postulate some hypothetical social and
political contract.

Furthermore, Ferguson's line of reasoning justified each
of the numerous types of governments which differing situations require.[161] As the following passage makes clear, not
even the illegitimate foundation of many governments can
deny to them the full range of governmental authority:

Political establishments, in many instances, originate in
force, and prerogatives are assumed which in the first
exercise of them were manifest violations of right. Men
nevertheless in process of time, or at least in the succession
of a few ages, acquire the habits of their situation; and
succeeding generations may be reconciled to forms that
were forced on their ancestors. They adopt as a custom,
and willingly submit to conditions which owed their first
imposition perhaps to violence. In such cases, we are not
always to look back to the origin of a custom or practice, in
order to judge of its validity. If it be such as the mind of
man may by habit be reconciled to, and willing to adopt, it
becomes binding on those who have availed themselves of
the custom, where it is favourable to themselves; and are
therefore fairly understood to adopt the conditions of it,
where those conditions are reciprocally favourable to others.[162]

The concluding portion of this statement, however, points
to the one exception which Ferguson persistently made:

Nothing can ever justify despotic rule. Qualifying his notion of tacit consent, Ferguson wrote:

> But if want of consent, in one age, will not preclude the obligation of compact on succeeding ages, or on those who in the sequel voluntarily accede to a practice, no more will the consent of ancestors, with whom a practice originate, bind their posterity, or those who in the sequel refuse their assent; and, if an institution, however willingly adopted by a former age, prove in the sequel a mere abuse; if it be a continued exercise of injustice and wrong, supported by force on the one part, and a continued series of suffering and reluctant compliance on the other; and practices, however long continued, as they are never ratified by consent, they are never established on the foot of customary practice, nor do they obtain the force of convention. The oppressed, even after any indefinite period of oppression are free to procure a relief by such means as they are enabled to employ for that purpose.[163]

Admittedly, he could provide no certain guide for distinguishing those illegitimate situations which are bound to be legitimized in time and those which are completely corrupt and unworthy of any regard. It is for this reason, and in this context, that he abandoned the attempt to formulate any precise definition of a "right to revolution." [164] This much, however, is clear: except for the most glaring examples of oppressive despotism, every government wields power which is, in fact, authorized by the consent of its subjects.

Over and above this general justification of non-despotic governments, Ferguson's theory of rights serves to provide special justification for that form which is better qualified than any other to preserve individual rights and which has the requirement for consent built into its very legislative procedures.[165] In preserving liberty, then, a mixed monarchy displays, not only the greatest perfection in the performance of governmental functions indispensable to social life, but

also the highest measure of moral authority which any governmental form is capable of displaying. Ferguson believed,
therefore, that the demands made by the power of physical
and social necessity are wholly reconcilable, in genuinely
progressive societies, with the demands made by the authority of moral good and that true danger results only from a
failure to understand the true structures of power and authority, a failure which can lead to the total destruction and
corruption of human nature.

In the light of his analysis of social and political variety
and change, Ferguson reinterpreted both the promise he
believed inherent in society and the dangers which he believed confront particular societies. The first can be shown
most readily by recalling his reassessments of the Roman
democratic republic; the second can be summarized through
a re-examination of those features of British society which, it
has been contended, appeared most dangerous to Ferguson
from the standpoint of virtue. With regard to Rome, then, it
is clear that the analysis served, first of all, to deny democratic institutions all claim to universal applicability.
Secondly, Ferguson became increasingly convinced that the
existence of democracy in Rome depended on a near-savage
level of human progress. Thirdly, insofar as Roman virtue
rested on Roman militarism, it was, according to Ferguson,
destined to liquidate itself. Finally—and most importantly—Ferguson came to believe that Rome's vaunted
equality was built on the labor of slaves, that the system,
in short, was basically unjust. Although Ferguson did not
maintain all of these objections at all times and although
nothing could ever completely extinguish his ardor for
the republic, it is eminently clear that he rejected all
thought of using Roman democracy as a universal yardstick
for measuring any society's contribution to human virtue.[166]

1. spare for sety rules
2. +g lows
3. installing gcd t olN
            vile

VIRTUE IN SOCIETY   279

Ferguson's reassessment of British conditions can best be described by showing how he redefined each of the critical elements—"interestedness," division of labor, and political institutions geared to the maintenance of order rather than virtue—in terms of the necessities, possibilities, and translated values inherent in the concrete social situation. It will be recalled that men's interested devotion to commerce had seemed to Ferguson to threaten the preservation of the society, as well as the integrity of the men. At the conclusion of his analysis, Ferguson was prepared to argue that interest and commerce are both inevitable concomitants of a progress which can only be averted at the price of despotism, that the concern for property and wealth leaves room for considerable development of whole-hearted devotion to the rights and liberties of one's party and to the defense of the nation against external enemies, and that property and commerce occasion substantial progress in the development of men's human faculties, while the prevalence of interested habits among men contributes materially to the existence of a free and active society.

Secondly, it has been shown above that Ferguson feared the emergence of a structure of subordination based on the "separation of arts and professions" because such a phenomenon seemed to threaten men with a narrowing and stifling of human capabilities. This challenge, too, Ferguson felt he could meet after a full consideration of all social factors. The division of labor, he believed, arises necessarily in a progressive, commercial society; it cannot be substantially altered because, by its very effects, it disqualifies men for the performance of tasks other than those to which they are assigned. Furthermore, since the structure of subordination in an advanced society can only rest on the division of labor and since no society (except the most primitive) can be maintained without some pattern of subordination, it is impossible materially to alter this system without, at the same time, collapsing the social structure. Men—particularly in the lower orders—must be made aware of the indispensability of social subordination: they must and can be taught the happiness available to them from a cheerful performance of their assigned tasks. The alternative is misery, chaos, and universal destruction.

The only range of possible action—and it is, according to Ferguson, a substantial one—lies in the direction of making available to men opportunities for varied activity which are not incompatible with their assigned social role. This meant, for Ferguson, requiring all citizens to spend some time in military training and on militia service in case of national emergency. It meant, moreover, eliminating the pointless differentiation between the civil and military functions of the ruling group and thereby providing them with the kind of varied experience which is likely to promote their general capabilities. Such alleviation of the rigid division of labor can and ought to be instituted; no other is either possible or desirable.[167]

Ferguson, in the last analysis, decided that the system of subordination resting on the division of labor has much intrinsic value. Not only is it intimately bound up with that enhancement of human capabilities resulting from commercial progress, but also it corresponds (far more closely than, say, a subordination resting simply on inequalities of wealth) to the distribution of influence and rewards in proportion to talents and merit. Conditioned by their circumstances, activities, and habits, the men of each class are men who are neither competent nor worthy to occupy any other position—no matter how ideal or abstract a conception of human worth may be applied. When properly understood, therefore, the division of labor is wholly consistent, according to Ferguson, with a concern for human virtue and happiness.

The third apparent basic danger which Ferguson espied in his own society was the restriction of governmental positions to a relatively small group in society and the direction of governmental activity toward the maintenance of order and prosperity, instead of the promotion of virtue. The apprehensions aroused by the observation of this phenomenon Ferguson could also quiet through a reappraisal of its meaning and significance. Most importantly, as has been shown, he stressed that all government necessarily rests on power and that—except in very unusual circumstances—it is inconceivable that power should be equally distributed or that the experiences enjoyed in the exercise of power should be equally shared by all.[168] Still referring to factors he considered necessary in all social circumstances, he maintained that all political institutions must (by virtue of the conditions of their origin and the conditions of societies sufficiently advanced in the sense of property and interest to spawn political institutions) use their power to order the conflicting and competing interests of diverse social groups, as well as to preserve the physical and economic existence of all its members. Moreover, the specific form in which these necessary functions are performed must reflect the actually existing conditions within the society: the activities of government must be such as to preserve the society as it is, permitting it to progress along the lines of its natural development. As for the inculcation of virtue—this is basically a task to which the instrumentalities of government are wholly inappropriate; to the limited extent that rulers can mold social habits, they must be contented to direct themselves to the strengthening of those opinions on which the social structure rests.

282

But this last, in Ferguson's view, presents both rulers and subjects with a genuine opportunity to enhance virtue. The British political system, after all, rests on opinions of self-assertion and ambition. Moreover, it does provide almost all men with some opportunity to participate in public life, even if that opportunity is restricted, for most, to the support of the party which represents their interests. Through the exhortations to preserve their liberty, most men can be led to expose themselves to some political experiences and thereby be encouraged to develop their talents and their sense of fellow-feeling. Due to the liberty and conflict which form an integral part of the British mixed monarchy, Ferguson believed, there is no reason to suppose that British society need ever relapse into a torpid and static order destructive of all virtue, particularly if the foregoing principles are supplemented by the adoption of the militia scheme.

The values which Ferguson found expressed in Britain's rule of law through mixed monarchy are so clearly implied in what has just been said and have, in any case, been discussed so recently that there is no need for an extended summary here. It needs only to be recalled that Ferguson considered mixed monarchy to be the surest possible guarantee of liberty and justice, in the sense of the preservation of rights and the prevention of abuses of power; he also believed it to be uniquely equipped, through its institutionalized provision for consent to legislation, to claim that its authority rests on explicit, as well as tacit, consent. Britain's political institutions, therefore, presented to him the picture of a form of government ideally suited to the basic legitimating functions and conditions of government and directed (because it presupposes and integrates party competition and commerce) as much as is humanly possible to the stimulation of positive virtue as any governmental system.

As a result of these reinterpretations, then, Ferguson felt

free to assert that British society is in fact capable of making those contributions to human virtue which society in general is supposed to make, if also in a manner appropriate to its particular circumstances. It does, within the limits set by necessity, go far to meet the description of a "state to be valued from its effects in preserving the species, in ripening their talents, and exciting their virtues." [169] The shortcomings which appeared to Ferguson as possible precursors of despotism turn out instead to be, in several cases, virtues in disguise, and, in others, relatively minor inconveniences or certainly remediable flaws. The danger of despotism, then, does not lie in any of the major tendencies of British social development: it stems primarily from actions taken in ignorance of the true significance of those tendencies, and only to a minor extent from failure to take the remedial steps indicated by the situation. A measure of the extent to which Ferguson succeeded in alleviating his fears is supplied by the fact that, although his last work does not represent any substantial revision of his principal arguments, the *Principles of Moral and Political Science* excludes altogether the extended discussion of the causes of despotism which occupies a sizeable portion of the *Essay on the History of Civil Society*. It is unquestionable that Ferguson believed that he had solved the major problems he set himself.

From this point of view, it is possible to re-examine Ferguson's several responses to his situation without encountering the bewildering confusion which resulted from the earlier view that considered each as a total response. It can now be seen that Ferguson withdrew from those circumstances which seemed to him irremediable and that he counseled Stoical indifference to all who believe themselves victimized by them. Thus, he despaired of ever seeing his society integrated by some principle of benevolent fellowship because he denied that such a principle could possibly arise in

advanced societies in a form strong enough to weld the
society together; he withdrew, in most respects, from the
attempt to overcome the narrowing of human capabilities
attendant on the division of labor because he was convinced
that this could not be achieved without destroying society;
and he abandoned all hope of democracy because he did not
believe that the conditions necessary for it could any longer
exist. Correspondingly, he urged the lower classes to accept
the inhuman indifference, the debasing drudgery, and the
grinding poverty which falls to their lot as inescapable
consequences of their situation.

The reform response, it is clear, Ferguson applied to those
situations which, in his view, are within discretionary human control. With regard to self-respect, he exhorted all
men to assert the rights and privileges inherent in their
persons and their stations and in general to maintain a sense
of their own integrities.[170] In the area defined by the division
of labor, he exhorted the rulers to blend, both for themselves
and for their subjects, some measure of military experience
into the normal civil careers of men—taking care to do so
with minimal disturbance to the normal economic pursuits
and class relations of society. The reform measures he proposed in the specifically political sphere were largely limited
to exhortations to rulers not to forget the importance of good
men for the strength of a nation's defense.[171]

Ferguson's denial of problems took place wherever his
reinterpretation showed him that some situation, which
originally appeared dangerous or bad is, in fact, benign and
good. Thus, selfish interestedness can be translated into
progressive ambition and vigorous concern for rights; degrading constriction of capacities can be seen as a just reflection of unequal talents and merits or, at worst, as an incon-
venient sacrifice made to the progressive common good; and
a state devoted to the stifling of un-routine talents and the

routinizing of affairs can be recast as an instrumentality of
the wisest men available and a sterling defender of liberty.
The denial of problems, in short, corresponds to contending
either that progress is irrelevant to virtue, which flourishes
in every social situation, or that it actually enhances man's
capacities and virtues. In either case, it points up those
situations where, Ferguson maintained, a completely satisfactory translation of values has taken place.

When Ferguson's differing responses are placed in full
context in this way, most of the confusion is cleared away.
But this does not mean that they are altogether adequate, as
measured by Ferguson's own moral principles, by Ferguson's
standards of descriptive accuracy, or by the criterion of
Ferguson's basic task. It does mean that the way has been
prepared for the definition of a small number of fundamental difficulties in his work, and the identification of these
difficulties can provide the most comprehensive explanation
of the dilemmas confronting Ferguson as an intellectual, as
well as of their consequences for his activities.

The first difficulty which emerges from a scrutiny of his
responses is the differential treatment accorded the lower
classes and the upper classes. One simple way of putting the
matter might be that the former are told only things they
presumably do not want to hear, while the latter are told
only things they do want to hear. This is a clear and important characterization of Ferguson's conclusions, but it does
not state a contradiction of principle. It is also true that the
advice directed to the lower classes is largely couched in
terms of the passive conception of virtue, while that directed
to the higher ranks consists of activist calls to self-assertion
and ambition. No doubt Ferguson urged all ranks to assert
the rights and privileges of their stations, but, equally certainly, he gave no leave to those classes having no rights
beyond those of their persons and no safeguards except those

against enslavement to demand as rights anything they did
not then possess. In effect, then, he applied different criteria
to men at opposite ends of the social scale and treated them
as not even equal in principle.

His reasons for doing this—even if he could not consistently admit that he was doing it—are neither insubstantial
nor dishonorable. He was persuaded that the lower classes
are so debased by their situation that they are progressively
more incapable of advancement and that the only hope for
society is to keep them working and quiescent. But this does
not alter that, in line with Ferguson's own observations, any
success he might have in quieting their unrest would not
materially improve the moral condition of these men, except
upon a very narrow interpretation of the passivist conception of virtue. His attempt to justify the situation by reference to the inequalities of capacities created by that very
situation can only be met by the scornful judgment which
his teacher, Montesquieu, passed on attempts to justify slavery: "Bad laws having made lazy men, they have been
reduced to slavery because of their laziness." [172] Ferguson
could not resolve this difficulty and was, in the last analysis,
compelled simply to sacrifice the poor upon the altar of social
necessity.

Secondly, it is equally clear that, however manfully Ferguson struggled to do so, he could never satisfactorily reconcile himself to the existence of a society integrated by power
and the ties of interest. Unquestionably his defense of rights
and commerce was quite sincere and wholly compatible
with virtue in its activist sense. But the total translation of
"virtue" into "liberty" was a coup de mot, rather than a
solution of the problem created by the decline of conditions
compatible with social love. The attempt to salvage social
feeling by an appeal to party spirit was an ingenious one, but
Ferguson himself pointed out that the extent to which a

liberal government succeeds in protecting individual rights leads to an increasing sense of security and a decreasing willingness to engage in political controversy. Furthermore, Ferguson also refused to grant the legitimacy of any new claims of rights. The political process, then, was bound (within the limits set by Ferguson's conception of governmental functions and by virtue of its very successes) to become an administrative process which could in no way engage the energies of the vast majority in party conflict.

As if in recognition of this, Ferguson placed his greatest hopes on the militia scheme. This embodies his one frank exception to the general approbation he bestowed on progress. Many of the arguments he adduced in favor of the militia reached straight back to his adulation for the Roman republic, militarism and all, and the end he hoped to achieve by it was the stimulation of moral virtue, without any qualifications to take into account the alleged relativity of "political characters." Nothing about the social situation as he described it makes the proposal congenial to existing activities, structures, or opinions. It represents, in fact, a clear and deliberate break with the spirit of the age as he saw it. In consequence, the established legislative procedure— geared to the settlement of controversies over rights— cannot be expected to introduce it. Only if, in response to special pleas, those intrusted with the national defense decide to demand the measure is there any possibility of its adoption. Consequently, Ferguson cannot treat his proposal as a normal political matter: he must make it an object of exhortation to the rulers. The implications of this will be considered in a moment; the important point for the present is that Ferguson's militia scheme stands as a symbol of his never fully resolved difficulty in accepting commercial and liberal society in place of a community of dedicated men. Here, too, as in the case of human talents, Ferguson's conclusion represents more of a bowing to necessity than a full reconciliation.

The third important difficulty—and this one provides a key to all of Ferguson's work—is revealed by Ferguson's inability to conceive of any way by which he can himself affect the course of events except through the exhortation of others—either rulers, or the poor, or men in general. But this conclusion manifests Ferguson's ultimate failure to achieve the tasks he set himself. This is true for three fundamental reasons. First of all, Ferguson repeatedly denied the efficacy of exhortation as a means of directing human conduct. Time and again he insisted that, although information about the means to desired ends may well be accepted, the ends themselves are determined by nature and habit, not reason or persuasion. To urge the poor to seek tranquillity instead of plenty, to urge the contented to seek strife instead of peace, to urge the rulers to promote virtue instead of order—all of these undertakings are, by Ferguson's own findings, doomed to failure.

As the following passage shows, Ferguson was aware of this and sought a solution. He wrote:

We hazard being treated with ridicule, when we require political establishments, merely to cultivate the talents of men, and to inspire the sentiments of a liberal mind, we must offer some motive of interest, or some hopes of external advantage, to animate the pursuits, or to direct the measures, of ordinary men. They would be brave, ingenious, and eloquent, only from necessity, or for the sake of profit: they magnify the uses of wealth, population, and the other resources of war; but often forget that these are of no consequence without the direction of able capacities, and without the supports of a national vigour. We may expect, therefore, to find among states the bias to a particular policy, taken from the regards to public safety; from the desire of securing personal freedom, or private property;

seldom from the consideration of moral effects, or from a view to the genius of mankind.[173]

He set out, in short, to persuade rulers to pursue a virtuous course by a more or less disingenuous appeal to the ends they already had in view. With regard to others, Ferguson's solution was less clear-cut. Some suggestion is offered by the following passage, although the context there is somewhat more limited than the present discussion:

> The reform, indeed, of false notions once taken up, on the grounds of religion, is not to be looked for in the effects of mere reason on the minds of ordinary men. These are engaged in their superstition by the horrors they feel, as well as by their habits of thinking, and require the impulse of an opposite doctrine, urged with similar passions, to have any considerable effect. Wild systems of enthusiasm or superstition, accordingly, have been required mutually to supplant one another: Reason has operated only in the minds of a few. . . .[174]

On the evidence of this statement, as well as on the accumulated evidence of the present study, it can be asserted that Ferguson solved his dilemma by assuming the roles of ideologist and moral preacher. In these capacities, he was able to rely on various manipulative techniques: playing on existing superstitions and fostering new ones, gaining a hearing from the upper orders through flattery and services, and in general shifting and adjusting his argument to achieve effects, not to set forth simple truth or to clarify his own thought. It is for these reasons that Ferguson's writing is so circuitous and verbose and that the structure of his basic argument must be laboriously dug out of his text.

None of this is intended to suggest that Ferguson deliberately decided all of this. That is a question which can never be answered, and it is not even particularly interesting. The interpretation here offered, like the whole of the foregoing analysis, is an attempt to reconstruct the logic of Ferguson's situation and to assess both his orientation and his role in the light of such a reconstruction. Ferguson's attempt to relate himself as an intellectual to his social situation is, accordingly, here considered a failure in the second place because it entailed a shift from the standpoint of the intellectual to that of the moralizer and ideologist, although the shift is explicable in terms of his role as intellectual.

This raises the third and final reason. If it is correct to say that, as an intellectual, Ferguson sought above all an orientation to practice, than it must be said that his work (insofar as it does not involve moralizing and ideologizing practice) fails to serve the most important task he set for it. Instead of an orientation to practice, his activities brought him practice in orientation; instead of a guide to activity in a wider social context, he produced essentially a justification for abstinence—on his part at least—from social practice, other than the clarification of his situation.

It may be argued that to deny the name "activity" to "orientation" simply flies in the face of Aristotle's dictum that contemplation is the highest form of activity, that the present judgment overlooks the extent to which Ferguson was committed to the classical ideal of the philosopher's task—a commitment manifested by the repeated distinction he drew between those few capable of reason, and the many subjected only to their passions and habits. Certainly it cannot be denied that Ferguson did, at times, align himself with such a classical ideal of contemplation. But several considerations serve to support the basic contention implicit in the judgment of failure; viz., that a most accurate statement of the demands which Ferguson made of his writings must stress his commitment to effectual, beneficent action. First must be recalled Ferguson's charge of treason against the Epicureans, a charge actuated precisely by their contemplative aloofness from the world of practical affairs. Secondly, it must be noted that Ferguson again and again insisted on the primacy of the Baconian motto that knowledge is power and on a pragmatic criterion for defining the scope of human knowledge, as well as the means to its attainment. Finally—and this is perhaps the most significant point—it must be borne in mind that Ferguson most frequently urged the contemplative attitude upon those who, according to his classical sources and his own convictions, were wholly incapable of it. That is to say, he counseled the poor and miserable, the mass of men, to disregard their external conditions and to give thought only to their own serenity of mind. This reveals that, whatever appeal the classical notion may have held for him as a final retreat, its basic function was ideological. In its main direction, Ferguson's work sought for practical efficacy, and in this respect it clearly failed.

In the final analysis, then, Ferguson proved unable to answer the questions posed at the very beginning of this chapter about the relationship between the virtuous man (a concept interpreted there as an ideal projection of his own role) and social reality. Despite his heroic efforts, Ferguson the intellectual was compelled to withdraw from the political sphere of effective actions into the private realm of contemplation, conversation, and intention. Just as his other withdrawals can be explained as the response to some ineluctable necessity, so this one—the most crucial of all because it represents an abandonment of the activist conception of virtue most congenial to the intellectual for the passivist one—can be seen to rest on unalterable fact. As an intellectual in his time, he was divorced from the main repositories of social power, and there was simply nothing that he could do.

But it would be absurd to equate the judgment that
Ferguson failed in his central task with a conclusion that his
was a contemptible or negligible achievement. It must first
be recalled that even the force of the necessities which
wrecked Ferguson's construction of a viable orientation to
practice was partly derived from his hatred of despotism as a
system destructive of all human integrity. At every crucial
point of his argument, he was faced with the conviction that
the only available alternative to acquiescent withdrawal was
a course of action involving grave risks of despotism, that the
only mode of power within the grasp of those not possessed
of it through the operation of the normal laws of social
development was one resting on force and fear. Given Ferguson's role and situation, his withdrawal from activism is at
least explicable in a manner consistent with, and perhaps
even an inevitable concomitant of, his humanistic commitments. Not even his abandonment of the intellectual's role
for those of ideologist and homilist makes him an easy target
for the contempt of those for whom such an abandonment
constitutes the greatest possible abomination. It must be
appreciated how deeply this fate was rooted in the logic of
his situation. At the risk of exaggeration, it can be said that
Ferguson's work and life manifest the unfolding of a tragic
destiny.

This characterization is certainly overdrawn. Ferguson
himself was, after all, no hero of tragic stature, and he lived
his life, in so far as can be seen, in chipper and cheerful
ignorance of the somber meanings ascribed here to his activities. But the issues here raised transcend the subjective
awareness of Adam Ferguson. If the basic thesis of the
present analysis is correct, if Ferguson can, indeed, serve as a
prototype of many modern intellectuals, then the conclusions here suggested may help to explain the undeniably
tragic career of frustration and betrayal displayed by the

history of so much of the modern intelligentsia. The paradox involved in viewing the optimistic professor as a tragic hero is, perhaps, no greater than that evinced by the contrast between modern intellectuals' sharp intelligence directed to high ideals and their fumbling and even vicious practices.[175] It is, however, not necessary to insist too strongly on this suggestion in order to show the significance of Ferguson's work.

Despite the ultimate inadequacy of his orientation as judged by its own criteria, Ferguson's orientation reveals the basic dilemmas confronting many modern intellectuals and foreshadows many of the approaches and solutions which have been proposed for them. Some of these have been pointed out in earlier chapters. Thus, it has been shown that Ferguson's struggles with technical philosophical problems were actuated by the conflict between his commitment to science and his commitment to the humanistic tradition. Then it was seen that the difficulties in his definition of virtue reflect his dual commitments to a notion of man as a striving, conquering creature and a notion of man as a tranquil being, harmoniously and lovingly related to his fellows and to nature. In summary of the foregoing examination of Ferguson's social and political ideas, it can now be noted that his inability to solve basic problems involving the division of labor, the commercial spirit of society, and the interested tenor of political life also rests upon conflicting commitments. He was torn between a conception of human activity as an expression of high vigor and ingenious power, and a view which stresses the richness, variety, and fullness of the active life: he could neither reject nor embrace specialization. Fluctuating between an image of society as a medium for securing individual satisfaction and physical well-being and an image of social life as a community devoted to the spiritual and cultural enhancement of hu-

man experience, he could neither damn nor bless industry
and trade. Finally, unable to choose between a conception
of the state as a guarantor of individual liberty and a conception of politics as a school for virtue, he could neither
abandon nor embrace the constitutional state. If one wishes
to denominate the first part of each of these antithetical
pairs as "modern" and all of the second ones as "classical,"
there can be no objection.[176] The present point is, however, that both sets of elements are included in the heritage
of the modern intelligentsia and that it has by no means
ever been demonstrated that the attempt to integrate both
is a mark either of ignorance or of depravity.

Two consequences may be drawn from a consideration of
Ferguson's dilemmas. The first is that, although they proved
to be insoluble, they were not fruitless. Many passages of his
analysis, when stripped of their verbal excrescences, are
found to contain insights not unworthy of comparison with
those of men generally acknowledged to be great. His attempt to reconcile his conflicting commitments produced a
body of social and political analysis which defines critical
problems and identifies significant characteristics in a way
which cannot be dismissed as meaningless or absurd. It is
true that he drew heavily on his predecessors; it is also true
that he frequently combined their observations into an interesting and suggestive whole, and that he considered, however inadequately, a wider range of problems than most.
Without seeking to exaggerate his capacities, then, it is
possible to consider Ferguson among the substantial contrib-
utors to modern understanding of social and political phenomena. This is true to a degree sufficient to raise the question of whether a social and political science not spurred by
the concerns and commitments which generated his thought
can, in fact, match the achievements of Ferguson and those
of his precursors, contemporaries, and successors who were,

like himself, intellectuals committed to a humanistic conception of man's dignity and integrity.[177]

In conclusion, then, it is necessary to return to the theme
of integrity. Whatever his inconsistencies, whatever his
compromises, whatever his failures, Ferguson never ceased
to portray a man of fundamental integrity; and it was to the
assertion of his integrity that Ferguson withdrew at the very
end of his attempt to resolve the problems inherent in his
role and circumstances. The peroration of his last book
opens with the following words:

> If we have not mistaken the interests of human nature,
> they consist more in the exercises of freedom, and in the
> pursuits of a liberal and beneficent soul, than in the posses-
> sion of mere tranquillity, or what is termed exemption
> from trouble. The trials of ability, which men mutually
> afford to one another in the collisions of a free society, are
> the lessons of a school which Providence has opened for
> mankind, and are well known to forward, instead of im-
> peding their progress in any valuable art, whether commer-
> cial, elegant, or political.

After extended praise of the "diffusion of political delibera-
tion and functions to the greatest extent that is consistent
with the wisdom of its administration," "party divisions,"
"freedom of conversation," it sums up "the argument relating to the felicity of nations . . . in these comprehensive though vague expressions":

> That the felicity of nations is proportioned to the degree in
> which every citizen is safe; and is most perfect where every
> ingenious or innocent effort of the human mind is en-
> couraged: where government devolves on the wise; and
> where the inoffensive though weak is secure.

But the closing words read: "Every one indeed is answerable
only for himself; and in preserving the integrity of one

citizen, does what is required of him for the happiness of the whole." [178]

This author's words cannot be dismissed as worthless antiques. The difficulties and uncertainties which they contain must be taken seriously by those whose own work is distinguished from that of Ferguson largely by the skill with which those same problems are concealed; the dilemmas which they reveal cannot be scorned by those who are not prepared to abandon commitments which they share with the wordy old Edinburgh professor.

1. Ferguson, *Essay on Civil Society*, p. 5.

2. *Ibid.*

3. Ferguson, *Institutes*, pp. 90–95; Ferguson, *Essay on Civil Society*, p. 16.

4. Ferguson, *Principles*, I, 121–22.

5. Ferguson, *Essay on Civil Society*, p. 23.

6. *Ibid.*, p. 19; see also Ferguson, *Institutes*, pp. 115–16, where Adam Smith's *Moral Sentiments* [sic] is cited as the authority for a similar reinterpretation of "self-interest."

7. Ferguson, *Essay on Civil Society*, p. 25.

8. *Ibid.*, p. 23.

9. *Ibid.*, p. 48.

10. *Ibid.*, p. 35.

11. Ferguson, *Principles*, II, 33.

12. The most striking affirmation of this viewpoint occurs in the following passage: "Without the rivalship of nations, and the practice of war, civil society itself could scarcely have found an object or a form. Mankind might have traded without any formal convention, but they cannot be safe without a national concert. The necessity of a public defense, has given rise to many departments of state, and the intellectual talents of men have found their busiest scene in wielding their national forces. To overawe or intimidate; or, when we cannot persuade with reason, to resist with fortitude, are the occupations which give its most animating exercise, and its greatest triumphs, to a vigorous mind; and he who has never struggled with his fellow creatures, is a stranger to half the sentiments of mankind" (Ferguson, *Essay on Civil Society*, pp. 35–36; see also *ibid.*, p. 154, where Ferguson wrote, "The frequent practice of war tends to strengthen the bands of society").

13. *Ibid.*, p. 47; Ferguson, *Institutes*, p. 95; *Principles*, I, 235.

14. Ferguson, *Principles*, I, 235.

15. *Ibid.*, p. 56; *ibid.*, II, 238–39.

16. *Ibid.*, I, 269.

17. *Ibid.*

18. *Ibid.*, p. 210.

19. Ferguson, *Essay on Civil Society*, p. 27.

20. Ferguson, *Principles*, I, 218.

21. Ferguson, *Essay on Civil Society*, pp. 27, 6–8; Ferguson, *Principles*, II, 411.

22. The anonymous reviewer of Small's biography, for example, stated that Ferguson "was a politician even more than a moralist" (in review of Small, *op. cit.*, p. 79).

23. Ferguson, *Institutes*, p. 284. Although the term "external" serves to qualify this statement, the qualification gains real significance only when combined with the passive view of virtue, and then, because mere externals are all unimportant, the whole statement becomes meaningless.

24. *Ibid.*, pp. 262–63. This passage, like the one last quoted, presents some difficulties to the interpreter. Bryson has argued that it must be understood to read, "the state of their [being in] society," and "the state of their [being in] communities" (Bryson, *Man and Society*, p. 39). Although this interpolation points up one side of Ferguson's study of society, the side which is presently under consideration, it also destroys Ferguson's ambiguity and therefore his meaning. As will be seen below, Ferguson did not usually claim for every society the beneficent effects he ascribed to society in general. The explanation and assessment of differing states of society was precisely one major objective of his writings.

25. Ferguson, *Essay on Civil Society*, p. 237; see also Ferguson, *Principles*, I, 265.

26. *Ibid.*, p. 266–67.

27. Adam Ferguson, *The History of the Progress and Termination of the Roman Republic* (Edinburgh: Bell and Bradfute, 1805), V, 77, 278.

28. Ferguson, *History*, V, 77; see also Unpublished Essays, "Of History and its appropriate Style," p. 7; but compare *ibid.*, pp. 8–9.

29. Ferguson, *History*, V, 75.

30. *Ibid.*, p. 74.

31. According to Ferguson, not even absolutist rule by those he considered the most virtuous men of all time could create a proper social setting for virtue. Needless to add, he denied that any progress of prosperity or order could compensate men for the loss of a social climate

conducive to goodness. He wrote: "The wisdom of Nerva gave rise to a succession which, in the persons of Trajan and the Antonines, formed a counterpart to the race of Tiberius, Caligula, Claudius, and Nero; and it must be admitted, that if a people could be happy by any other virtues than their own, there was a period in the history of this empire, during which the happiness of mankind may have been supposed complete. This however is but a fond and mistaken apprehension. A People may receive protection from the justice and humanity of a single man; but can receive independence, vigour, and peace of mind, only from their own" (*ibid.*, p. 418).

32. "Of History and its appropriate Style," Unpublished Essays, pp. 5–6.

33. In marveling over the Roman Empire's survival into the fifteenth century despite its corruption, Ferguson exclaimed: "So long was it before the lights of civil, political, and military wisdom, erected by the Roman commonwealth, though struck out by the Goths and Vandals in the West, and continually sinking in the East, were entirely extinguished" (*History*, V, 414).

34. Ferguson, *Essay on Civil Society*, p. 88.

35. *Ibid.*, p. 235; see also pp. 230–31.

36. *Ibid.*, pp. 28–29.

37. *Ibid.*, pp. 280, 285; see also p. 42.

38. *Ibid.*, p. 353.

39. *Ibid.*, p. 346. Even literary and scientific activities were, in Ferguson's view, afflicted with the prevailing disorder, and abilities were suppressed by an excessive emphasis on specialized knowledge and scholarship. See *ibid.*, pp. 45, 274.

40. *Ibid.*, pp. 84–85.

41. *Ibid.*, p. 414; see also p. 412 n. Ferguson's remarks on China appear particularly remarkable when contrasted with the enthusiasm for China widespread among his contemporaries. Cp. François Quesnay, *Le Despotisme de Chine* (Paris, 1767), translated and discussed in Lewis A. Maverick, *China, A Model for Europe* (San Antonio: Paul Anderson Co., 1946). For this reference, I am indebted to the research of a student, Miss Marianne Eaton.

42. *Essay on Civil Society*, p. 230.

43. *Ibid.*, p. 111.

44. *Ibid.*, p. 335.

45. *Ibid.*, p. 333.

46. *Ibid.*, pp. 392–93, 423.

47. *Ibid.*, pp. 319–20, 330, 350.

48. *Ibid.*, p. 343.

49. "Proper occasions alone operating on a raised and happy disposi-

tion, may produce [the virtuous man], whilst mere instruction may always find mankind at a loss to comprehend its meaning, or insensible to its dictates. The case, however, is not desperate, till we have formed our system of politics, as well as manners; till we have sold our freedom for titles, equipage, and distinctions; till we see no merit but prosperity and power, no disgrace but poverty and neglect. What charm of instruction can cure the mind that is tainted with this disorder? What syren voice can awaken a desire for freedom, that is held to be meanness, and a want of ambition? Or what persuasion can turn the grimace of politeness into a real sentiment of humanity and candour?" (*ibid.*, pp. 59–60).

50. *Ibid.*, pp. 187–88. In his later book, Ferguson reiterated this point in the following words: "Among the circumstances which lead in the progress and decline of nations, that of political situation may be justly reckoned among the first or most important. And in this the most favourable conjuncture is sometimes obtained, or the reverse is incurred, with perfect blindness to the future, or ignorance of the consequences which are likely to follow. The parties would always better themselves: But they are often driving they know not whither. Thus the Barons of England, in times of high feudal aristocracy, knew not that the charters which they extorted from their sovereign, were to become foundations of freedom to the people over whom they themselves wished to tyrannize. No more did the Roman people foresee, that the support they gave to Caesar, in reducing the Senate, was in effect to establish a military despotism, under which they themselves were to forfeit all the advantages of a free nation" (Ferguson, *Principles*, I, 314).

51. *Ibid.*, II, 291. The significance of this passage, as well as the following one, is underlined by their having been written during the French Revolution and published by Ferguson during the great anti-Jacobin hysteria in Britain (compare pp. 95 f.).

52. *Ibid.*, pp. 497–99.

53. *Ibid.*, I, 251.

54. *Ibid.*, II, 481–82.

55. *Ibid.*, I, 253–55.

56. Compare *ibid.*, pp. 301–4.

57. *Ibid.*, I, 200–201.

58. *Ibid.*, p. 194.

59. The only response which was always and everywhere out of the question for Ferguson was a withdrawal born, not of confident or resigned submission to a greater power, but of indifference. This was precisely the crime with which he charged the Epicureans and for which he castigated them as follows: "The Epicurean was a deserter from the cause of his fellow-creatures, and might justly be reckoned a traitor to the community of nature, of mankind, and even of his country, to which he owed his protection" (*Ibid.*, II, 5).

60. The following two summary statements of Ferguson's contributions to social theory (although they are both inclined to honor some dubious claims made in Ferguson's behalf) stem from the works of two reputable historians of sociological theory and may serve as a useful contrast and introduction to the present discussion. William C. Lehmann wrote in the introduction to his detailed survey of Ferguson as sociologist: "We rather count it sufficient to claim that Ferguson appreciated the fact and the meaning of society and brought it into the center of his field of vision and attention in a way that was certainly illuminating and we believe essentially new, and that he applied to its analysis a method that was at least remarkably realistic, critical, and essentially empirical; that he keenly appreciated the organic nature of society or the socio-historic process in its static and still more in its dynamic aspects, and treated it from a point of view that was at once psychological and historical; that as a result he presented a thoroughly evolutionistic analysis that at least deserves our attention; that he developed a concept of a division of labor in society in a way that would logically call for sociology as a science more comprehensive in its scope than the other social sciences; that he moved on a plane of humanistic or psycho-cultural interpretation that might still challenge many a writer in sociology today; and finally that he anticipates such specific theories as in particular the conflict theory of human society in a way that should alone give him a place in the history of social theory if not of sociology itself" (Lehmann, *op. cit.*, pp. 26–27). As if in response to Professor Lehmann's closing suggestion, Albert Salomon outlined Ferguson's sociological achievements in the following words: "Firstly, he anticipated Max Weber's discussion of the methodological problems: a) he studied the subjective elements in the use of documents and foreshadowed the critical method of Niebuhr in dealing with the mythology and religious foundations of primitive societies; b) he discovered the specific character of sociological generalizations as presenting a rational construction in abstractions, not reality.

"Secondly, he used the suggestions made by Thucydides and investigated the early history of the Greeks and Romans in the light of the discoveries of anthropology. . . .

"Thirdly, he anticipated problems of formal sociology with the repeated efforts to emphasize the relevance of size (population, territory) for the character of social groupings. He was aware that in positive or negative values, the optimum of social organizations may depend upon marginal situations.

"Fourthly, he anticipated Toynbee's category of 'challenge and response' with his thorough investigations of the conditions of great social accomplishments. Virtues are indispensable for establishing and maintaining wealth, power, and continuous improvements. And they come into existence only under the conditions of danger, pressure, and conflict.

"Fifthly, he developed the problems of the division of labor as interdependent with those of social stratification.

'Sixthly, he discarded the organic theory of history as cycle and suggested a spiral theory which made it possible to combine the unending continuity and interpenetration of civilizations with categories of corruption and decay as sociological generalizations.

"Seventhly, he prepared the way for the sociological analysis and description of historical processes and situations as the empirical science which made it possible to present the most comprehensive typology of human behavior patterns in social action as the self-realization of man. For this reason, he was eager to give an account of the advantages and disadvantages of progress in the diverse spheres of man as far as the completeness and happiness of man and society are concerned. In this respect he anticipated the work of Jacob Burckhardt. . . .

"Eighthly, he vigorously described the relevance of military virtues for perfect societies as the only guarantee for the maintenance and survival of progress in societies. He assumed that human perfection and social happiness were possible only if the political-philosophic and military-pragmatic virtues were not separated from each other.

"Ninthly, he traced the first outline for a doctrine of man on the basis of empirical investigations and the elaboration of types of social behavior which are recurrent in different situations and show the identity of human nature in its dynamic adjustments to a variety of situations. The inclinations of human nature remain the same; however, they look different in different situations. . . ."

In conclusion, Salomon states, "His work points out . . . the transformation of the science of the Law of Nature into a sociology of the social and historical process with the philosophic intent to reestablish a scientific knowledge of man" (Albert Salomon, "History of Sociology Abstracts," No. 4, pp. 5–6. The author is indebted to Professor Kurt H. Wolff for access to these interesting notes. Further discussion of some of the problems raised by both of these passages must be reserved for another place).

61. Ferguson, *Principles*, II, 418–19.

62. Ferguson, *Essay on Civil Society*, p. 15.

63. *Ibid.*, p. 38; see also Ferguson, *Principles*, I, 231–32.

64. *Ibid.*, p. 166.

65. Ferguson, *Institutes*, pp. 17–18; Ferguson, *Essay on Civil Society*, p. 182.

66. Ferguson, *Institutes*, p. 266.

67. Ferguson, *Essay on Civil Society*, p. 182.

68. Ferguson, *Principles*, I, 58.

69. Ferguson, *Essay on Civil Society*, p. 180. Ferguson here seems to be following David Hume's critique of Montesquieu (compare Hume, "Of National Character," in *Essays: Moral, Political and Literary*, ed. T. H. Green and T. H. Grose [2 vols.: London: Longmans Green and Co., 1882]).

70. Ferguson, *Essay on Civil Society*, pp. 167–68.

71. Ferguson argued: "The inquiry [into the original character of mankind] refers to a distant period, and every conclusion should build on the facts which are preserved for our use. Our method, notwithstanding, too frequently, is to rest the whole on conjecture; to impute every advantage of our nature to those arts which we ourselves possess; and to imagine, that a mere negation of all our virtues is a sufficient description of man in his original state. We are ourselves the supposed standards of politeness and civilization; and where our features do not appear, we apprehend, that there is nothing which deserves to be known. But it is probable that here, as in many other cases, we are ill qualified, from our supposed knowledge of causes, to prognosticate effects, or to determine what must have been the properties and operations, even of our own nature, in the absence of those circumstances in which we have seen it engaged" (*ibid.*, p. 114).

72. *Ibid.*, p. 129.

73. The following passages describe Ferguson's method of drawing historical inferences. One valuable source of information, he maintained, is the legend and lore of any society. He wrote: "It were absurd to quote the fable of the Illiad or the Odyssey, the legends of Hercules, Theseus, or Oedipus, as authorities in matter of fact relating to the history of mankind; but they may, with great justice be cited to ascertain what were the conceptions and sentiments of the age in which they were composed, or to characterize the genius of that people, with whose imaginations they were blended, and by whom they were fondly rehearsed and admired. In this manner fiction may be admitted to vouch for the genius of nations, while history has nothing to offer that is intitled to credit" (*ibid.*, pp. 116–17). In his history of Rome, he extended this argument more daringly to apply also to the writings of Livy and other sources of information about the Roman monarchy and even the early republic (Ferguson, *History*, I, 77 n.). Another part of his historical method is illuminated in the following discussion of Roman prehistory: "That the Roman state was originally a small one, and came by degrees to its greatness, cannot be doubted. So much we may safely admit on the general analogy of human affairs, or infer, from the continuation and recent marks of a progress which this people were making, after they became an object of observation to other nations, or began to keep records of their own: That they had been as an assemblage of herdsmen and warriors, ignorant of letters, of money, and of commercial arts, inured to depredation and violence, and subsisting chiefly by the produce of their own herds, and the spoils of their enemies, may be safely admitted; because we find them, in the most authentic parts of their story, yet busy in supplying these defects, and coming forward in the same direction, and consequently proceeding from the same origin, with other rude nations . . ." (*ibid.*, I, 8).

74. Ferguson, *Institutes*, p. 28.

75. Ferguson, *Essay on Civil Society*, p. 123.

76. *Ibid.*, p. 127.

77. *Ibid.*, pp. 136–37; see also Ferguson, *History*, I, 240–41. For a contrary view of the influence of "superstitions" and "rites," however, compare *ibid.*, p. 118, for the case of Carthaginian habits and *ibid.*, p. 418 n., for a comment on Christianity.

78. Ferguson, *Essay on Civil Society*, pp. 133–34.

79. Ferguson remarked: "Mankind, in very early ages of society, learn to covet riches, and to admire distinction; they have avarice and ambition, and are occasionally led by these passions to depredation and conquest: but in their ordinary conduct, are guided and restrained by different motives; by sloth, or intemperance; by personal attachments, or personal animosities; which mislead from the attention to interest" (*ibid.*, p. 191).

80. *Ibid.*, p. 146.

81. He wrote: "With all these infirmities, vices, or respectable qualities, belonging to the human species in its rudest state; the love of society, friendship, and public affection, penetration, eloquence, and courage, appear to have been its original properties, not the subsequent effects of device or invention. If mankind are qualified to improve their manners, the materials to be improved were furnished by nature; and the effect of this improvement is not to inspire the sentiments of tenderness or generosity, nor to bestow the principal constituents of a respectable character, but to obviate the casual abuses of passion; and to prevent a mind, which feels the best dispositions in their greatest force, from being at times likewise the sport of brutal appetite and of ungovernable violence" (*ibid.*, p. 143).

82. *Ibid.*, pp. 123–24.

83. *Ibid.*, p. 258.

84. *Ibid.*, p. 149.

85. See, e.g., *ibid.*, p. 17.

86. Ferguson, *Institutes*, pp. 28–29.

87. *Ibid.*, p. 30.

88. Ferguson, *Essay on Civil Society*, p. 276.

89. *Ibid.*, p. 277; see also Ferguson, *Institutes*, pp. 31–32; Ferguson, *Principles*, II, 423.

90. *Ibid.*, p. 424.

91. Ferguson, *Essay on Civil Society*, p. 282.

92. *Loc. cit.*

93. The few passages in which Ferguson tended to equate the roles assigned in the division of labor with the distribution of natural talents occur in discussions seeking to justify this arrangement (*ibid.*, pp. 94–95, 280). See also Ferguson, *Principles*, I, 250–51.

94. Ferguson, *Essay on Civil Society*, p. 147.

95. Having described some of the characteristics of the Roman

emperors, Ferguson set forth the following interesting note: "These extremes scarcely gain credit with the modern reader, as they are so much beyond what his own experience or observation can parallel. Nero seems to have been a brute of some mischievous kind, Aurelius of an order superior to man; and these prodigies, whether in the extreme of good or evil, exhibited, amidst the ruins of the Roman republic, are no longer to be found. Individuals were then formed on their specific dispositions to wisdom or folly. In latter times, they are more cast in a general mould, which gives a certain form independent of the materials. Religion, fashion, and manners, prescribe more of the actions of men, or mark a deeper track in which men are constrained to move. The maxims of a Christian and a Gentleman, the remains of what men were taught by those maxims in the days of chivalry, pervade every rank, have some effect in places of the least restraint; and if they do not inspire decency of character, at least awe the profligate with the fear of contempt from which even the most powerful are not secure. Insomuch that if human nature wants the force to produce an Aurelius or a Trajan, it is not so much exposed to the infamies of a Domitian or a Nero" (Ferguson, *History*, V, 418 n.). For an extension of this argument, citing the influence of chivalry on the "law of nations" as well as domestic manners and displaying the same touch of regret as the preceding passage, see Ferguson, *Essay on Civil Society*, p. 311.

96. Ferguson, *Principles*, I, 393. The passage from which this phrase is drawn is actually a sketch of the history of literary art showing that various styles of art, too, correspond to differing stages of social development. Ferguson wrote: "The scenery of heroic action is to be found in the rudest times; in such times, danger is encountered with courage, friendship preserved with fidelity and ardent affection. Wrongs are resented with extreme animosity. If a genius be found that is fit to seize the sublime in human character, he will not need the leading of former examples to engage him in the relation of actions, or the description of objects, already brought home to his feelings in the examples of that life in which he himself is engaged. The circumstances that may induce men to become poets or artists of any other description upon a lower pitch of conception or sentiment, and with the merit of correctness and elegance, rather than that of magnificance and elevation, may come afterwards, and in the rear of many other arts, according as they are attended with the advantages that give to men of ingenuity leisure from the pressing cares of human life, and give to the people in general a relish for the entertainments provided for minds otherwise vacant and unemployed. Such circumstances we may conceive to arise from the distinctions of rank and profession, which accompany a certain state of the commercial arts; from the security which regular governments bestow, and the other accompanyments of what are commonly termed the polite ages of mankind, characterized by mildness of manners, and abounding at once in the practice of commercial, literary arts of every sort" (*ibid.*, pp.

292–93). Elsewhere, Ferguson made another observation on the relationship between social circumstances and literary style; he remarked: "In rude ages men are not separated by distinctions of rank or profession. They live in one manner, and speak one dialect. The bard is not to chuse his expression among the singular accents of different conditions" (*ibid.*, p. 267).

97. *Ibid.*, I, 252.

98. *Ibid.*, pp. 247–50.

99. *Ibid.*, II, 268.

100. *Ibid.*, p. 269.

101. *Ibid.*, I, 239; see also p. 256.

102. Ferguson, *Essay on Civil Society*, p. 17.

103. *Ibid.*, p. 152.

104. *Ibid.*, p. 207.

105. Ferguson, *Principles*, II, 461. Later in the same discussion Ferguson offered the following definition for liberty: "Liberty consists in the security of the citizen against every enemy, whether foreign or domestic, public or private, from whom, without any provision being made for his defence, he might be exposed to wrong or oppression of any sort: And the first requisite, it should seem, towards obtaining this security, is the existence of an effective government to wield the strength of the community against foreign enemies, and to repress the commission of wrongs at home . . ." (*ibid.*, p. 465).

106. Ferguson, *Essay on Civil Society*, pp. 401–2. Ferguson also distinguished the several phases in the development of law when he commented: "Law in some instances is an article of custom, and a part in the manners of the people to whom it relates. In other instances, it is the will of the powerful, requiring compliance on the part of the subject. And in constitutions provided for the freedom of the people, it is the deliberate convention of parties, respecting the terms on which they are to live in society, and the securities they are to enjoy for their persons and property" (Ferguson, *Principles*, I, 302).

107. *Ibid.*, II, 286.

108. At the very outset of his comments on political forms, Ferguson exclaimed: "When I recollect what the President Montesquieu has written, I am at a loss to tell, why I should treat of human affairs: but I am instigated by my reflections, and my sentiments; and I may utter them more to the comprehension of ordinary capacities, because I am more on the level of ordinary men. . . . In his writings will be found not only the original of what I am now, for the sake of order to copy from him, but likewise probably the source of many observations, which, in different places, I may, under the belief of invention, have repeated, without quoting their author" (Ferguson, *Essay on Civil Society*, p. 98). It has not been considered necessary, in the present study, to call attention to Ferguson's dependence on Montesquieu (as

well as other writers, especially Hume) on the occasion of every one of innumerable illustrations for two reasons. In the first place, since no great claims for originality have been made, it is not necessary to specify contrary instances. In the second place, and this is the most important reason, the present study seeks to explicate the significance of Ferguson's peculiar combination of ideas in relationship to his role and situation. Ferguson himself offered, in the following words, a fair statement of the assumptions actuating this procedure: "This much however may be said with assurance, that although the Romans and the modern literature flavour alike of the Greek original, yet mankind in either instances would not have drank [sic] of this fountain, unless they have been hastening to open springs of their own" (ibid., p. 261).

109. Ibid., p. 94.

110. See ibid., pp. 102–7. Since Ferguson was convinced that most of the nations of Europe were monarchies in Montesquieu's sense and since Montesquieu had affirmed the appropriateness of such monarchies to the conditions of his time, it is interesting to note that, in concluding his discussion of the monarchical form, Ferguson expressed considerable fear about the future of European monarchies and—inferentially—dissented from the judgment of his mentor. He wrote: "If those principles of honour which save the individual from servility in his own person, or from becoming an engine of oppression in the hands of another, should fail; if they should give way to the maxims of commerce, to the refinements of a supposed philosophy [addressed to the Enlightenment philosophers?], or to the misplaced ardours of a republican spirit [directed at Rousseau?]; if they are betrayed by the cowardice of subjects, or subdued by the ambition of princes; what must become of the nations of Europe?" (ibid., p. 107). If Ferguson was indeed convinced that the progress of advanced societies drove them irresistibly toward ever greater commercialization, then his apprehensions about the future of Europe—especially France—must have been great indeed. This may help to account for the mildness of his reaction to the French Revolution.

111. Ferguson, Institutes, p. 295.

112. Ferguson, Essay on Civil Society, p. 101.

113. Ibid., p. 151.

114. Ferguson, History, I, 19–20; compare Charles Secondat, Baron de Montesquieu, Considerations on the Causes of the Grandeur and Decadence of the Romans, trans. Jehu Baker (New York: D. Appleton and Co., 1882), esp. pp. 180–87.

115. In this context, it is significant (if also quite usual) that, next to Rome, Ferguson's favorite example of a democratic state was Sparta, not Athens. See, e.g., Ferguson, Institutes, p. 316; Ferguson, Essay on Civil Society, pp. 242–45.

116. Compare Ferguson's analysis of the post-Revolutionary

French government, *supra*, pp. 80–81 n. 63. The following passage, in which Ferguson described the intensification of class conflict in Rome—although it does not state explicitly that Rome was compelled to expand in order to maintain itself—does reveal Ferguson's conviction that the consequence of expansion inevitably precluded democracy. When this discussion is juxtaposed to the passage about the first Roman revolution, the paradoxical conclusion suggested in the text is strongly supported. Ferguson wrote: "In this time of suspence, the controversy began to divide the colonies and free cities of Italy, and was warmly agitated wherever the citizens had extended their property. The rich and the poor took opposite sides. They collected their arguments, and mustered their strength. The first had recourse to the topics that are commonly urged on the side of prescription, urging that in some cases, they had possessed their estates from time immemorial. . . . The poor, on the contrary, pleaded their own indigence and their merits; urged that they were no longer in a capacity to fill the station of Roman citizens or freemen, nor in a condition to settle families or to rear children, the future hopes of the commonwealth: that no private person could plead immemorial possession of lands which had been acquired for the public. . . . This mode of reasoning appears plausible; but it is dangerous to adopt by halves even reason itself. If it were reasonable that every Roman citizen should have an equal share of the conquered lands, it was still more reasonable that the original proprietors, from whom these lands had been unjustly taken, should have them restored. If, in this, the maxim of reason and justice had been observed, Rome would have been still a small community, and might have acted safely on the principles of equality, which are suited to a small republic. But the Romans, becoming sovereigns of a great and extensive territory, must adopt the disparities, and submit to the subordinations, which mankind in such situations universally have found natural, and even necessary, to their government" (Ferguson, *History*, I, 394–96; see also Ferguson, *Essay on Civil Society*, p. 417).

117. *Ibid.*, pp. 100–101.

118. *Ibid.*, pp. 286–87. It is impossible to take seriously Ferguson's frequent hesitancy to put his pronouncements in unequivocal terms. Thus, in the second paragraph here quoted, the qualified phrasing of the first sentence is wholly incompatible with the firmness of the conclusion drawn. The principle of interpretation followed here considers the meaning of the passage in its entirety rather than weighing each sentence in isolation. Unless qualifications are clearly intended and their implications pursued, Ferguson's circumlocutions will be treated as precisely what they are: manifestations of a poor style.

119. The following excerpt, drawn from Ferguson's Roman history, shows that existing patterns of opinion tend, in his view, to defy change even when that change is appropriate to changed social conditions and when the alternatives are chaos and despotism. This underlines the forcefulness with which he denied the possibility of

altering political forms to suit some abstract principle when social conditions and social habits unite to support the existing order. Ferguson wrote: "The Roman republic had, for some time, subsisted in a very disorderly state; citizens having dominion over many other nations, scarcely admitted any species of government among themselves. The inhabitants of Rome, assuming the prerogatives of a collective body, of which the members now not only extended all over Italy, but were dispersed throughout the empire, generally assembled in tumults, whose proceedings, at every convulsion, nothing but force could regulate or control; accordingly, the immediate prospect was that of a government of force, either in the hands of a multitude that could not be resisted, or in the hands of those by whom such disorders had been suppressed. All who wished to preserve the republic, endeavoured to extend the ordinary prerogatives of the Senate, and to prevent, as much as possible, these ill constituted assemblies of the people from deliberating on matters of State; and it might, no doubt, have been still better for the empire, if the spirit of legal monarchy could at once have been infused into every part of the commonwealth; or if, without further pangs or convulsions, the authority of a prince, tempered with that of a Senate, had been firmly established. But men do not at once change their habits and opinions, nor yield their own pretensions upon speculative notions of what is suited to the state of their age or country. Caesar aspired to dominion in order to gratify his personal vanity, not to correct the political errors of the times; and his contemporaries, born to the rights of citizens, still contended for personal independence and equal pretensions to power, however impossible it might be for the future to preserve any species of republic among such a people, or at the head of such an empire" (Ferguson, *History*, IV, 139–40; see also Ferguson, *Institutes*, p. 297). When it is recalled that the habits which, according to Ferguson, precluded timely change in Rome are precisely those which Ferguson most virtuous, it becomes even more clear that, for Ferguson, the destruction of the Roman republic was a paradoxical—and even genuinely tragic—event. It is not only true that, in his view, the military progress which underlay Roman virtue was doomed to destroy the conditions under which virtue could integrate Roman society, but also that the virtue which remained among the best men in the new circumstances contributed materially to Rome's failure to solve its new problems in time to avert despotism.

120. Ferguson, *Essay on Civil Society*, p. 204.

121. Ferguson, *Institutes*, pp. 296–97.

122. Ferguson, *Essay on Civil Society*, pp. 102, 202–3.

123. Ferguson, *Principles*, I, 264.

124. Ferguson wrote: "Where the citizens of any free community are of different orders, each order has a peculiar set of claims and pretensions; relatively to the other members of the state, it is a party; relatively to the differences of interest among its own members, it may

admit of numberless subdivisions. But in every state there are two interests very readily apprehended; that of a prince and his adherents, that of a nobility, or of any temporary faction, opposed to the people" (Ferguson, *Essay on Civil Society,* pp. 248–49). This description differs slightly from that presented in the text, in that the nobles are assimilated to the king; elsewhere, however, Ferguson made it clear that he envisioned a tripartite division as well.

125. Ferguson stated the matter in the following words: "In governments properly mixed, the popular interest, finding a counterpoise in that of the prince or of the nobles, a balance is actually established between them, in which the public freedom and the public order are made to consist. From some such casual arrangement of different interests, all the varieties of mixed government proceed; and on the degree of consideration which every separate interest can procure to itself, depends the equity of the laws they enact, and the necessity they are able to impose, of adhering strictly to the terms of law in its execution" (*ibid.,* p. 252).

126. *Ibid.,* p. 253.

127. He explained this in the following words: "Amidst the contentions of party, the interests of the public, even the maxims of justice and candour, are sometimes forgotten; and yet those fatal consequences which such a measure of corruption seems to portend, do not unavoidably follow. The public interest is often secure, not because individuals are disposed to regard it as the end of their conduct but because each, in his place, is determined to preserve his own. Liberty is maintained by the continued differences and oppositions of numbers, not by their concurring zeal in behalf of equitable government. In free states, therefore, the wisest laws are never, perhaps, dictated by the interest and spirit of any order of men: they are moved, they are opposed, or amended, by different hands; and come at last to express that medium and composition which contending parties have forced one another to adopt" (*ibid.,* p. 196).

128. Ferguson explained: "But under the simplest governments of a different sort, whether aristocracy or monarchy, there is a necessity for law, and there are a variety of interests to be adjusted in framing every statute. The sovereign wishes to give stability and order to administration, by express and promulgated rules. The subject wishes to know the conditions and limits of his duty. He acquiesces, or he revolts, according as the terms on which he is made to live with the sovereign, or with his fellow-subjects, are, or are not, consistent with the sense of his rights" (*ibid.,* p. 253).

129. The second of these advantages is particularly valuable in advanced commercial societies because "when interest prevails in every breast, the sovereign and his party cannot escape the infection: he employs the force with which he is intrusted, to turn his people into a property, and to command their possessions for his profit or his pleasure. If riches are by any people made the standard of good and of

evil, let them beware of the powers they intrust to their prince"
(*ibid.*, pp. 156–57).

130. Ferguson remarked: "It is the nature of human things to
advance in accumulating the good or evil to which they tend. And
there is ever accordingly either a progress or a decline in human
affairs" (Ferguson, *History*, III, 152; see also Ferguson, *Essay on Civil
Society*, p. 321; Ferguson, *Principles*, I, 194–95).

131. Ferguson, *Essay on Civil Society*, pp. 427–28. Of the two
qualifications stated in the first sentence, the second is the dubious
one. The first one clearly reflects Ferguson's conviction that external
threats can knot together the social bonds of any society and invigorate
its spirit. The second one, however, runs counter to the general tenor
of the passage, which certainly suggests that despotism, once established, cannot be eliminated—a suggestion which is bolstered in other
parts of Ferguson's text as well. See, e.g., the passage cited earlier, in
which Ferguson likened the despotic state to a Hobbesian "state of
nature" (*ibid.*, pp. 110–11). A few other passages, on the other hand,
seem to support the implication embedded in the qualification: viz., its
corruption through force of will (Ferguson, *Principles*, II, 235, 417).
The question is not of first importance, although it is of some interest
to discover whether Ferguson considered despotism to be a remediable
condition. The best answer would appear to be that he normally did
not believe that it can be overcome, except where the despotic forms
are newly established and the basic integrity of the social order is still
intact.

132. Ferguson did not argue that every despotism arises from the
failure to solve problems which are inherently soluble. Some, in his
view, are based on irresistible physical factors—the case with most
non-progressive nations. Others result from unfortunate combinations of
physical and social factors, as, for example, Ferguson suggested in the
following passage: "It were happy for the human race, when governed
by interest, and not governed by laws, that being split into nations of a
moderate extent, they found in every canton some natural bar to its
further enlargement, and met with occupation enough in maintaining
their independence, without being able to extend their dominion.
There is not a disparity of rank, among men in rude ages, sufficient to
give their communities the form of legal monarchy; and in a territory
of considerable extent, when united under one head, the warlike and
turbulent spirit of its inhabitants seems to require the bridle of
despotism and military force" (Ferguson, *Essay on Civil Society*, p.
157). Ferguson never explained whether he believed that such necessary
despotisms are also incompetent to maintain the social order for an extended period of time. Still other despotisms (like that of Rome) result
when a society is trapped in some peculiar variety of social progress.

133. In expressing this distrust, Ferguson warned: "The best constitutions of governments are attended with inconvenience; and the
exercise of liberty may, on many occasions, give rise to complaints.
When we are intent on reforming abuses, the abuses of freedom may

lead us to incroach on the subject from which they are supposed to arise. Despotism itself has certain advantages, or at least, in times of civility and moderation, may proceed with so little offence, as to give no public alarm. These circumstances may lead mankind, in the very spirit of reformation, or by mere inattention, to apply or to admit of dangerous innovations in the state of their policy" (*ibid.*, p. 415).

134. *Ibid.*, pp. 219–20. In a note to a comparable passage occurring in his later work, Ferguson referred his readers to Adam Smith's *Wealth of Nations* (Ferguson, *Principles*, II, 427).

135. Ferguson, *Essay on Civil Society*, pp. 241–48. For further arguments asserting the impossibility of using law to revert to an irrevocably lost state of simplicity and equality, see Ferguson, *History*, I, 374–75, 390–91; for an argument against any attempt to legislate against "usury," see *ibid.*, IV, 305.

136. Ferguson, *Principles*, II, 422. This statement is particularly interesting for two reasons. First, it maintains that Roman democracy and equality presupposed slavery—a notable qualification of the praise which Ferguson normally bestowed on them. Secondly, it tends to make inequality of wealth a universally necessary phenomenon, instead of one bound up with a certain stage of historical development. The extent to which this was, in fact, Ferguson's later judgment is indicated by the following passage, which immediately precedes the one quoted above: "The source of supply which nature has provided for man, in any given situation of climate or soil, is labour. . . . The wealth of the citizen is measurable by the quantity of labour he can employ. If he can command the labour of others, he may dispense with his own; but, to enable one person to obtain the labour of others, it is necessary that the one should be able to pay the hire of that labour; and that the other should be in need to receive that hire. If all men were equally rich, every one might be willing to pay the hire of the labour, while no one would be willing to labour for hire; But as labour is necessary to supply the consumptions of life, on the supposition of equal riches, every one would be reduced to labour for himself; and thus a supposed equality would reduce the fortune of every person to the fruits merely of his own labour, and in fact would be to render every person alike and equally poor" (*ibid.*).

137. Not surprisingly, Ferguson was also prepared to defend the remaining privileges accorded to men of high birth. In a statement wholly consistent with his interpretation of modern subordination and habituation, he wrote: "Families, who have long occupied the highest places in the ranks of society, alarmed at the intrusion of those who would partake in their state, endeavour to set a bar in the way of more recent pretensions, by contending for birth as necessary to constitute rank. And we may observe, by the way, that it is perhaps fortunate for mankind that any thing is devised to prevent estimation from becoming the appendage of mere riches alone. Persons born on a certain elevation if disposed to worthy pursuits, are more likely to receive impressions and to entertain sentiments becoming their station,

than they who have recently arrived at their supposed distinction by
sordid or mercenary arts" (*ibid.*, I, 245).

138. Ferguson, *Essay on Civil Society*, p. 88.

139. Ferguson, *Principles*, II, 418–19; see also Ferguson, *History*,
III, 212.

140. Ferguson indicated the kinds of differences he had in mind
when he wrote: "The members of a republic, and the subject of a
monarchy must differ; because they have different parts assigned to
them by the forms of their country: the one destined to live with his
equals, or to contend, by his personal talents and character, for pre-
eminence; the other, born to a determinate station, where any pretence
of equality creates a confusion, and where nought but precedence is
studied. . . . The republican must act in the state, to sustain his
pretensions; he must join a party, in order to be safe; he must lead one
in order to be great. The subject of a monarchy refers to his birth for
the honour he claims; he waits on a court, to shew his importance;
and holds out the ensigns of dependence and favour, to gain him
esteem with the public" (Ferguson, *Essay on Civil Society*, pp.
291–92). For the development of the distinction between "political
character" and "moral character" and for a lengthy survey of the
different types of "manners" appropriate to differing constitutions, see
Ferguson, *Principles*, II, 413–15. To indicate how far Ferguson was
prepared to have political character depart from his description of
virtue, the following excerpt may suffice: "Under monarchies,
whether absolute or fixed, the scale of subordination may be further
extended; or the extremes of high and low much further removed
from each other than they are in republics of any sort. . . . Under
such institutions, accordingly, equality may be altogether unknown;
the habit of individuals may be in every instance either to yield or to
assume superiority. And these habits of subordination, or precedence,
or deference, are necessary to give the people their value in the
different ranks they are destined to hold" (*ibid.*, p. 416). Compare
elsewhere where some of these passages are cited in another connection without reference to Ferguson's distinction between political
and moral character. This is believed to have been permissible because, in the last analysis, the distinction does not hold; i.e., it cannot
safeguard Ferguson's urgings to private virtue from the corrosive effects
of the concerns and attitudes endorsed in this discussion. No one can
be, at the same time, a man actuated by virtue in any of Ferguson's
primary senses and a man motivated by the considerations Ferguson
deemed appropriate, for example, to the subject of an absolute monarch.

141. Ferguson, *Essay on Civil Society*, p. 398.

142. *Ibid.*, pp. 404–5. More strikingly he asserted: "The history of
England, and of every free country, abounds with the example of
statutes enacted when the people or their representatives assembled,
but never executed when the crown or the executive was left to itself.

The most equitable laws on paper are consistent with the utmost despotism in administration" (*ibid.*, p. 255).

143. Ferguson, *Principles*, II, 492–93. The last sentence reflects a basic doubt whether such an institution will or can be established in his own time, a doubt whose significance will be made clearer below.

144. It should, however, be added that Ferguson was also concerned with the proper conduct of foreign policy and that he incorporated much of his discussion of the means requisite to the maintenance of commerce and national character under the general heading of population policy. Moreover, he did devote some space to a discussion of various systems of taxation. But, except for some comments in support of a balance-of-power foreign policy, none of the other topics yield any information important for present purposes; and the summary offered in the text presents all of his key counsels.

145. *Ibid.*, II, 144; see also 146.

146. *Ibid.*, p. 220. It is interesting to compare this argument, which seems to base man's obligations on nature's nurturing care, with Ferguson's general denial that a right to command can be founded on unsolicited benefits. He wrote: "As to . . . the right to command; if it be asked whether this may not result from labour? We must answer in the negative; for although one person may have taken pains to qualify another for the performance of some particular service; yet we must contend, that no right to his service can be founded on this plea. Labour employed by one on the person of another, without his consent, may be an injury, and cannot be the foundation of any right" (*ibid.*, pp. 209–10).

147. *Ibid.*, I, 257.

148. *Ibid.*, II, 180.

149. Ferguson, *Essay on Civil Society*, p. 96.

150. Ferguson, *Principles*, II, 318; see also p. 180.

151. The concessions which Ferguson made to his more general view of the relationship between virtue and social activity, in the second paragraph of the quoted passage, deserve further consideration—and this will be offered below—particularly in light of Ferguson's beliefs about the relativity of political characters.

152. The connection between the harmonistic assumption ultimately underlying Ferguson's passivism and his defense of the "rule of law" is suggested in the following passage: "It is congenial to the nature of intelligent being that the scene in which he is to act should be governed by fixed and determinate laws, either obvious, or scrutable by the faculties with which he is furnished. Such accordingly is the scene prepared for man in the system of nature. It is also essential to the liberties of the people, that their rights should be defined in well known and permanent regulations, from which the citizen may know his condition without consulting the caprice or uncertain will of any person whatever" (*ibid.*, II, 476–77).

153. *Ibid.*, pp. 184–85.

154. *Ibid.*, II, 198–253 *passim*; Ferguson, *Institutes*, pp. 195–222 *passim*.

155. David Hume, *A Treatise of Human Nature*, ed. L. A. Selby-Bigge (Oxford: Oxford University Press, 1888), pp. 49–92; Hume, *Essays*, I, 443–60; compare Hume, *Enquiries*, p. 306.

156. Ferguson, *Principles*, I, 462.

157. *Ibid.*, pp. 463–65. Unlike the inequality of property, the institution of slavery can never be consistent with original rights. Ferguson asserted: "[A] slave, according to the definition adopted, where the institution of slavery took place, and agreeably to the practice of purchase and sale, established in the market of slaves is considered as a thing, and not as a person. The supposition is impossible, and cannot be realized by the consent of any party, even relating to himself. He may consent to do what another commands, within the limits of possibility; but must continue to be a person, having original if not acquired rights, and inspired by nature with a disposition to revolt, whenever he is galled with the sense of insufferable injury or wrong" (*ibid.*, p. 243). To grasp the full significance of this point for Ferguson's self-consolation about the irretrievable loss of classical democracy, compare *supra*, pp. 197 f.

158. The passage cited above to illustrate Ferguson's argument on the right to resist wrong continues as follows: "But will this consideration which confirms the title to sovereignty, where it is exercised by the society in its collective capacity, or by those to whom the powers of the whole are committed, likewise support the claim to dominion, wherever it is casually lodged, or even where it is only maintained by force? This question may be sufficiently answered, by observing, that a right to do justice, and to do good, is competent to every individual or order of men; and that the exercise of this right has no limits but in the defect of power" (Ferguson, *Essay on Civil Society*, p. 96).

159. Ferguson, *Principles*, II, 240.

160. *Ibid.*, pp. 245–46.

161. See *ibid.*, II, 272–73.

162. *Ibid.*, II, 233.

163. *Ibid.*, p. 235.

164. See *supra*, pp. 213 f.

165. This does not mean that mixed monarchies rest completely on explicit consent manifested in elections. In the first place, such consent by majority rule cannot, in itself, bind minorities. The rule of the majority, too, ultimately rests on power; its right can only be ascribed to a tacit contract (Ferguson, *Principles*, I, 263). Secondly, no modern state can, in Ferguson's view, or ought to extend the suffrage to all; its authority over disenfranchised inhabitants, however, cannot be questioned. He wrote: "In modern Europe, we are happily every where rid

of that distinction of free man and slave, which in antient times
excluded so many of the human species at once from any means of
defending themselves, in forming the laws to which they were
subject. But even here, and where the spirit of political establishment
is most favourable to public liberty, there are still considerable exclusions from the political meetings of the people, whether for police or
election. . . . In the first attempts of the French Revolution to
equalize the rights of man, a certain though very small census was
required to entitle the citizen to vote at elections. In subsequent
appointment this census was dropped; but still those who are to be
governed by the law exercise their discretion, and menial servants are
excluded. In Great Britain, a certain census * is required, together with
some circumstances of freehold and burgess qualification (*Distinctions
of rank, for the most part, are taken from birth or property; and we may
censure the rule, but cannot reverse it. It is even fortunate for mankind
that a foundation for subordination is laid, too obvious to be overlooked
by the dullest of men, or by those who stand most in need of being
governed. But, though property sometimes overpowers both ability and
every other merit, yet there are occasions in which it must give way to
either. At elections and country meetings, men of fortune predominate;
but armies are commanded, and states are governed by men of
ability.). . . . But, notwithstanding these exclusions, the liberty of
the subject is more secure perhaps than it has ever been under any
other human establishment. And if any one plead that, being excluded from a vote at elections, he is not bound by the laws to which
the people assent by representation, his plea may be admitted, and he
is at liberty to withdraw from the influence of these laws; But while
he remains within the precincts to which they extend, and continues
to take the benefit of them, he is not at liberty to counteract or to
disturb the order of things established" (*ibid.*, II, 472–73).

166. In some places, in fact, he did not consider Rome as a
democratic republic at all, characterizing it, rather, as a "mixed republic" with qualities closely akin to a mixed monarchy. See, e.g., Ferguson, *Essay on Civil Society*, pp. 249–50; Ferguson, *Institutes*, p. 296;
Ferguson, *History*, I, 390–91. Although the precedent for such a
designation dates back to Ferguson's favorite Roman authors, Polybius
and Cicero, and although it may therefore appear surprising that
Ferguson did not employ this designation throughout, it must nevertheless be insisted that Ferguson normally and usually (as is borne
out by numerous citations offered above) viewed Rome as the model of
a democratic republic; the revised designation occurs at only a few
places, and then never in an unambiguous way. The basic spirit of the
republic was, for him, a virtue based on equality; and the crisis of the
republic appeared to him basically as a crisis of equality.

167. Ferguson stressed the importance of this proposal in the
following words: "It is difficult to tell how long the decay of states
might be suspended by the cultivation of arts on which their real
felicity and strength depend; by cultivating in the higher ranks those
talents for the council and the field, which cannot, without great

disadvantage, be separated; and in the body of a people, that zeal for their country, and that military character, which enables them to take a share in defending its rights" (Ferguson, *Essay on Civil Society*, p. 348).

168. As the following passage shows, he did not believe this to be possible even in the unlikely event of a viable democratic constitution: "If popular assemblies assume every function of government . . . the public is exposed to manifold inconveniences; and popular governments would, of all others, be the most subject to errors in administration, and to weakness in the execution of public measures. To avoid these disadvantages, the people are always contented to delegate part of their powers. They establish a senate to debate, and to prepare, if not to determine, questions that are brought to the collective body for a final resolution. They commit the executive power to some council of this sort, or to a magistrate who presides in their meetings. Under the use of this necessary and common expedient, even while democratical forms are most carefully guarded, there is one part of the few, another of the many. One attacks, the other defends; and they are both ready to assume in their turns" (*ibid.*, pp. 249–50).

169. *Ibid.*, p. 88.

170. See *ibid.*, pp. 134, 256, 284–85, and 408–10.

171. *Ibid.*, pp. 92, 222–23, 340–41, 345.

172. Charles Secondat, Baron de Montesquieu, *The Spirit of the Laws*, trans. Thomas Nugent, ed. Franz L. Neumann (New York: Hafner Publishing Co., 1949), p. 241.

173. Ferguson, *Essay on Civil Society*, p. 209.

174. Ferguson, *Principles*, I, 185.

175. The difficulties and failures of the modern intelligentsia have received extensive treatment in philosophical and sociological writings, and they have been subjected to searching examination in twentieth-century literature as well—particularly by European novelists. Illustrative of the first category are such diverse works as Konrad Heiden's *Der Führer*, Max Horkheimer's *The Eclipse of Reason*, Julien Benda's *The Betrayal of the Intellectuals*, Raymond Aron's *The Opium of the Intellectuals*, Erich Kahler's *The Tower and the Abyss*, and Albert Camus' *The Rebel*. As examples of the second group can be cited Thomas Mann's *The Magic Mountain*, Nikolas Kazantzakis' *Zorba the Greek*, Simone de Beauvois' *The Mandarins*, and Lionel Trilling's *Middle of the Journey*.

176. This corresponds in a general way to the approach of the school of Leo Strauss. See Leo Strauss, *Natural Right and History* (Chicago: University of Chicago Press, 1953); Cropsey, *Polity and Economy*.

177. For a conflicting judgment, compare Gladys Bryson, *Man and Society*, *passim*.

178. Ferguson, *Principles*, II, 508–12.

Afterword
*Civil Society and Politics: Learning from Ferguson**

I

IN disputes about present-day issues in which the concept of "civil society" figures, Adam Ferguson is often
invoked as "authority," although his work is rarely given a
place among the "classics" of political thought.[1] Several intellectual generations of the recent past recalled Ferguson
primarily because of a favorable citation by Karl Marx, in
connection with Ferguson's elucidation of the human costs
of division of labor, which was taken as authority in the
"materialist" critique of the society comprehended by the
Marxist exposé of civil society as "bourgeois" society. In an
argument more influential in recent years, Ferguson is cited,
following the lead of Friedrich Hayek, as authority for the
proposition that "nations stumble upon establishments,
which are indeed the result of human action, but not the

execution of any human design," which is in turn glossed as an authoritative endorsement of the thesis of the market and the common law as "spontaneous social formations" possessing unique qualities of rationality and individual freedom.

Marx and the Marxists overlook the extent to which Ferguson's unhappiness with the division of labor has much more to do with the separation between civil and military roles in the governing class than it has with the discomfort he shares with Adam Smith about the negative effects of repetitive tasks on workers, not to speak of his conviction that a militia ordered by the established social hierarchy would be the appropriate remedy for both. Hayek and his followers, in turn, disregard the awkward circumstance that Ferguson's own authority on the point cited are the *Memoirs* of the Cardinal de Retz, and that his formulation consequently has more to do with uncertainties that confront Machiavellian calculations, which were well known to Machiavelli and that are in no way antithetical to Machiavellism, than it has with the origins of the comparatively autonomous systems of economics or law operative in "polished and commercial societies." The key term is "design," which De Retz certainly does not mean to abandon in favor of anything like "spontaneous formation." The question is always about the qualities of foresight and prudence that may strengthen control. Ferguson's own illustrations of stumbling, in context, are, first, a surprising paraphrase of Rousseau's point about the consequences of the first appropriation ("laying the foundation of civil law and political establishments") and, second, the unintended link between voluntary and forced subordination.[2]

These experiments in treating Ferguson as "authority" on questions about "civil society" do not encourage me to follow this track. Then too, the debate about the dynamics and inner logic of civil society, understood by both Marx and Hayek to center on capitalism and its ancillary institutions, is not the sole or even principal arena of present-day dispute about the concept. When a political scientist like Omar Encarnacion speaks of "civil society as a political celebrity," he is talking about a range of conceptions that centers on the grid of voluntary associations, almost always excluding the economic and legal entities at the heart of the concept at issue between Marx and Hayek. Voluntary associations in this sense, moreover, were absent from Ferguson's *Essay* and a source of considerable unease to Ferguson, insofar as he was called upon to comment on the Yorkshire Association or the American Committees of Correspondence, generally regarded as precursor of the breed. This class of uses of the term is the offspring of ideologically dissimilar parents. On one side, there is a recently revived tradition of moderately conservative commentary derived from Tocqueville's claims about the part supposedly played by voluntary associations in the shaping and moderation of American democracy (typically condensed in a concept of "social capital"), and on the other side, there is a younger tradition derived from political movements of the decades between 1960 and 1990, East and West, where the emphasis was on non-state organization as a locus of resistance to the state apparatus and as agent of self-help and mutual aid for individuals subject to regimes of indifference or oppression in matters of urgent collective goods. With different versions of the concept resembling one or the other parent, "civil society" has attained political celebrity as a precondition for democratic transition, a foundation for democratic consolidation, and a preliminary to global governance.

And, like all celebrities, civil society has also attracted doubters and carpers. Encarnacion, for example, thinks that he can show empirically that the thesis of civil society as "miracle worker on behalf of democratic consolidation. . .amounts to a myth." He compares Spain and Brazil, and he finds an inverse relationship instead of the predicted correspondence between a vibrant civil society, as this is consensually defined by political scientists, and the quality of democratic rule.[3] Similarly, there is a mounting skeptical literature about sanguine expectations that non-governmental organizations on behalf of human rights, ecology, anti-corruption, and the like may be able to ground a new type of non-state global citizenship.

Notwithstanding the rich ambiguities of the term and the uncertainties attending various explanations in which it is perhaps prematurely invoked, it does not seem possible to dispense with the inquiry in which "civil society" in all of its uses is engaged, the attempt to clarify the interrelationships among non-state formations whose operations interact decisively with those of the state, affecting both the form and content of politics. I suggest that a review of Ferguson's treatment of civil society can be instructive, not because I propose to treat him as an authority but because I consider him a thinker with whom a negotiation is still worthwhile, from whom we can learn. As befits such an exploratory encounter, I will proceed without definitive claims to dissolve ambiguities.[4] I will offer a reading of Ferguson on civil society against an unexpected historical backdrop, the "civilizing of the Highlands" after the Jacobite Rising of 1745, a sequence of events at the time of his young manhood linked to Ferguson mainly by his role as military chaplain at the time of the '45 (but not in that theater) and by the role of his acquaintances and sponsors. I shall argue that Ferguson's strongly political conception of "civil society" becomes clearer in the light of the political discourse attending these events and that we can learn from that conception, as so understood.

The prime civilizing processes, on this view, depend on reciprocal relations between state and non-state institutions, a conjuncture of entities that operate by distinct logics, but that cannot be understood without a common (often tacit) constitution. Pointing the argument, with reference to Hayek's interpretations, I would say that it is the state rather than the market (or the other dimensions of civil society) that may be seen as chief among the "establishments, which are indeed the result of human action, but not the execution of any human design." At issue are acts of power and resistance, no less than buying and selling. If the latter individual measures precipitate a system of economic relations, usually as important to civilization as similarly generated systems of legal relations, the struggles for power constitute a whole that is never settled into a system, drawing ever-new energies from the other relations of society and exerting ever new influences in return. The disorder in order, as well as the order in disorder are Ferguson's topics. I intend this study as a modest contribution to the contemporary discussion of civil society, but I would also be quite happy to have it serve simply as a contribution to the appreciation of Ferguson.

II

Ferguson's *Essay on the History of Civil Society* has generally been read, quite properly, in the context of the Scottish
Enlightenment and of the surging economic and social
modernization of Scotland during the last three or four
decades of the eighteenth century.[5] Ferguson's childhood
association with the Highlands, where he was born in 1723,
has of course been noted, sometimes in disregard of the fact
that his father was a Presbyterian clergyman furiously hostile to the manners and politics of his parishioners, but this
peculiarity has been given weight only in connection with
Ferguson's supposed proto-Romantic reservations about
commercial society, somehow derived from the warrior
world in which he was supposedly raised.[6] I would like to
take note of quite a different dimension of the Highlands
of his time, to which he was sensitized by the most forma-
tive experience of his young manhood, and to suggest that
the political realism of his concept of civil society is indebted to the discourses associated with the complex of
events characterized by contemporaries as the "civilizing of
the Highlands."

To situate Ferguson in that context, I begin with a vi-
gnette of his service as chaplain to a Highlands regiment
stationed in London in December, 1745. I follow with an
account of a key element in the civilizing process, after the
suppression of the Jacobite Rising of 1745, the expropria-
tion of the heritable jurisdictions held by feudal grandees in
the Highlands and the establishment of a uniform King's
justice in the region. This is important for my project of
learning from Ferguson because it highlights the conjunc-

tion between law, commerce, and the confrontation between power and resistance in civil society and because it
helps me to understand what Ferguson means when he
makes civil society depend on constant political actions to
assert and sustain the two more or less autonomous "systems"—law and commerce— crucial for its civility. Civil
society, in brief, is a function of a constant effort of deliberate but inherently insecure and uncertain civilization.[4]

For Ferguson, as for many of his contemporaries, civilization meant first of all the substitution of civilian rule for
the military rule, which is, in their view, the defining characteristic of the feudal age[5] – an accomplishment which
might itself well require the use of force. The history of this
conception in the age of the second overseas empire of the
nineteenth century is a matter of continuing research interest.[6] But it was first crystalized in the context of the pacification of the Highlands, notably after the risings of 1715
and 1745. This civilizing mission of the British army is
made exceptionally clear by Ferguson himself, in the "hard
case" of a Highlands regiment. On December 18, 1745, on
the occasion of a solemn fast to rededicate the nation against
the Jacobite army, which had just crossed into England,
Adam Ferguson addressed the First Highlands Regiment of
Foot, of which he had been made deputy chaplain by the
influence of his patroness, whose son had been a schoolmate of Ferguson and was now the youthful commander.
The regiment was deployed in the continental war against
France rather than in the anti-Jacobite campaign, yet on
this solemn occasion Ferguson found it necessary to explain
to the troops why they should "oppose [their] own acquaintances... [and] oppose [their] own relations." The crux of

the matter is that "by a man's country is meant that society or united body of men, of which he is a member, sharing all the advantages that arise from such a union. Not merely the soil or spot on which he was born, as is too often understood by many. . . .No: the name of country bears a meaning more sacred and more interesting. It was not for the place of their nativity that Jacob exhorted the Israelites to play the man [in my scripture]: it was for their people and for the cities of their God."[7] To counterpose the society united by advantages to the locality of birth and home of acquaintances and family, and to enact that confrontation in military action makes it unmistakable that civilization is not simply a "spontaneous social formation." Neither commerce nor law can flourish without state intervention in the social arrangements, and a harsh overriding of beliefs that Romantic writers, by contrast, considered invaluable because organically rooted in the deepest layers of human experience and spirituality. However Romantic the image of Ferguson as fighting chaplain at the Battle of Fontenoy, Ferguson's sermon shows how far he was removed, already as a very young intellectual, from all pre-Romantic conceptions of the Highlands.

The implications of Ferguson's alignment with the "civilization of the Highlands" become clearer from the story of events in which Ferguson himself played no part. It is my claim nevertheless that the decisions and justifications of the main actors in the mid-eighteenth-century struggle over the heritable jurisdictions illuminate Ferguson's presuppositions when he speaks of the actions requisite to the establishment and maintenance of civil society.

The historian among the eighteenth-century Edinburgh intellectuals, Chancellor William Robertson, puts the issue in context in his discussion of the "restoration" of monarchical power after the long "anarchical" interregnum between the barbarian dismemberment of the Roman Empire and the epoch that culminated on the continent in the rise of Charles V. According to Robertson, baronial jurisdiction is the third obstacle to civil order in the law, ranking only behind private wars and trial by combat.[8] It should be noted that Robertson does not abstract the authoritative measures taken against feudal practices from the cumulative effects of the rise of cities, commerce, and other social processes that converge to weaken the feudal lords and to create new classes of social actors to strengthen the kings. Like Ferguson, he sees the emerging civil society as both source and beneficiary of appropriate political action, and he credits both the effects of "progress" and policy for the civil outcome.

To deal with the conjuncture between the conjoint dimensions, Robertson provides an analytical tool for distinguishing between the "political" and "civil" consequences of a given legal order. In speaking about the canon law, for example, he charges that its political consequences in strengthening the usurped power of the clergy or the domination of the popes make it "one of the most formidable engines ever formed against the happiness of civil society." He continues, "but if I contemplate it merely as a code of laws respecting the rights and property of individuals, and attend only to the civil effects of its decisions concerning these, I must view it in a different, and a much more favourable light."[9] Just this distinction is presupposed throughout his treatment of the correlation between the centralization of state power and the establishment of a unified system of justice, and it enters as well into his observation that the

reformed legal system brings into being a new order of influential political actors, in the persons of lawyers. Ferguson's
treatment of "Civil Liberty" invokes a similar conjunction
between political and civil dimensions of the legal order,
although in that context his emphasis is on the political
resolution of the people.[10] In the language of Ferguson's
late treatises, the facts of the "history of the species" and the
wills of purposive actors must both be considered, with
outcomes determined by neither alone.[11]

Our turn from a fairly high level of generality to a detailed historical case study next conforms to Ferguson's practice in his teaching, when he generalized on comparative
developments but narrated British constitutional history as
exemplary object lesson, as he did with Rome in his *History
of the Progress and Termination of the Roman Republic*. A
contemporary noted in a private letter to a friend, that "the
most prevalent" opinion of this book "is rather not so high
as the former character of the author would have led people
to form." He explained:

> He has treated his subject rather in a narrative than in a reflective
> way, & has been sparing of those general & philosophic views of
> the subject which is the great distinction between Modern His-
> tory, since the time of Montesquieu & the ancients.[12]

The unknown critic recognized an important ambivalence in Ferguson's management of Bacon's distinction between natural history, which assembles materials for natural philosophy, and civil history, which provides, according
to Bacon, the "foundation" for wise commentary and discourse, to guide judgment and public conduct.[13] While
Ferguson certainly looked reflectively at the "history of the
species" in the manner of Montesquieu in his *Essay*, he nev-

ertheless reserved the option of narrating events in detail in order to capture the complex interplay of civil circumstances and political actions. This was Ferguson's world, as he observed it, and his analytical distinctions between the civil and political constituents of civil society, as well as its political form, are designed to comprehend it in a way comprehensible to the actors as well as the spectators.

III

> "An Afghanistan could no longer
> be tolerated within fifty miles of
> the 'modern Athens.'"
>
> —*G. M. Trevelyan*[14]

The Act of Union between Scotland and England in 1707 had expressly reserved the distinctive Scottish system of law and the administration of justice. With the transfer of ultimate political control from Edinburgh to London, in fact, the political importance of Scottish lawyers and judges as resident agents of public authority increased substantially. But the order they helped to shape and administer extended into the Highlands only so far as it was upheld by certain great families, notably by the Campbells under the Duke of Argyll. And even in this portion of the domain, legal and political order assumed a distinctive character, shaped by the varying amalgam of clan loyalties, feudal privileges, and modern legal, political and estate-management practices which the dominant families put in place. The westernmost "civilized"—portions of the Highlands controlled by Argyll, for example, were governed as much by Argyll's personal influence over the clan members retained in key loca-

tions within his holdings as by the extension of improved
agriculture and commercial relationships in his estates. With
this came hereditary judicial and military offices, an important share of Scottish electoral management and patronage,
and an influential part in the deliberations of government
in London.[15] The widespread rising of the clans beyond
Argyll's control in the '45, as well as the lack of effective
Scottish resistance to Charles Stuart, determined Lord Chancellor Hardwicke to bring the Highlands more effectively
within the more conventional British constitutional and
political system.

Four months after Culloden, then, in August, 1746,
Hardwicke secured from the House of Lords a formal request to the Lords of Session in Edinburgh, asking them to
draft a bill to eliminate the heritable jurisdictions, which
reserved the administration of criminal justice in and around
the Highlands to feudal superiors who were also often clan
chiefs. This was part of a package of five proposals which
Hardwicke had already outlined several months before the
initial move in Parliament, and which was to include pro-
hibition of arms and Highland dress, dissolution of most
Episcopal meeting houses, and elimination of wardholding,
a form of tenure requiring military service or quite arbitrary
penalty payments. But Hardwicke hoped to strengthen his
proposal by gaining a detailed formulation from the Scottish justices. In putting the case to the Lords, he placed it in
the context of "two formidable rebellions," and remarked
that "the cause must arise from some peculiar defect in the
constitution of government of that kingdom." The unde-
sirability of leaving "a great part of Scotland...absolutely
exempt from the authority of the Crown" had already been

remarked by James II of Scotland in 1455, he noted, but it had not been remedied either at the Union of the Crowns in 1603 or the parliamentary union of 1707.[16]

Despite the order from the House of Lords, the President of the Lords of Session in Scotland, Duncan Forbes, replied that he and his fellows "have judged it improper" to draft a bill taking away the "several kinds of Heritable Jurisdictions," since these "are secured to the proprietors" by the Articles of the Union "as rights of property" which "cannot without due satisfaction be taken from them." Instead, Forbes offered some suggestions to improve the "regular administration of justice in this part of the kingdom" which would not infringe the proprietors' rights. He noted first of all that the high jurisdiction had been lodged "in powerful families" originally because of "the great difficulty the government was under of bringing offenders to justice, and executing the law, when that country was yet uncivilized, and the necessity of committing that charge to such as were able to execute the same." The Highlands continue "in a state so unsettled, that offenders are not from thence easily amenable to justice, nor can process of law have free course through it." The country must first be brought "under subjection of the law" before regular administration of justice could be put under the king's courts and judges. To further this process of civilization then, he proposed annual circuit courts in several towns near the Highlands, where justices might either hear or perhaps only review cases involving loss of life or limb, but he urged the retention of the lesser criminal and many civil causes in the lower jurisdictions and baronies where they were lodged, provided only that the actual justices would be given regular salaries in place of the poundage now provided and appointments for life, upon good behavior. Forbes went on to regret that the Lords of Session also could not satisfy the request for detailed information about existing titles to heritable jurisdictions, since the records are radically incomplete, partially destroyed, or otherwise unavailable.[17]

Forbes was a very old, independent, and respected man, who had watched with dismay from his estate at Culloden first the ineffectiveness of the resistance to Prince Charles and then the harshness of Cumberland's pacification of the Highlands, and it is a risky business to seek ulterior reasons behind his stated conviction that it was still "impracticable... to give the Law its course among the mountains" without great courage "and a greater degree of power than men are generally possessed of"[18]; and that therefore consideration of policy as well as rights of property militated against Hardwicke's design. But there is, to say the least, no inconsistency between this and Forbes' long-standing ties to the second as well as to the third Duke of Argyll. Forbes had been the agent of the second Duke and the close collaborator of Islay, who became the third Duke in 1743, during the 1720s and 1730s, when the Campbells of Argyll were first revising their leases to make them more attractive to improving tenants, and he remained closely connected with the family in subsequent years. When Ferguson wrote, "In every society there is a casual subordination, independent of its formal establishment, and frequently adverse to its constitution,"[19] he had such situations in mind.

The crucial fact is that the greatest holder of heritable jurisdictions was Argyll himself, and that indeed the rebellious clan chiefs possessed few, if any. Hardwicke certainly

knew this, if only because his son-in-law, Lord of Glenorchy
and heir to the estate and title of the Campbells of
Breadalbane, had asked Philip Yorke to tell him so the previous June, after being asked to comment on the original
package of proposals. It seems likely indeed that Hardwicke's
cautious turn to the Lords of Session on this matter was his
response to Glenorchy's claim that the proposed abolition
of jurisdictions will affect none but the friends of the Government."[20] Glenorchy went on:

> If that power is taken away from those who are attached to the
> Government, 'twill be exposing me to continual robberies, and
> thieves will start up every day in my own estates . . . . The loss of
> rent occasioned by poor tenants being robbed is not near so great
> as prosecution before the Court of Justiciary. This law appears to
> me to be giving greater liberty to the common people when they
> ought to be curbed, and to encourage those who were in the
> Rebellion and famous for thieving, to pillage the friends of the
> Government by taking from them the power of punishing them.
> Eighteen armed men came two days ago and plundered a farm in
> the corner of this estate. If any of those can be catched, I can try
> them at my father's Court and can imprison them or hang them;
> but if they must be prosecuted at the Justiciary Court, as the law
> now stands, I would not be at the trouble to take them if I could.[21]

When Hardwicke was presenting his original request to
the House of Lords for an order to the Lords of Session in
Scotland, he did so, according to an authoritative contemporary account, "without the least support from the Duke
of Argyll, who sat by in a corner silent, and complained of
the head-ach[e]."[22] Forbes' reluctance, in short, may not be
unrelated to Argyll's headache. But neither of them can be
associated with nostalgia for the old clannish ways. Islay, in
fact, had written vehemently against the heritable jurisdictions some twenty years earlier, when his attempts to col-

lect debts from the bankrupt Earl of Cromarty were stymied by the fact that the Earl was hereditary Sheriff of the
county to which he had retreated from his creditors:

> The Highlands can never be civilized so long as any person is
> tolerated in the giving publick defiance to the courts of the Law,
> and the difficulty that attends the execution of the processes of the
> Law in the Highlands seems to be the very essence of their barbar-
> ity.[23]

There is no reason to suppose that Argyll and Forbes
were less dedicated to "civilizing" the Highlands than
Hardwicke. But neither is it sensible to assume, with a number of historians, that Hardwicke was proceeding on a mere
misconception of Highlands circumstances, and that he
imagined a greater direct causal link between the authority
of rebellious clan chiefs and the feudal jurisdictions than in
fact subsisted.[24] At issue between Hardwicke and Argyll, so
far as issues can be reconstructed when contests are so dis-
creetly managed, was a considerable difference in political
conception. Rosalind Mitchison has explored one important dimension of this difference in calling attention to the
legalism and distrust of the coercive aspects of political power
that kept the British government from mustering "the force,
energy and resources before the '45 to substitute" a system
alternative to the one that had brought forth the Jacobite
rising in 1715.[25] She shows that Islay, despite his own dedication to modern law and economic improvement, pressed
the case for a transitional mobilization of the coercive capacities of clanship in order to establish the Hanover supremacy. This analysis can be quite plausibly extended to
include forceful use of heritable jurisdictions to push through
the new order after Culloden.

Yet Hardwicke's alternative approach in 1746 cannot be simply accounted for by reference to that "dislike of threats and force as acknowledged weapons of government," which Mitchison adduces to explain government policy between the '15 and the '45. Hardwicke's conception appears in his statements and actions after the report of Duncan Forbes' response. Although he was prepared to make some concessions with regard to minor jurisdictions comparable to those of English justices of the peace, Hardwicke immediately brought in his own bill "abrogating, and totally extinguishing, all heritable jurisdictions of justiciary, regalities, and bailleries in Scotland," resuming all sheriffships to the Crown, taking away most criminal and civil jurisdiction from the barons and all authority to maintain their own prisons, providing for procedures to compensate proprietors of these rights, and strengthening the capacities of the king's courts to take up those jurisdictions by various procedural changes. In presenting his bill, he insisted that the Rebellion was no more than the occasion for it and he denied that the measure implied any condemnation of Scotland or of the proprietors of the jurisdictions. His reasons were "drawn from known and allowed maxims of policy," he avowed: "men are mortal; governments, in the view and contemplation of lawgivers and founders of states, are framed to be perpetual."

Hardwicke based his argument on the claim that "the administration of justice" is "the principal and essential part of all government," first, because "the people know and judge of it by little else," and, second, because "the chief office of government" is, after all, " to secure to me the regular course of law and justice." "When the king therefore grants away jurisdiction," he maintained, "he parts away with so much of his government." The people will enter into "a dangerous and unconstitutional dependence" upon "those who have the power to protect or hurt them, and this dependence will operate most strongly in the uncivilized part of any country . . .." This is a capital instance, according to Hardwicke, of the "confusion" which must follow if any of the powers balanced in the constitution "exceed their due proportion." Correcting the "wrong and dangerous model of government" established in Scotland with the heritable jurisdictions will "secure that proportion of authority to the Crown, which the law intends," he concluded, and will assist materially "to fix the allegiance of the people, where alone it ought to rest, upon that sacred object."[26]

Notwithstanding the references to the Whig theory of the constitutional balance, Hardwicke also linked his argument to earlier "maxims of policy." The *Parliamentary History* prints a footnote, presumably also taken from the earlier text published by Hardwicke himself, quoting the *Basilicon Doron* of James VII, who was to be James I of England. Writing for the guidance of his heir in 1599, James had said:

> But the greatest hindrance to the execution of my law in this country are their heritable Sheriffdoms and Regalities, which being in the hands of the great men wracks the whole country: for which I know no present remedy but by taking the sharper account of them in their offices, using all punishment against the slothful that the law will permit: and aye as they vaik [Scots for "become vacant"] for any offences committed by them, dispose them never heritable again: pressing (with time) to draw it to the laudable custom of England, which ye may the easier do being King of both, as I hope in God ye shall.[27]

In a confidential letter, Hardwicke resorted to authority in a manner no less paradoxical than in this citation of the first Stuart king of England, if also a complementary one. Writing to the Duke of Cumberland on April 16, 1747 (the first anniversary of the Battle of Culloden) to explain his reasons for revising the heritable jurisdictions bill so as to retain some jurisdiction in baronial courts, Hardwicke offered an "argument from history which has some weight with me, though it comes from a hand not to be quoted in public nor scarce mentioned to any Prince below your Royal Highness's discernment and largeness of thought." The argument derives from the precedent of Cromwell, who had, according to Hardwicke, "abolished all the great heritable jurisdictions at once, without giving any compensation for them; but at the same time preserved and established in the Barons' Court the same jurisdiction which is left to them by this bill." "Nobody can imagine he would have done it," Hardwicke concluded, "if it would have left an influence capable of giving disturbance to his government."[28] There is doubtless irony in this citation of the regicide Cromwell to a royal prince widely assailed for a harshness in Scotland comparable to that of Cromwell in Ireland, as there was in the citation of the first Stuart king to a parliament assessing penalties for a rebellion on behalf of that family. But first to be noted is Hardwicke's decisive location of his measure within a context of constitutional lawgiving. His aim is to new-model the basis of government in the Highlands and, indeed, in Scotland.

The ironies also have their significance. Hardwicke represents a *politique* conception of great sophistication. Unlike James I or Cromwell, he has no illusions about replacing feudal disorder and oppression with a regime of sovereign righteousness. His proposal to expropriate the heritable jurisdictions possessed by the great Scottish families forms integral part of a complex of political moves to adjust the structure of politics in Scotland, to bring it more effectively within the calculable and manipulable "system" established throughout Great Britain. It may seem strange that this should have been thought necessary, since Scottish parliamentary politicians were already notorious for their lack of independence, but Hardwicke and Newcastle were forcibly reminded by the events of the Rising that their control over Scottish politics was at the mercy of key individuals. As the heirs of Robert Walpole, who had been undone in 1741 in considerable measure because the second Duke of Argyll turned against him, they did not require much prodding. Islay, the third Duke, had himself played an important part in shaping Walpole's system and had remained loyal when his brother went into opposition. Moreover, Hardwicke probably conceded that Argyll could not be replaced in the management of Scottish affairs. But his position was to be decisively redefined. He could not be denied command over the normal political resources of the time, accumulated and organized with great skill; but he was no longer to be able to claim an independent and unique source of power in being the only one able to muster, or at least to hold in check, the irrational forces of the old Highlands.[29] To an extent hard to measure, the assumption by the Dukes of Argyll of the traditional royal office with regard to the Highlands (where they had earlier been agents of the King), recognized by many contemporary references to Argyll as "king of Scotland," also doubtless affected the extent and quality of their influence in the Lowlands. Hardwicke undertook to centralize the ultimate provision of the symbolic as well as of the material resources upon which political authority rests, and he proved quite willing to pay a considerable price, in his own coinage, for this change. Under the circumstances after 1746, Argyll could not refuse the offer.

Hardwicke set out in 1746 to combine the regimes of coercion and monetary accommodation in the Highlands which had already been explored as alternatives in 1691, in the first confused aftermath of the Glorious Revolution, and which had both been frustrated at that time by a Duke of Argyll. Attempts had then been made to implement first a policy of stringent military pacification, with provision for permanent policing, and then a policy of financial subsidy for chiefs, combined with realignment of the feudal superiorities, which fostered incursions upon the clan territories of others by the great chiefs who were also feudal magnates. These designs were foiled by a series of maneuvers culminating in the massacre of Glencoe.[30] In 1746, the military force had been applied by Cumberland. Hardwicke never accepted the conception of a continuing military regime for the Highlands (and perhaps for Scotland) which was at least implicit in the sweeping distrust of all Scottish political figures and arrangements professed by Cumberland, Chesterfield, and others. But neither did he regret or try to stay the punitive campaign conducted by Cumberland after Culloden.[31] His conduct of the treason trial in the House of Lords, his part in the other exemplary capital prosecutions, his design of effective coercive legislation for disarming the Highlands and his support for its effective enforce-

ment all testify that he was not afflicted by that diffidence
about rule by coercion which Mitchison finds in British
governments after the Union and before the '45. As soon as
possible, however, this rule was to be regularized in an orderly system of administration run by officers of the crown.
The greatest obstacles to such administration, according to
William Ferguson, were the heritable jurisdictions, which
"had helped to promote feuds and to debase the administration of justice."[32] That the problems were not limited to
the Highlands may be suggested by the situation in
Lanarkshire, where there were eight hereditary regalities and
two baronies, in addition to the hereditary sheriffship of
the Duchess of Hamilton, four commissary courts and two
sets of justices of the peace. Above all, though, it was necessary to attack the symbolic as well as material attributes
that distinguished the power of Argyll and others who amal-
gamated clan chiefdomship, feudal superiority and political influence. The alternative was a more unified administrative and judicial structure subject to the dual disciplines
of the law and of the "system" of political dependencies.

The parliamentary opposition challenged Hardwicke's
proposal, charging that it represented an assault on established property rights, a new aggrandizement of monarchical power, and a further extension of electoral corruption.
They denied that there was any evidence that the Heritable
Jurisdictions contributed to rebellion or otherwise created
disturbance and they warned that the organization of judicial power under ministerial control jeopardized the authority
of parliament and the "free enjoyment of the people's liberties and properties."[33] Although these are the familiar and
recurrent themes of the old "country" party, often abused

for merely factious purposes, the charges indicate that the political component of Hardwick's reordering of civil "justice" was widely recognized, if also in simplified stereotypes, and that the preservation of property, which everyone accepted as the core of justice, could nevertheless involve a choice among properties, with the property in jurisdictions readily dismissed. As the opposition expected, the selection of replacements for the hereditary sheriffs, after enactment of the legislation, was a highly political process, with lists of nominees carefully scrutinized for political loyalty and skill by the government's managers. "Every effort was made to find men who were thoroughly loyal," writes a nineteenth–century historian, "as it was hoped that the new officials would be of use in spreading a spirit of attachment to the government."[34] What was not acknowledged or, perhaps, recognized by the opposition was, first, that the government's politics displaced a politics of feudal and clannish dependencies, not a benign management of self and estates by independent gentlemen, and, second, that the feudal superiorities being eliminated were being replaced by arrangements to foster commercial property as well as more impersonal authority. In the end, Hardwicke's conception cannot be understood apart from his design for "civilizing" the Highlands in another sense.

George Lyttleton, speaking for the ministry in the House of Commons, indicated the connection:

> Can there be a better or happier fruit of the Union than an active communication of the generous, free, and noble plan of the law of England, in the room of those servile tenures and barbarous customs, which in Scotland deform the system of government, and by the effects which they have over that part of the people, which

being least civilized is consequently more prone to disorder, disturb the peace and endanger the safety of the whole constitution? When this is accomplished...the way will be open to many other improvements, to the introduction of arts, of manufactures, of industry, of all the virtues and sweets of civil life, in the wildest parts of that country, but all these blessings must be the gifts of good government.... Before (those people] can be mended by the instructions of government, they must be protected by its power and relieved by its care. Authority and justice must take the lead in this great work of reformation: discipline, peace, and civility, will follow after.[35]

The political and legal change appear here as preconditions for the creation of a "civil life" understood as one which is not only no longer barbarous or military, but also devoted to "improvement" in the eighteenth-century sense. It was in this context, then, that Hardwicke also moved to abolish the military tenure known as "wardholding" because of the conceptions of authority and property which it represented.[36] But "improvement" was not an end in itself: the new civil order was to serve together with the political "system" as foundation for the constitution of government. Hardwicke put it succinctly some years later, in a letter to the general commanding in Scotland:

I have proceeded and shall continue to proceed, upon the uniform principles of extending the vigor and benefit of the laws over the whole country; Of suppressing all private power that tends to obstruct the due course of these laws and the proper influence of His Majesty's government, of civilizing and improving the country and making them feel the advantages of property, and upon these solid foundations to build up loyalty and good affection to the King and his family.[37]

The care for commercialized agricultural property and life, then, formed integral part of Hardwicke's *politique* conception.

The most striking demonstration of this is Hardwicke's scheme for the estates forfeited by rebels, which he did not present to Parliament until 1752 but which he expressly linked to the abolition of heritable jurisdictions at that time. In Hardwicke's "notes of the debate for annexing the forfeited estates in the Highlands to the Crown unalienably," which took place on March 17, 1752, Hardwicke asserts that "this scheme" was already "in view at the time of the Jurisdiction Bill" and anticipated in earlier legislation. The scheme proposed to put management of the estates in the hands of royal commissioners, to prevent any recapture of the estates or their incomes by the attainted rebels through various subterfuges, and to apply the income remaining after proper debts are paid "to civilize the highlands; – Correct the spirit of barbarity, disorder and rebellion; to introduce submission to government and law." The latter objectives are to be attained, first, by substituting a "dependence on the king their sovereign supreme lord" for "dependence on their [clan] chiefs," by "teaching them to hold their estates and tenancies from the crown," and, second, by measures which will "teach them the more civilized arts of life–industry–manufactures," and thus "give them a taste of property" so that they "will desire to keep and enjoy it."[38]

The major speeches in opposition accepted the linkage alleged between the political objective of breaking the political power of clan chiefs and the social objective of bringing "improvement" to the Highlands, but they charged that the government's design would give unwarranted and dangerous powers to the government itself and to the great families considered loyal to the Crown, whose political influence would be so greatly enhanced by the management to be in effect delegated to them. The Duke of Bedford spoke derisively of the "chimerical and impractical project, which is that of planting industry, religion, and loyalty among the people of the Highlands of Scotland, by trustees appointed by the Crown for that purpose" and he insisted at length, citing the history of English improvement as precedent, "that the best way for improving the islands and reforming the people, would be to sell these forfeited estates at any price to gentlemen of England, or the low country of Scotland, whose interest would be to root out that clannish spirit which prevails in the Highlands and to propagate the spirit of industry among the people."[39] The Earl of Bath is also recorded as emphasizing "that the great improvements of all my lands in England has arisen from their being made alienable, and in consequence thereof divided amongst a vast number of private men, every one of whom took all possible care to improve that part which properly belonged to him, and which with its improvement he had a power to transmit to his posterity, or to such other persons as he pleased to name." Although this line of argument, with its implicit dismissal of the Scottish entails, which Hardwicke did not dare to touch, takes a strongly modern line, Bath's characterization of the government's proposals for crown ownership and public management resorts to the conventional "country" rhetoric: government is proceeding with this measure in undue haste and virtual secrecy at the end of the session, he charges, because "a part of Scotland is to be in some degree subjected to a Turkish sort of government: "the inhabitants are to have no property in the lands they possess, nor any representative in the national assemblies of their country; and they are in the first instance at least, to be under the jurisdiction of a bashaw appointed by, and removable at the pleasure of the crown."[40]

In reply, Hardwicke and Newcastle argue, first, that only ownership by the crown and collaboration in due form with well-affected Scottish interests can counteract the insidious influence of the old proprietors and their clannish authority. Citing the experiences of 1715, they denied that effective new landlords could be found to take the estates, especially since misguided traditions of honor would bind Highlanders to complicity in fictitious claims and other devices calculated to let agents for the rebellious forfeiters outbid all competitors for the estates, if they were put up for sale by auction. If the land were held by the crown, however, long-term leases could be designed in such a manner that "every such lessee's self-interest will operate directly against his clannish spirit. Instead of following their chief into any future rebellion, the cheapness and the certainty of their leases will induce all, and probably prevail with most of them, to assist the government in opposing his return; and a spirit of industry and improvement will be propagated among them, not only by the certainty of holding their estates for a long term of years, but by all the methods that can be contrived by the managers under the crown."[41] Under such management, moreover, it should be easily possible, through suitable inducements, "to get a few intelligent and industrious farmers and masters of manufacture, with some servants and journeymen, and a few who understand fishing and curing of fish, to go and settle there, in order...to instruct and employ such of [the people] as may incline to be industrious, which I am persuaded will be the greatest part, as soon as they are made sensible of the plenty and independency that attend industry." And this combination of leases and "industrious strangers," Hardwicke concluded, "is certainly the most effectual method for giving a turn to the spirit of the natives, both with respect to industry and loyalty."[42]

It is striking that in this matter, as in the related question of heritable jurisdictions, Hardwicke claims continuity with the historical authority of both James I and Cromwell. The model, odd as it may now seem, is the "foundation for the spirit of industry and improvement, now so prevalent among the people of [Ireland]" as a result of "introducing more industrious strangers from England and Scotland into [that island]."[43]

He could have cited James on the Highlands themselves, drawing on a passage in the *Basilicon Doron*, which is only a few pages removed from the one he had cited in 1746:

> Here now speaking of oppressors and justice, the purpose leadeth me to speak of Highlands and Border oppression. As for the Highlands, I shortly comprehend them all in two sorts of people: the one, that dwelleth in my main land are barbarous, and yet mixed with some show of civilitie: the other, that dwelleth in the Isles are and are all utterly barbarous, without any sort or shew of civilitie. For the first sort, put straight to execution the laws already made by me against their overlords and the chiefs of their clans, and it will be no difficulty to daunt them. As for the other sort, think no other of them at all, than as wolves and wild boars: and therefore follow forth the course that I have begun, in planting colonies among them of answerable inlands-subjects, that within a short time may root them out and plant civilitie in their room.[44]

Hardwicke's design for planting civility was more conciliatory in intent, if not in effect, than James' vehement projection, but there is clear continuity in the primacy of state requirements. Civility is integral to the "domestic peace and good order" which must be, according to Hardwicke, the ultimate goal even when "statesmen" pursue "remote interests" at home and abroad, which are visible only to those with "more extensive political views" than the people. With the help of the notion of "interest," Hardwicke commands a more elaborate account of the connection between industriousness and civility than James,[45] but both agree that the political regime must forcefully assert itself to strengthen and to draw strength from the reformed state of the spirit they call civility.

It is this central place assigned public power that separates Hardwicke from the opposition in this debate. While Hardwicke's opponents manifest considerably more awareness of contrasts between Highlands possessors and English landlords than they had shown in the debate over heritable jurisdictions, they now proposed drastic measures for taking control out of public hands and expressed a generalized distrust of the Scottish political class, which may well confirm the report that they were "secretly encouraged by the Duke of Cumberland."[46] Hardwicke instead worked to cultivate a political class in the English sense, and, perhaps, to move it incrementally towards an administrative class, reorienting the organization which Argyll had developed and redefining offices.

In speaking of a contest between the respective political conceptions of Hardwicke and Argyll, then, it is necessary to focus quite narrowly on the politics of justice as an element of public authority. They agreed that the welfare of the nation and the security of the state required destruction of the clan system and the "civilization" of the Highlands, and they also agreed that the introduction of commercial society would decisively advance both objectives, by reorienting proprietors from the accumulation of military force to the accumulation of wealth and by fostering pacific interests and industry among the lower classes. On the political side, they agreed that such changes could only come about by means of firm management in the hands of advocates and others tied to the government's design by office and by their own prospects of advancement through this course. What separated them, and what makes this special case relevant to the wider inquiry into the British administration of justice in the eighteenth century, was Hardwicke's conviction that the systematic institutionalization of the king's justice as the pervasive reference point for every interesting and contested issue in social life was essential to the constitution of domestic authority.

The interesting nuance that distinguished Argyll's political conception from Hardwicke's concerns the precise political character of justice. While Hardwicke saw justice as a prime practical and symbolic instrument of the sovereign state taking institutional form around the crown and as a counter to unofficial personal dependencies, Argyll saw it more nearly as a special sort of political weapon to be wielded by the friends of government. Across the broad spectrum of cases covered by well-established legal doctrine, this difference would not affect the contents of justice; we are only talking about the assignment of political benefit from the conduct of judicial functions and about the contents of justice in that uncertainly delimited subset of cases that are said to involve "political questions." Hardwicke sought political means to further institutionalization, rationalization and strategic control from the political center;

Argyll inclined more nearly to a politics of contestation. At issue are "political" rather than "civil" dimensions of the legal system (Robertson).[47] Both positions, as well as the contest between them, illustrate the fluid and permeable boundaries between state and civil society, which it has been the objective of this case study to illustrate.

IV

The lengthy case study of "civilizing the highlands" illustrates the political uses of civil relations and the civil consequences of political actions, as they were understood by participants in the events and as Ferguson knew and appreciated them. More broadly, then, I argue that Ferguson's concept of civil society presupposes just such a dialectical interplay between political interventions and non-state social development in several dissimilar and bounded domains, including the histories of literature and morals, as well as the "systems" of law and economics; and that the "constitution" that is the dynamic product of these exchanges provides the highest level of politically relevant analysis, transcending both politics in the narrow sense and civil society. In "learning from Ferguson," the aim is not to offer the one final interpretation of one or another of his texts, and this exempts me as well from limiting myself to the *Essay on the History of Civil Society*. Ferguson's primary aims as teacher were not identical with his aims in writing this essay, but his lecture notes, as well as his textbook treatises, can be drawn upon for important glosses to clarify his suggestive ideas.

Above all, reading Ferguson in the context of the complexities of the "civilizing process" shows that he is not read productively or well when he is taken as "authority" for either Marxist or Hayekian critiques of constitutional democracies of the modern type, with their characteristic reliance on political mediation between social initiatives and constraints, on the one hand, and, on the other, the state's mechanisms for formalization and legitimate coercion. Ferguson is better read as a theorist of such regimes. This does not make Ferguson a democrat, of course, but it may make him a valuable teacher of democrats.

Here are what seem to me to be the basic elements of Ferguson's conception, much as I wrote them down almost thirty years ago.[48] Human beings find themselves in some state of the progress of the arts whereby they secure subsistence, accommodation and ornament. When they are in an advanced state of those arts, as in Ferguson's time, they occupy different places within a commercial system that produces great wealth. In Ferguson's usage, the term system indicates that this is a complex "partial society" whose principles of interconnection are relatively stable and can be stated in fairly general terms. Ferguson's choice reflects his respect for Adam Smith's account of the sources of the wealth of nations. Accordingly, it is important to note that individuals each have a distinct profession, with the vast majority compelled for the sake of livelihood to occupy themselves with one of the professions producing material goods. Among the professions is that of tradesman, and his activities actually bring the diverse other activities into a system. Through commercial exchange, individual producers are supplied with what they want and are able to dispose of their surplus.

A peculiar character of this system or partial society is that its principle of union does not require any of its mem-

bers to look to a common cause, beyond his private interest. Ferguson points out that the diverse partial societies,
which are together comprehended within what he calls the
"universal confederation" of the nation, have diverse principles of intercourse. In one of his lectures, he offers examples of partial societies held together by love, by friendship, by shared fear, by shared interests, and even, in the
case of a company of gamblers, by mutual antagonism. The
confederacy of the arts, as he sometimes calls the commercial system, fits between the last two of these societies on
the scale of social affection among members requisite for
existence. Ferguson defers to Harris and then to Smith's
Wealth of Nations for an account of the laws governing this
system, but reserves to his own interpretation questions
about the relationship between the system and other factors in the life of the nation.[49]

Two consequences of the advanced state of the commercial arts connect it with other aspects of life. First, like all
circumstances delimiting and directing man's activities, the
professions educate and habituate their votaries. They refine certain of the talents to a very high degree and stultify
others. Since the various specialized tasks are unequally challenging and since the tendency of the system is to narrow
the scope of occupations ever more, as ever more inducements and opportunities arise for intensifying production
by particularizing tasks, many individuals will be rendered
very limited indeed. This source of inequality combines with
another inevitable concomitant of advanced arts, the unequal distribution of property.

Where there are such palpable differences among men as
those produced by the radically disparate social education

of diverse professions and by the steep inequality of wealth, the scheme of social subordination, which is bound to exist, will be defined largely by these factors. Ferguson distinguishes this "casual" pattern of subordination from the "political establishment," with its order of offices. Both arrangements play a vital part in society and in the history of the nation. Ferguson considers the pattern of casual subordination associated with the commercial system an essential aspect of power in modern nations, but he does not deem a theory of that pattern a comprehensive or satisfactory treatment of power in the nation. It is incorrect to suppose that Ferguson has it in mind, in the Marxist manner, to penetrate the appearances of political arrangements to the social power relations beneath. The interplay between the casual and the political patterns of power cannot really be brought within a single theoretical formulation because they are to be comprehended in terms of different vocabularies. There is distortion in seeing the relationship as one where the casual determines the political; there is comparable distortion in talking simply about the ends which political action ought to pursue and the power relationships appropriate to those tasks. The tension between these provides the dramatic action of the *Essay.*

Similar considerations apply to two other constellations of social factors and partial societies also found in nations, and which should be briefly described before returning to the central political theme. Men find themselves at some state in the progress of literature and science. The former comprises a state of the language, habitual ways of seeing things, accumulations of information, and modes of inquiry. All these will strongly affect what a man can say and what he can find out. In an advanced state, the language is subtle and discriminating, many facts are available, and the techniques of productive science are known. But access to these resources is unequally distributed in society and there is a tendency for the cultivation of knowledge to be segregated within a particular profession, so that it ceases to be a shared social capability.

Related to the state of knowledge as well as to other aspects of civil society are the manners of the people. Ferguson speaks of advanced societies as marked by a general refinement and gentility, especially among the higher ranks. At the same time, there is concentration on private interest incident to the commercial system and a brutalization of the lowest ranks, in consequence of the separation of professions. More generally, Ferguson worries about a dangerous narrowing of aspirations and channeling of ambitions into competition for riches and recognition that tend, in turn, to generate servility and arrogance.

Vital to all the relationships depicted so far are the political establishments. In his writings Ferguson tries several different formulations to express the distinction between the comparatively settled arrangements of the legal and constitutional order, which are like the facts I have already considered, and the "political operations of state,"[50] which give effect to these arrangements and are constantly creating the universal confederation of the nation. However expressed, there is always special provision for the established relationships of rights comprehended by the system of jurisprudence. As use of the term system in this connection as well indicates, the legal relationships, including the powers of officials, are seen to form an integrated, rule-governed, comprehensible whole. In an advanced state of the progress of polity, this system will provide security of personal and real rights, including above all the rights of property and legitimacy of office, equal protection under the law, and stability of expectations. Force is a monopoly of the magistrates and any subject employing it in his relations with others is properly punished to the extent necessary to repress such occurrences. This condition Ferguson calls civil liberty. Yet, political establishments "continue in a state of gradual formation."[51] What appears regular and established from one point of view, proves to be something being regulated and in the process of establishment. Some persons, in government and out, must pursue political purposes, must actively engage themselves to the task of ordering society in one way or another. That the *consequences* of their actions will not conform to their designs doesn't affect this point. It is the *effects* that are wanted, for the sake of their own moral integrity but also for the sake of political community. Only where some at least are "citizens" prepared to constitute and will the force of their community, can there be national felicity. Political establishments in an advanced state of the arts must work to protect the various partial societies and to enforce the conventions among them. They must also protect the confederation as a whole against external enemies.

The deliberate actions of leading men do in fact produce political consequences that none of them intends. That is because of the contests among them and because of the interplay with circumstances, and this is the stuff of the history of nations. For Ferguson, political judgment is a matter of wise choice between options defined by circum-

stances. Political events depend on the interacting consequences of the choices made and effectuated by all the powerful political actors. The political world is a world of conflict, not settled lawfulness. Without a will to counter abuses
and without active engagements in political actions, outcomes will not be determined by some logic of the situation or requirements of a system, but rather by the will of
those who relate to circumstances in a corrupt and exploit-
ative way, or simply by those who are left with the power
by the casual operations of things but cannot perform the
corrective and integrative tasks which must be carried out if
the nation is not to stagnate, decline, and fall. "Spontaneous social formations" can neither obviate these actions nor
guide them.

The warning example is China. Montesquieu had already
contested the widely held view that China is a model of
excellence, and he repeatedly placed his discussions of China
next to his discussion of England, as if to invite comparison
between these two opposite ways of managing a society
devoted to commerce.[52] He had depicted the rule of emperor and mandarins as despotic, and he had portrayed a
society in which all conduct is extorted from people by
some ritual or regulation backed by force, except only commercial activity which is spurred on by tolerated dishon-
esty. Ferguson seizes upon Montesquieu's themes of tranquility, self-interest, and compulsion; but he dispenses with
Montesquieu's physicalist explanation of the case. China
shows what becomes of civilized societies when they order
their conduct exclusively by the norms appropriate to commercial and related spheres in societies in an advanced state
of the arts. Duncan Forbes has already called attention to

the fact that the catalogue of objectives Ferguson ascribes to Chinese national character corresponds very closely to David Hume's leading values.[53] According to Ferguson, the terms "polished" and "civilized" confuse judgment when they are taken to refer to proficiency in arts and commerce, scholarship or fashionableness. They refer properly to an effective political condition and citizenship. Even the qualities prized by those who use the terms in the misleading way cannot subsist without political spirit and its effects.[54] Ferguson excoriates the mandarin, depreciates the legislator, and vindicates the statesman who is a party politician.

In the last analysis, Ferguson differs politically from Hume and Smith, to whom Hayek seeks to assimilate him, because he believes that political life is primarily about power and the assertion of will, and only secondarily about property and the satisfaction of interest. Two passages in Ferguson's lecture notes confirm this. While talking about political establishments as the "results of human art applied to human society," he turned to the "inconveniences" which make it impossible for men to govern themselves only by means of the informal power generated in diverse social relationships and which require political establishments. As numbers of men rise and riches increase, competition intensifies. Then, Ferguson wrote, "The first object of competition is property. The second is eminence and power."[55] The note is corrected in the same hand, to put power first and property second. Political institutions are occasioned by the struggle for power and are designed to render it nondestructive and, in fact, to render it a capital social good. A similar revision can be found in the following note:

> Amidst parties contending partially for their respective advantages
> the choice will be determined by the character and interests of
> those who are in condition to make it.

The word "interests" is crossed out and replaced by "will."[56]

The struggle for power is not seen to have the demonic
implications it has for Hobbes because it is not seen to take
place in a social vacuum where all is always at risk: the competition arises on the basis of things achieved and relationships established, and the existing systems and structures
provide boundaries within which it takes place. That consideration accounts for the great importance Ferguson at-
taches to the casual subordination of ranks. There is a passive resistance in things as they are that inhibits and cau-
tions the actor without immobilizing him. Political power
serves above all, according to Ferguson, to remedy abuses in
the casual system or in previously established political establishment. But these serve in turn to provide the limiting
scene and determinate place within which the political actor plays his part. It can happen, of course, that political
power takes the form of pure force and breaks beyond the
limiting conditions to proceed without limit. But that presupposes a corresponding weakening and narrowing of the
entire "confederation," as well as the failures of the other
political actors. On my reading, Ferguson attempts to develop a dynamic conception of the constitution-forming
interplay between civil society and state institutions, an
understanding that is dialectical not in the sense of the
Hegelian logicistic formulas but in the sense proposed by
Kenneth Burke, where a conception is dialectical if it ac-
knowledges the multiplicity of perspectives required to comprehend human action and the merely provisional and

"ironic" superiority enjoyed by the perspective that is taken
as most representative. It provides an aid to serious reflection on and bargaining with a writer like Ferguson.[57]

If we follow the lead of these reflections on Ferguson,
civil society appears as an open concept rather than as an
ambiguous one, the summative expression of some vital
research questions, rather than an answer. The questions are
about social formations whose effects and actions bear to a
measurable extent on the effective constitution of the political system under study without being agencies of the
state. The qualities and configurations of such social formations will differ from place to place, and the researchable
issues are not about the consequences of the presence or
absence of "civil society," as in the arguments derived from
neo-Tocquevillean models of various kind, but about
regularities relating to their various types, about changes
in the patterns, about diverse modes of interaction between civil society entities, so broadly defined, and state
formations. Instead of a conceptual debate about the inclusion of economic, religious, cultural, or interest group
formations within the reach of "civil society," to take some
examples cited earlier, we have a common reference point
for empirical investigations that take place under disparate
headings. The point of the concept is to fix the interplay
between non-state and state formations as a vital area of
both social scientific investigation and political reflection.
It outlines a research agenda and a topic for normative ex-
ploration.

In relation to the present state of the question, I can
modestly conclude from my fresh encounter with Ferguson,
first, that there is no good reason to limit civil society to

spontaneous social order selected by a supposed evolution-
ary process, although such constituents cannot be excluded;
second, that it is arbitrary to identify the concept with socially benevolent entities or modes of proceeding. Against
the idea common to both libertarian and Marxist thinkers
that capitalist markets form the anatomy of civil society, it
seems more productive to link newer research into civil society with the recent revival of interest in the work of Karl
Polanyi. While the differentiation between state and civil
society remains fruitful, the idea of categorically distinct
political and social realms is undermined by a consideration
of the work that civil society can reasonably be asked to do.

* This paper originated in joint planning with Patricia Nordeen, whose
Yale dissertation on Adam Ferguson makes an important contribution
to situating Ferguson in present-day political philosophy. Because the
paper had to be ready in May for the 2004 interim meeting of the
Research Committee on the History of Sociology in Marienthal, Aus-
tria, where it was presented, the press of time forced us to abandon the
collaboration. I am nevertheless in debt to Dr. Nordeen and look
forward to her own half of this project.

1. David Kettler, *Adam Ferguson: His Social and Political Thought*. New
Brunswick NJ and London: Transaction, 2005. This is a reprint, with addi-
tions, of *The Social and Political Thought of Adam Ferguson*. (Columbus: Ohio
State University Press, 1965).

2. *Essay on the History of Civil Society* III, II (122); *MEMOIRS OF JEAN
FRANCOIS PAUL de GONDI, CARDINAL DE RETZ, Being Historic Court
Memoirs of the Great Events during the Minority of Louis XIV. and the Adminis-
tration of Cardinal Mazarin.*.

3. Omar Encarnacion, *The Myth of Civil Society: Social Capital and Democratic Consolidation in Spain and Brazil*. New York: Palgrave Macmillan, 2003. In
her dissertation, Nordeen offers an extensive critique of what she calls "market-
exclusive" conceptions of civil society, focused on the work of Juergen Habermas,
as expanded upon in Jean Cohen and Andrew Arato, *Civil Society and Political
Theory*. Cambridge: MIT Press, 1992.

4. With malice, Conal Condren writes: "There is a simple but complicat-
ing conjunction which above all else makes the successful use of authorities a
creative and uncommon skill. On the one hand, over time and across societ-

ies, the substantive living tissues of politics change. On the other hand, the ideas of those I call 'classics' of political thought are fixed in the mordant of ink. They are dead and dyed. It is overcoming their fixity in the face of new problems and possibilities that is difficult for even the most willing of authority exploiters.... [The] means of transcendence is to be found not in any edifying catalog of academic and literary virtues, but in the sleazy ambit of the most venerable of literary vices, ambiguity. This is not only, or even mainly, because what may be deemed ambiguous, vague, uncertain, or unclear provides a flux for the mordant of ink, mechanisms for the diverse relationships into which texts can be seen to enter when proffered to posterity; it is also partly because ambiguity in particular and by definition suggests a balance between interpretive options.... Authorities, like ambiguities, are essentially contestable." *The Status and Appraisal of Classic Texts* Princeton: Princeton University Press, 1985: 259-60.

5. Kettler [1965] 2005; Nordeen 2003.

6. See, for example, Duncan Forbes' otherwise excellent "Introduction" to his edition of Ferguson's *Essay on the History of Civil Society*. Edinburgh: Edinburgh University Press, 1966: xxxiii-xl.

7. Ferguson is clear that the link between civilization and commerce is real but not essential. "The success of commercial arts, divided into parts, requires a certain order to be preserved by those who practice them, and implies a certain security of the person and property, to which I give the name of civilization, although this distinction, both in the nature of the thing and the derivation of the word, belongs rather to the effects of law and political establishment, on the forms of society, than to any state merely of lucrative possession of wealth. Civilization has been conspicuous in nations, who made little progress in commerce, or the arts on which it proceeds. The Romans had formed a very accomplished republic, and exhibited many an illustrious character; whilst, in respect to family estate, and manner of life, they were nearly in the condition of peasants and husbandmen. The policy of Sparta arose from a principle directly opposed to the maxims of trade, and went to restrain and to suspend the commercial arts in all their effects." *Princples of Moral and Political Science* 1.3.9 (252)

8. "A feudal kingdom resembled a military establishment, rather than a civil institution." William Robertson, *The Progress of Civilization in Europe* (Chicago: University of Chicago Press, 1972 [1769], 17. Chancellor Robertson was a friend of Ferguson and the leader of the Moderate group in control of the Scottish church assembly. I are citing a modern republication of the first and prefactory volume of his *History of the Reign of the Emperor Charles V*, which originally appeared two years after Ferguson's *Essay*.

9. See, for example, Jennifer Pitts, *A Turn to Empire*. Princeton University Press, 2005

10. *A Sermon preached in the Ersh language to his Majesty's First Highland Regiment of Foot, Commanded by Lord John Murray at their Cantonment at Camberwell on the 18th Day of December, 1745, Being appointed as a Solemn Fast, by the Reverend Adam Ferguson, Chaplain to the said Regiment: and Translated by him into English, for the Use of a Lady of Quality in Scotland, at whose Desire it is now published.* London: A. Millar, 1746.

11. Robertson, *op. cit.* 37-52.

12. *Ibid.* 52.

13. Ferguson writes, "It is not in mere laws, after all, that I are to look for the securities to justice, but in the powers by which the laws have been obtained, and without whose constant support they must fall to disuse. Statutes serve to record the rights of a people, and speak the intentions of parties to defend what the letter of the law has expressed: but without the vigour to maintain what is acknowledged as a right, the mere record, or the feeble intention, is of little avail." *Essay on the History of Civil Society,* III. vi. (166)

14. Ferguson's ambivalence and the resulting ambiguities on these matters is clearest in the texts and revisions of his lecture notes, archived at the University of Edinburgh. For a preliminary analysis, see David Kettler, "Ferguson's *Principles*: Constitution in Permanence," *Studies in Burke and His Time,* vol. 19, no. 3, 1978: 208-222. The issues are somewhat smoothed over in Ferguson's retrospective textbook, Adam Ferguson, *Principles of Moral and Political Science* (Hildesheim and New York: Georg Olms Verlag, 1975 [1792]).

15. Author and date unknown. National Library Mss, No. 646.

16. Bacon, *De Augmentis Scientiarum,* 2.1-2.4; 2.7; 2.10; 8.2. See Lisa Jardine, *Francis Bacon. Discovery and the Art of Discourse.* Cambridge: Cambridge University Press, 1974: 135f.

17. G. M. Trevelyan, *History of England,* III. New York, 1953: 52

18. Eric Cregeen, "The Changing role of the House of Argyll in the Scottish Highlands"; Rosalind Mitchison, "The Government and the Highlands," and John M. Simpson, "Who Steered the Gravy Train, 1707-1766- in N. P. Phillipson and Rosalind Mitchison, eds., *Scotland in the Age of Improvement.* Edinburgh, 1970: 5—72.

19. *The Parliamentary History of England,* vol. 13, 1416-1418.

20. *Op. Cit.* vol. 14, 2-9.

21. *The Culloden Papers,* ff. 33-35. Quoted in John Prebble, *Culloden.* London, 1967: 35.

22. *Civil Society, 133*

23. Lord Glenorchy to Hon. Philip Yorke, June 26, 1746, in Philip C. Yorke, *The Life and Correspondence of Philip Yorke, Earl of Hardwicke, Lord High Chancellor of Great Britain.* Cambridge, 1913. vol. I, 604—605.

24. *Ibid.*

25. Letter from Dr. Birch to Philip Yorke, London, August 9, 1746. Printed as a note in *Parliamentary History,* vol. 13, 1416.

26. Letter of October 17, 1725. Quoted in Mitchison, *loc. cit. 35.*

27. E.g., George S. Pryde, *Scotland from 1603 to the Present Day.* London, 1962.

28. Mitchison, *loc. cit.,* 44.

29. *Parliamentary History*, vol. 14, 20-22.

30. James I, *Basilicon Doron.* Menston, 1969: 58-59. Spelling has been modernized. Hardwicke quotes the passage in the original Latin: *Parliamentary History*, vol. 14: 25-26n.

31. Lord Chancellor to HRH The Duke of Cumberland, April 16, 1747. Philip Yorke, *Op. Cit.* 607-8.

32. William Ferguson, *Scotland. 1689 to the Present.* London, 1968: 147.

33. *Ibid.* 15f.

34. Cumberland wrote repeatedly to Newcastle before and after Culloden, that the whole of the governent of Scotland, including Argyll and all associated with him, had to be replaced. "All in this country are almost to a man Jacobites: and mild measures will not do," (April 4, 1746) A week after Culloden, he wrote: "If I had destroyed every mann of them, such is the soil, that rebellion would sprout out again, if a new system of government is not found out for this country." (April 23, 1746) And some months later: "I am sorry to leave this country in the condition it is in; for all the good that I have done has been a little blood— letting which has only weakened the madness, but not at all cured. ... (July 17, 1746). William Coxe, *Memoirs of the Administration of the Right Honourable Henry Pelharm.* London, 1829, vol. I, 300— 303. Chesterfield, with an important positjon in the ministry, shared Cumberland*s views: "The Duke*s report from Scotland verifies the opinion I have always had, and declared, of that country; and while that favourable distinction remains of loyal and disloyal, the rebellion will never be extinguished. Recall your Scottish heroes, starve the whole country indiscriminately by your ships, put a price upon the heads of the chiefs, and let the Duke put all to fire and sword." (Letter to Duke of Newcastle, March 11, 1746. Bonamy Dobree, *The Letters of Philip Dormer Stanhope, 4th Earl of Chesterfield.* Vol. III. London, 1932: 750. See also 671-3, 692-4, 711-12. Hardwicke at times spoke of Cumberland as a "physician," especially when writing to his young son, Joseph, serving with the army, but he always rejected the view of the rebellion as a Scottish national movement.

35. Ferguson, *Op. Cit.* 157

36. *Parliamentary History*, Vol. 13, 30-43.

37. George W. T. Ormond, *The Lord Advocates of Scotland.* Edinburgh, 1983, Vol. II, 42.

38. *Parliamentary History*, Vol. 13, 50.

39. *Parliamentary History*, vol. 13, p. 1417n. Dr. Birch writes to Philip Yorke that Lord Chancellor Hardwicke showed wardholding "to be very opressive of the people in general and consequently very necessary to be

redeemed by the people for the establishment of freedom and encouragement of industry. . ."

40. Lord Chancellor to General Bland, February 7, 1754. Philip Yorke, *Op. Cit.*, 622.

41. *Parliamentary History*, vol 14, 1237-38.

42. *Loc. cit. 1248*

43. *Loc. Cit.* 1260-61. Yorke reprints some materials bearing on Hardwicke's views on Scottish entails. *Op. Cit.* 424 and note.

44. *Parliamentary History*, vol 14,1267.

45. *Loc. Cit.* 1252-3.

46. *Ibid.*

47. James I, *Op. Cit.*, 41-43.

48. Albert O. Hirschman, *The Passions and the Interests. Arguments for Capitalism before its Triumph.* Princeton: Princeton University Press, 1977.

49. Ormond, *Op. Cit.*, 49.

50. For Argyll's last use of his "feudal" jurisditional privileges, in order to crush resistance to his redevelopmental strategy, see George W. T. Ormond, *The Lord Advocates of Scotland.* Edinburgh, 1983. II: 57 and T.B. Howell, ed., *A Complete Collection of State Trials*, Vol. 19, London, 1816. The Lord Advocate, who appeared before him as prosecutor in this murder case, eventually decided on uncertain grounds and with the help of Argyll's clansmen on the packed jury, was clear about the stakes. He said that news of the murder of "the king*s factor upon certain of the forfeited estates that had been but a few weeks before annexed to the crown unalienably, and the produce of them appropriated by law. . . for the future tranquillity of the united kingdom in general, and for the immediate advantage and improvement of the highland parts of Scotland in particular..." had determined him to take an active part. Because the murderers "as far as in them lay, had endeavoured to make the world or the public believe, that the civilizing of the Highlands was a vain and impracticable attempt," he had made up his mind "to do all that in me lay, consistently with law and justice, to convince the disaffected part of the Highlands of Scotland, that they must submit to this government, which they have several times in vain endeavoured to subvert." Howell, *Op. Cit.*, 59; see also 173-4.

51. David Kettler,"History and Theory in Ferguson's *Essay on the History of Civil Society.* A Reconsideration." *Political Theory*, 5.4 (November, 1977) 437-460.

52. Lecture Notes, University of Edinburgh Manuscript Collection, Vol. 1, Lecture 15 (1784), 170 ff. Ferguson introduced a reference to Smith's *Wealth of Nations* in the 1773 edition of the *Essay*, evidently on the basis of advance manuscripts, and he praised it as "equal to what has ever appeared on any subject of science whatever." But he adds immediately that all must agree that wealth must not be "the principal object of any state," and that consequently this science cannot be taken directly as a guide to conduct." 287.

53. *Principles of Moral and Political Science*, Vol. I, 265.

54. *Ibid.* Vol II, 269.

55. Montesquieu, *Spirit of the Laws*, 8.21. Compare the laudatory articles on "la Chine" and "Chinois philosophie de" in the *Ecyclopedie*. The latter does not acknowledge that Chinese "tranquility" is antithetical to scientific progress.

56. Duncan Forbes noted this in his "Introduction" to the *Essay*, xxxvi. Ferguson warns against "tranquility," "pretended moderation," "politeness," "sensibility," and so on.

57. *Essay*, 205, 288. Ferguson rejects unpolitical renderings of the terms "polished" and "civilized."

58. Lecture Notes I, Lecture 25 (December 14, 1779) 262b

59. Lecture Notes I, Lecture 30 (December 24, 1779) 291b.

60. Kettler, "Ferguson's *Principles*: Constitution in Permanence," *Studies in Burke and His Time*, 19, 3, 1978.

Index

Activism, 99, 141, 152, 177, 198, 212, 271; *see also* Ambition, Progress, Virtue

Administration, 312–13 n. 142; *see also* Conflict, Laws, Political life

Agricultural society, 234

Allegiance, 161; *see also* Authority

Ambition, 5, 150 f., 164, 191, 220; *see also* Activism, Commercial society, Moral theory, Perfectionism, Progress, Virtue

America, 37; *see also* American Revolution, Carlisle Commission

American Revolution, 18, 63 f., 85–86, 89–90; *see also* Price, Stamp Act Crisis

Anthropocentrism; *see* Christian religion, Human dignity, Immortality

Aristotle, 7, 122, 125, 253; *see also* Classical tradition, Contemplation, Perfectionism, Teleology

Army; *see* Militia

Arrian, 147

Athole, 43, 44, 47

Aurelius, Marcus, 7, 61, 141 f.; *see also* Stoicism

Authority, 23, 269, 275, 313 n. 146; *see also* Political theory, Revolution, Rights

Bacon, Francis, 7, 119, 126, 134, 147; *see also* Empiricism, Science

Barbarian society, 232 f.

Benevolence; *see* Fellow-feeling

Black, Eugene, 31 n. 27

Black, Joseph, 53, 65

Black Watch Regiment, 44, 69 n. 5

Blair, Hugh, 33, 40, 44

Britain, 24–25, 102 n. 13, 165, 202, 218, 245 f., 260, 278, 282; *see also* Commercial society, Despotism, Electoral reform, Militia, Progress

363